AUTO

BOOK 6

SUNSET AND EVENING STAR

Each volume in the evocative and richly entertaining autobiography of Sean O'Casey is essential reading for a proper appreciation of this major Irish dramatist whose plays were among the most exciting developments in modern drama.

Born in the back streets of Dublin, suffering from weak and diseased eyes, he lived in poverty and physical hardship for many years. In his late teens he became a manual labourer and after working on the roads or in the docks from five in the morning to six at night he would spend his evenings helping the cause of the Gaelic League and Sinn Fein. He became Secretary of the Irish Citizen Army and a founder member of the Irish Labour Party. Although his first published work was in 1907, not until the success of *Juno and the Paycock* in 1925 did he give up manual work and become a full-time writer.

While such plays as *Purple Dust* lay unheeded by West End theatre managers, O'Casey wrote his memorable sequence of autobiographies. In this final volume reminiscences of his friendship with Shaw and of life in Devon during World War Two mingle with rebellious indignation at organized religion and true concern for the people of Ireland.

The autobiography ends · eleven years before O'Casey's death from a heart attack in 1964.

By the same author in Pan Books

AUTOBIOGRAPHY (BOOK 1):
I KNOCK AT THE DOOR
AUTOBIOGRAPHY (BOOK 2):
PICTURES IN THE HALLWAY
AUTOBIOGRAPHY (BOOK 3):
DRUMS UNDER THE WINDOWS
AUTOBIOGRAPHY (BOOK 4):
INISHFALLEN, FARE THEE WELL
AUTOBIOGRAPHY (BOOK 5):
ROSE AND CROWN

AUTOBIOGRAPHY

BOOK 6

SUNSET AND EVENING STAR

SEAN O'CASEY

UNABRIDGED

PAN BOOKS LTD : LONDON

First published 1954
by Macmillan and Company Ltd.
This edition published 1973 by Pan Books Ltd,
33 Tothill Street, London, SW1.

ISBN 0 330 23499 4

Printed in Great Britain by
Richard Clay (The Chaucer Press), Ltd, Bungay, Suffolk

CONTENTS

A Drive of Snobs	9
Childermess	22
Cambridge	44
Deep in Devon	68
The Dree Dames	84
Rebel Orwell	99
Heavily Hangs the Broad Sunflower	113
Orphans of the Storm	128
Red Laugh of War	136
In Cellar Cool	145
Shaw's Corner	161
Sunset	191
Outside an Irish Window	206
And Evening Star	218

You cannot prevent the birds of sadness from flying over your head, but you can prevent them building nests in your hair.

CHINESE PROVERB

I'm gonna wash 'em all outa my hair.

To My dear Friend Hugh MacDiarmid
Alba's Poet and one of Alba's first men

A DRIVE OF SNOBS

BACK to London, New York lingering beside him still (Oh, linger longer, do), his hand still touching Rockefeller Center, his eyes still luminous with the myriad windows lighting up New York's night; here he was driving back with his boy, Breon, and their maid, Marion, back to their new home, a flat in Battersea; back with presents, nylons for his wife from Tessa, his agent's wife, more nylons from Lillian Gish, a padded silk bed-jacket for her from handsome Sylvia Sydney, a grand black-and-white silk scarf from George Jean Nathan, a set of pop-up books for his boy from Mimsie Taylor, a lass as lovely as his own wife, and that was saying a mouthful – a phrase he had learned in London, but which he had never heard in America; and his pockets jingling with enough dollars to keep things going for another year.

> Home is the sailor, home from the sea,
> And the hunter home from the hill.

Home safe from terrible dangers, too, as this letter, one of several, can show:

Hudson Theatre

Mr SEAN O'CASEY

Now Mr O'Casey, I attended your play, *Juno and the Paycock*, last night. I felt very discrossed also discoroged with it could you not make it any better than you have it, if not you are getting a warning to stop it at once or can you not make it any more pleasant for the Irish people who are delighted to hear something of their own country.

I have seen many plays throughout New York but I have never seen anything like what is in the Hudson theatre. Its redicilus and why dont you think so too you must remember that these disgraceful pictures and plays are condemned and *Thank God*. You are getting a very keen and good advise

now before you go any further with your work, dont you
think you would be better to be bricklaying than ridicaudling
the Irish, you are going to be Jumped upon some night and
you and your gang are not safe. The most prinsible thing
Stop the cursing and swaring for the players good. This is
only a warning.

KELLY, BURKE, AND SHEA

Heaven having a blast at him! He would have to amend his
The Bells of Mary's were bullying. He'd have to thank God for
the race and the sod, for Kelly and Burke and Shea. The members of the Legue of Dacency were out defending western
Christian culture. Sign your name, Kelly, sign your name,
Burke, sign your name, Shea – this'll put the wind up him! O
advocates of heaven. Their letter was a *cry di curé*. Comrades
of the great war against profunity. Oh, sweet and salient
natures! A chosen three, who carry great green banners in St
Patrick's Day Purrade, and are blessed by father Spiellman as
they go bye byes. Henceforth he, with Erinn, would remember
the days of old; he'd give three hours a day to mend the harp
the minstrel boy tore asunder; he'd seek out mother machree
and love the silver that shone in her hair, so that, at the last,
having kept the faith, his name might be written down from
everlasting to everlasting in the Book of the Green and Golden
Slumbers.

The O'Caseys had taken a five-roomed flat in forty-nine
Overstrand Mansions (the forty-niners), facing Battersea Park,
on the south side of the Thames. All the homes here, along
Prince of Wales Drive, were flats in groups of mansions, York,
Prince of Wales, and Overstrand, the line of them extending
from one end of the park to the other. A. de Blacam, who,
some time ago, used to write a daily column for De Valera's
paper, *The Irish Press*, excited himself and his readers by proclaiming one morning that the great democrat, G. K. Chesterton, had lived for years in forty-eight Overstrand Mansions
(next door, be God!), plump in the middle of the workers and
the poor. He did in me neck! Occasionally, he may have
caught a glimpse of a poor woman or a poor child coming
from the poor quarters to enter the park for a play or a rest;
but no fuller revelation of the worker's life comes before the
eyes or enters the mind of the select residents of the flats in the
select mansions of Battersea. These hoity-toity persons were

far more selective of their chance acquaintances than were the proper persons of Park Lane in the hey-day of its historical hallowed-be-thy-name period. The livers in these flats were of the higher-low middle class, a step or two down from the grade of the middle class who lived on the other side of the river in the Borough of Chelsea; so they had one more river to cross before they entered the land of Canaan. Battersea was, almost wholly, a working-class borough, and so the families of the mansion flats shoved themselves as far as possible, bodily and spiritually, to the edge of the district. All they knew of the workers was the distant glimpse of sooty roofs they got from a few of the higher windows at the back of their flats; or, during an election, when they went to give their votes for what Disraeli called 'The barren thing – Conservatism – an unhappy crossbreed, the mule of politics that engenders nothing'; though the workers' district barely loomed into view from where the votes were cast. The name of the borough rarely appeared on the notepaper of the residents, who hid the humiliation of Battersea under the simple postal symbol of London, SW11. Peek-a-boo, I see you, I see you hiding there! In conversation the name was never mentioned: it was as if they had innocently crossed the border of Chelsea, and had settled in Battersea without knowing it. They were not to blame: that was their life, and they lived it.

The first floor of the flats had a balcony going right across the façade, the second floor a concrete jut-out on which one could stand, but couldn't sit, and the upper floor had no balcony at all; so the rents sank as the flats mounted. As well as this distinction between the flats themselves, there was also a distinction between the blocks, Overstrand being ever so slightly more genteel than the York block; and York was careful to await an advance from Overstrand before assuming acquaintance with Overstrand, for fear of a snub; for it is almost unbearable for one snob to be snobbed by another.

Once a Mrs Black, living almost next door to him, wife of a civil servant, was presented at Court. She dipped the knees in a curtsy to kingship, and returned to the flat creaking with exultation. Her kingdom had come, and she entered gallantly into it; for that night, in her Court dress, feathers and all, her husband in white tie and tails, with a few select friends, she sat down in the flat's dining-room to a five-course dinner, done to a turn by a qualified chef, served by a footman in coloured coat and plush britches, and eaten by candlelight; a first-class offering of thanks to God for his regarding of the highliness of his handmaiden, who had now been magnified in the sight of all her neighbours.

There was a Mrs Green, too, her husband, Ben, their two children, Peter and Pauline, all rigid with fear of touching person, place, or thing beneath them, and quivery with desire to acquaint themselves with persons, places, or things they thought to be above them. Once a month, mother, son, and daughter went to ride in Richmond; and all the morning before departure there was a running-up-and-down parade of hard hats, whips, and jodhpurs (a lady goes apace apace, a gentleman goes a trit trot trittrot); though, as a matter of fact, each was taut with a constricting fear of canter and gallop, from the time they got on to the horses to the time they gladly got off again.

—No, said the mother once to Sean, they had never been in a stable; they mounted of course in the yard; and she was shocked when Sean told her a horse would never know what to do with her till she had spent a good deal of her time in a stable with him; till her nose had got used to the smell of dung and horse-sweat. Yet to those whom she believed to be her equals, she was a very pleasant woman, loved her children, and took good care of them. But no thought for other children troubled her, or any of the other residents. They all spluttered with indignation when the Battersea Council organized popular entertainments, flooding the park with poorer children, neatly dressed or tattered and torn, jostling the middle-class kids out of their way, the over-populated bodies of the rougher children transferring surplus vermin to the fresh and vacant bodies of the better-kept kids, making their flesh become delightful feeding-grounds for louse and flea. A-hunting we will go, a-hunting we will go, a-hunting we will go! No one could blame them for dividing their children from the louse and the flea; they were to be blamed, though, for raising no word against the conditions which inflicted these dangers and torture upon the children of others. Again, when a rough-and-tumble crèche, a roped-in patch of grass, surrounded by shade-giving trees, was founded so as to give working-class mothers a snatch of rest from their labours, by leaving their toddlers in charge of a woman there at tuppence an hour a head, the residents, as superior rate-payers, signed a complaint and sent it to the Borough Council, complaining that the crying of the children, in anger or in play, disturbed them, and that the crèche utterly destroyed the order and serenity of the park. And this was the rendezvous chosen by Chesterton in which to laugh and sing and clap hands with the workers!

Mrs Green sorted out her mansion-house flat into a greater eminence by giving all the corks drawn from champagne bottles emptied enjoyably by her and her husband, to the tune of a bottle a month, an honoured preservation. She fixed all the corks into a finely-made walnut frame, windowed with fine glass, enclosing a soft bed of cramoisie velvet on which the cosy corks lay; each cork crowned by its own patch of tinsel, green, gold, or silver, with an ivory-tinted card below each one telling the name of the wine and the district where the vine grew and the vintage year in which the wine was pressed from the grape; with the year, month, and day the wine was drunken. There they swung in their costly case on the wall of the dining-room, like dried-up, shrunken heads of enemies to be honoured and gloated over at seasonable times; honoured as Queequeg honoured, and departed from, the withered head he carried about with him, as told in the story of the White Whale. Wine of France and milk of Burgundy. No corks here damp with English ale or brown with the stain of Dublin's potent porter. No, sir. Fine bouquet, delicious aroma, Mrs Green; various vintages, but all excellent. You are honoured in your corks. There is nothing whatever vulgar about corks: they are graceful, and full of meaning. Quite: a soul is safe in a champagne bottle.

Here in the medley of middle-class dressing for dinner, of creaking jodhpurs; of grades in flats and grade in car; in assembly of champagne-bottle corks; in one-maid or two-maid establishments; in first-class or second-class convent school; in carat-weight of collar-stud or cuff-link; here, among all this middle-class tension and torture, *The Irish Press* was declaring triumphantly that Chesterton was living with, and plunging about, among the workers and the poor!

And yet these people were important to England and to life; intelligent, mostly kind in a limited way, and anxious about the future of their children in a mistaken way. Too anxious that they should get on in the world; anxious that they shouldn't do any new things, but that they win respect from others by doing all the old things that were fading out of life. The lady of the jodhpurs' son, Peter, was attending a school whose system was a preparation for the manner and method of a public school, imitating the public school in all it did, while the public school was itself imitating all that had been done by itself through all the years gone by for ever, ignorant of, and indifferent to, the new throb in the world's heart, the new beat in the world's pulse. Once, when Sean was sitting on a park bench with Mrs Green and her son, the mother complained to Sean that Peter didn't want to accept from Mr Lemon, the headmaster of his school, an invitation to spend a week's fishing with him during the holidays. Fancy, she had said, thinking of refusing such an invitation from such a man; and Peter, head hanging down, had mumbled, I don't want to go, Mother; I'd hate it. To which she: You mustn't say such things, Peter. Mr Lemon's your Headmaster, and, even if you do hate it, you'll have to like it; and you'll have to be nice to him, very nice to him all the time; all the time – do you hear? Don't you agree, Mr O'Casey?

—Well, Mrs Green, I can't see how Peter can hate and like a thing at one and the same time. You are asking too much of him.

—He'll have to like it, said Mrs Green, emphatically; have to learn to like it. Mr Lemon's his Headmaster, and quite a gentleman.

Sean, knowing that nothing he could say would change Mrs Green's attitude of mind, and anxious to make it as easy as he could for Peter, put his hand gently on the lad's shoulder, saying, Never mind, old boy; do your best. We old fellows are very trying to the young. You'll get used to him, and like him after a bit.

—No, I won't, said the lad, a little bitterly; I know I won't; I'll simply hate it all the time, all the time.

—All the time, all the time, thought Sean; tormented all the time. No choice for the kid. Lemon showing him how to fish, and the lad too nervous to take notice. Evidently a Headmaster wherever he might be. Aloud, Sean said, It won't be so bad, after a bit, Peter. You feel at ease with me, now; but if I asked you to come for a week's fishing with me, you'd be saying to your mother: I don't want to go; I'd hate it.

—No I wouldn't, burst from Peter. I'd simply love to go with you!

There was so much energy in the boy's exclamation, so

much sincerity in the look he gave to him, that Sean, for the first time he could remember, was at a loss for a word to say.

Sean felt sure that no one out of all the middle-class residents in Battersea had ever thrust a foot into a working-class district. And here was where and this was how Chesterton lived among the workers and the poor of Battersea Borough. Never in his life, Sean believed, did he smell the smell of a slum. In her life of him, *Gilbert Keith Chesterton*, Maisie Ward flips in a remark made by a journalist that G. K. C. was 'cultivating the local politics of Battersea; in secluded pubs, he drinks with the frequenters, and learns their opinions on municipal milk and Mr John Burns'. She doesn't halt to say what the frequenters said to Chesterton, or what he said to them; nor does she record any conversations held in the secluded pubs of Battersea; and, as a matter of fact, Battersea pubs are no more secluded than pubs anywhere else. These visits – if they ever occurred – were evidently part of those tip, touch, habits which coloured his whole life. Rushing round, he tipped Shaw, Dickens, Browning, John of Austria, breathless with running all the time; and as he ran past life, he shouted gee gee up to the white horse, dismounting for a while to chuck the roman catholic church under the chin. There's the brave horseman, there's his two min; there he goes out and here he goes in; chin chucky chin chucky under the chin. He never waited a second to sit down in any room of thought, contenting himself with peeping round the door, throwing in a coloured puff-ball of braggart doctrinal remark that went round the room of life till it fell into dull dust when some curious finger chanced to touch it. A whiff of his love for the workers is felt in his 'As far as personal taste and instincts are concerned, I share all your antipathy to the noisy Plebeian excursions. A visit to Ramsgate during the season and the vision of the crowded howling sands has left in me feelings which all my Radicalism cannot allay.' His instinct was to run from the worker, man of the lower class, when the worker was noisy. Lover of the worker's soul, let me from thy presence fly. He didn't like the noisy children just let loose from school. He never did. And his deep love of God, expressed in his deep love of humanity, is shown in his 'The guide showed me a cross given by Louis XIV to Mlle de La Vallière. I thought when reflecting what the present was, and where it was and then to whom it was given, that this showed pretty well what the religion of the Bourbon régime was and why it has become impossible since the Revolution.' In Chesterton's mind, the symbol couldn't come to rest in the hands of a whore. And Blake and Whitman were two of the higher souls this laddo tried to touch! Maybe, the king didn't give her the cross in levity; maybe, she didn't take it so. How did Chesterton know? Even if he gave it in levity and she took it in the same mood, what was that to him? The poor king and the rich whore – if Chesterton's religion was as true as he so heartily and so superficially made it out to be – would have to answer for it, and not Chesterton. It is difficult enough for us to judge the things of time; it is beyond us to judge the things of eternity.

In another way, we get a glimpse of his childish mind yielding to a visible dream of violence, for Maisie Ward tells 'His love of weapons, his revolver, his favourite sword-stick, remained with him all his life': till death did them part. Chesterton's bow of burnished gold, his arrows of desire. Bang bang! Not a hoe or a spanner, not a fiddle or a fife; no, a sword-stick and a gun. The cross and the gun; an up-to-date union. A film critic reviewing a film said 'We saw at once that the face of him who carried the cross for the Saviour was the face of Hopalong Cassidy'. And here we are again, for in a lot of ways Chesteron was the hopalong cassidy of the roman catholic church. No, this was no man for a symbol on a workers' banner. One could ne'er imagine this man striding along between Feemy Evans and Fluther Good. He knew far less about the workers than did Yeats or Lady Gregory, who mingled with them at a hundred feiseanna, sat in their homes, chatted with them, and recorded many things about them as their works do testify. In Battersea and Beaconsfield, Chesterton dwelt among the jodhpurs, worn, not for riding, but for display; among the gatherers of champagne corks; among those who graded life by size of flat and cost of car. His dive into a workers' district was similar to his dive into the country, when he went to live in, and wander through, the rural life of Beaconsfield, a village tongue-tied to London, with as much of the country in it as Wandsworth Common, Hyde Park, or Kensington Gardens. He figured finely in the drive of snobs. Decent people, important people, kindly in a limited way, intelligent, though over-anxious for their children to keep the perishing rules: these were his peers; and to associate him with workers or with the poor was but to upset the man's nature with a rosy libel.

The residents round, possessing no gardens, made Battersea Park one, and regarded it as their own, nearly as private as those green squares in cities where residents round them are provided with private keys, admitting themselves, and rigidly keeping everyone else out. The flower and the tree belong to you and to me, but no one else. Breeds without the law and without the railings. A broad path led to the sub-tropical gardens, and one passed through this into a wide, concreted, circular space, in its centre a bandstand, and surrounded with benches. On fine days, these benches and this circle were crowded with nannies, minding the children of the flats, or with middle-class mothers minding their children when their nannies were off for the day. The wide circle round the bandstand was usually crammed with children riding round on bicycles, tricycles, rolling hoops, or playing ball – an animated scene of wild innocence and joy.

Opposite to the path leading into this circle was another leading out of it, bringing one to the park's centre and towards the green sward that ran along parallel with the Thames. At this exit from the circle stood two enormous chestnut trees, their pink and white flowers flooding the circle with floral candlelight when a spring day grew gloomy. Sean often sat here watching his boy, Breon, careering round on his bicycle with Mrs Green's children; or sat with Eileen busy now with sewing things for the coming baby. Here, he met a Mrs Mellor, minding her young and intelligent son. He had noticed that she usually sat in a spot with a vacancy on either side of her, seeming not to wish to mingle in talk with the other mothers there. She looked sad and anxious, as, indeed, she might well be, for she told Sean, who had sat down beside her, that her husband, Editor of the *Tribune*, was seriously ill in hospital. She mentioned, half hopefully, that when her husband recovered, he would visit and work in the constituency he hoped to represent for Labour in the next election. A woman, Sean thought, bravely trying to live a middle-class life on scanty resources, determined to give more than she could safely spare to her little boy. How hard it was for all of us to bring them up in the way that they should go!

Here, too, he came across an old codger of seventy-two who was well in with all the more superior members of the flats, who admired him as a real, respectable working-man, one who knew his place, and fitted himself into life a long long way from theirs. They had given him gifts from what they possessed, and for which they had no further use, so that all he wore, inside and outside, from his socks and shoes to his bowler hat and walking-stick, had been worn and carried by a flat-resident some time before; a life going around in cast-offs. Whenever he came towards a lady watching her playing child, he swept off the bowler hat, and sat down near her, if, by a gesture of movement, she invited him to do so; leaving always a deferential space between his lesser body and the lady's loftier one, gracious to him so long as he kept his reverential distance. Once when Sean was chatting to Mrs Green, he appeared, came near; off came the bowler hat from the grey pow, and Mrs Green moving nearer to Sean, invited him silently to sit down and rest. After some words about his own health, which was fair, thank God, he asked about the health of Mrs Green's children, Miss Pauline and Master Peter; and, on being told they were fine, the old fellow burbled out a hand-some Thank God for that, Ma'am. Suddenly Mrs Green crossed over opposite to an acquaintance who had just arrived in the circle to give her child a chance to play; and Sean and the old man were left together. He had eyed Sean's untidy get-up and battered cap curiously, concluding, Sean assumed, that there was nothing there that could suit him; but as Sean had been talking amiably and easily to Mrs Green, he surmised Sean must be one that had been accepted, and so would make a safe buddy.

The old fellow leaned back on the bench, and crossed one leg over the other. Never before had Sean seen these old legs crossed. While sitting with his lady-friends, the old man in-variably sat upright, his legs demurely kept together, divided only by the walking-stick thrust down between them. Now the bottom of a trouser-leg was stretched high over a shoe, and Sean saw he was wearing a pair of vivid purple socks. The old face was almost handsome, gentle-wrinkled, still young-look-ing, the white hair and whiskers alone calendaring his age; a face, though, made too soft and pleasant by the torpor of sub-missive manners. Never another sky for him now but the sun-set and evening star, brightening into a star of the night.

—You know Mrs Green? he asked Sean, looking sideways at him, a little puzzled at his status still.

—Well, said Sean; her mother, father, uncles and aunts as well.

—Oh? came the comment; a puzzled query. A very kind

lady; very kind. Her children, too, are very genteel and respectful, treating me as if I was almost a gentleman myself.

—Yes, said Sean; a kind lady. Her little family is all her world.

Master Peter and Miss Pauline came by on their bicycles, jumping off in front of the old man to ask him how he was. The old bowler hat was lifted in a minor tribute as he said he was well, thank God, and inquired after their health, which being satisfactory, they said goodbye, mounted their bicycles, rode off, and the old bowler hat was carefully replaced on the old head.

—A very kind lady, he murmured. She thinks of me at times. He took off the hat, extending it towards Sean so that he could get a fresh look at it. Her husband gave me this; yes, indeed; her husband's hat.

—It still is, said Sean. Whenever Mrs Green looks at it, she knows it's her husband's hat. You know it, and I know it, for you've just told me so. If you tell it to others, they'll know it, till all Battersea will know it as Mrs Green's husband's hat. He patted the thin, bony knee of the old man. Don't be too grateful, friend. Your humbleness and respectability deserve more than an old hat from Mrs Green's husband.

—I should be grateful, and I am, he murmured, glancing curiously at Sean. I know my place, sir, though the kind ladies here treat me almost as an equal. Though poor, I was brought up proper to remember my place, and to be humble and respectful to my betters.

—Reared up in some Institution, thought Sean, and taught a damaging docility. His place in the universe, or his place in nature? Of no importance. What matters is his place among the kind ladies and gents. Ah, my friend, he said aloud, it isn't good to be always humble. The lower classes are busy casting humbleness aside, and are shedding their respect for those who rob and rot them.

—Oh, no, sir! I hope not, sir, looking at Sean in a puzzled way, as if to try to discern Sean's place among the ladies and the gents. They will only destroy themselves. Our class can do better by knowing their place and keeping it. Ruin themselves, they will, if they go on like that, sir; or talk about being as good as their betters. Oh, a bad sign, sir; a very bad sign! God never meant us to be equal.

—All will be equal one day, said Sean, but each will differ

from the other; but difference is very different from inequality.

—I dunno, sir, said the old man, bewildered by the talk. He sat silent, casting sidelong glances at Sean. Who was this fellow, talking this way, upsetting things? Yet he had often seen him talking so free and easy with Mrs Green, Mrs Black, and Mrs White. God help him – odd things were happening these days! He got up from the bench, fiddled with his tie, tapped the pavement with his stick; glanced at Sean, then at Mrs Green sitting opposite, chatting away with her friend. God help him! Treat the people above you as you should, he said, faintly, and they'll do the same to you. I must be going, now. At this time, I make a little cup of tea for myself. I don't need much. It isn't right to ask for things beyond us, or wish them either. I must be off. You must know I'm right, sir. He looked dazed, fumbling with his tie and tapping the pavement with his stick. I must go, he went on; I never miss a cup of tea about this time. It does me good. I look forward to it. Goodbye, sir.

He made off towards his tea, his eyes searching out Mrs Green opposite, chatting to her friend. She saw him, and waved a lily-white hand in farewell; and off came the bowler hat in a grand sweep of reverential gratitude. Sean saw Mrs Green pointing him out to her friend; telling her, doubtlessly, of the grand old working-man, so rare and so unlike so many of his class and station; and Sean knew that the old codger had won another client. The two ladies still kept looking after the old, upright figure, very likely wishing to God that all working-men were like this worthy old man, a real gentleman in his own humble way; yes. But workers were getting less and less like him. The old faithful retainer had become but a mummified memory. The bowed head before a master existed no longer, even in a picture. They had become conscious of their power, and as this consciousness grew, they saw less importance in those to whom they had been for so long such a comfort, such a stay. They were breeding importance within themselves. Yes, ma'am, a pleasant sitting-room, a wireless-set, my own bathroom, and every second evening off: sounds fairly fair. I'll think over it, ma'am, and let you know as is convenient. Of course, the first week'll be only a trial to see if you suit me, ma'am. You want to know by tomorrow? Oh, well, if you're in such a hurry, ma'am, you'd better look for someone else – goodbye.

The old man paused where the two trees stood, canopying the old bowler hat with chestnut blooms as they would canopy a crown concocted out of jewels; as they would carelessly canopy tinker, tailor, soldier, sailor, richman, poorman, beggarman, thief. There he paused, his head below the murmuring foliage, his feet touching fading petals on the ground; an old mind trying to bud old thoughts; an old man standing in the shadow of the trees as if he stood hesitant in the valley of the shadow of death. Here, he paused, turned, and looked towards Sean. Sean waved a hand; the old man took no notice, but turned and went his way, and his old world went with him.

CHILDERMESS

ANOTHER child was on its way into the world. A world
weird and wonderful. Well, it wouldn't know what was being
forged in front of it. Here was the new life pushing a way out
into smoke, into fire, into shouting; woven within the walk
of Ribbentrop among the roses of England and the lilies
of France; within the hearing of the cocksparrow chirrup of
Chamberlain charming away war, and the distant humming of
waiting Panzers, impatiently ready to make a rush at life. But
new life is careless of what may front it, and so a new life was
pulsing its way out of a peaceful darkness into a marring and
menacing light. A difficult time for man and woman; difficult
in the way of doing the right thing by life and making both
ends meet. It is an expensive thing to bring a life from the
womb into the world. Was then; worse now. The middle class
now die and are born beyond their means. Unto us a child is
born, unto us a son is given, is an alarming announcement
today, giving to the tenor of the joy-bell the ugly minor note of
the knell.

Through the stir of middle-class emotion, and by a middle-
class doctor's advice, Eileen had booked a berth in a London
wist-not nursing-home, many miles from the Monument, the
fee being twelve guineas a week, not counting extras, of course.
Adding the doctor's fee of fifty guineas, Sean saw in his mind
the mighty sum of a hundred pounds demanded of him, with
other costs lurking in dark corners ready to come out when the
bigger bill was paid. The uncertainty of how the common
claims of life are to be managed is the laocoön with which man
is for ever struggling.

Sean had no respect whatever for London nursing-homes,
nor for the middle-class emotion that kept the contemptible
things going. The knights and dames of low degree had to have
their tiny honours. Sean had visited three of these places to see
sick friends, and had been stabbed by amazement at their drab-
ness and dirt; how unsuitable they were for the needs of the
sick. On entering, he had run his fingers along the ledge of the

dado, and had shown them covered with thick dirt to the
friend that was with him. The rooms were heavy with old air,
and wore a weak look, as if they, too, were sick; and all he saw
seemed to whisper cynically of uncleanliness and of clumsy,
uncomely methods of management and care. He was to have
his surmises habited by proof. Eileen entered, and became a
patient. Sean went to see her settled there. As in the others,
here in this nursing-home the glamour was gloom. Rowland to
the dark tower came. The hall rimmed with dust; no sign of
surgical cleanliness or of that quiet alertness felt where doctors
and nurses are. The Home was joined on to a crowd of similar
buildings so that there was little air in the room, and whatever
air crept in was immediately swallowed up by the dusty-thick
curtains blotting the window, and the dustier and thicker carpet smothering the floor. Brown curtains, a browner carpet,
brown dado, sovereign effects to hide the clinging dangerous
dust. A grey-green bedspread covered the couch which was
soon to see the birth of a new life. In a glumly-grey jug on a
bedside table, a massive spike of crimson gladioluses flamed a
challenge to the bum-pomp of all the room's pattern: a
present from a friend, and no indication by the nursing-home
of any desire to brighten and sanctify the room.

Various kinds of ailments were tethered to this place; there
was a patient down with double pneumonia, a lady trying to
wriggle out of mental dementia through having nothing to do
and taking too much drink to pass away God's good time, a
duodenal-ulcer case, and another of appendicitis – not a merry
or a wholesome throng to greet a new-born babe. Britannia,
mother of jellabies, stretching out her generous hand to teach
children of Africa, Asia, and the West Indies, shoves her own
children behind her, and squanders the priming force of her
people. The thought given to the mind and body of the English
child is the thought, not of a cultural leadership, but one as
low as that given by a rude council pow-wowing under a cow-
hide wigwam. Childless with all her children. The middle class
are to blame. Caught in the glare of their snobbery, they strain,
not after knowledge, but after Eton; not after human development, but after a nameless name; suffering indignity and
danger, rather than give up a few pieces of silver, a good
address on their notepaper, and a badged blazer for a son or a
daughter. Ad ardua sed disastra.

The two housemaids seemed to have the minds of backward

ten-year-olds; they were untidily dressed, clumsy, and inco-
herent when asked a question; giggling rather than answering,
mouths sloppily open; a grin without a gusto. Cheap labour
out of some Institution, thought Sean. Besides the matron,
whom Sean never saw, there were two nurses – one for the
day, one for the night; each, from what was said, eager to find
another place. Won't find it easy, thought Sean, for they didn't
soothe his idea of what efficiency and carefulness should be.
Clearly the place was being run for profit; not clean or competent profit, but profit grimed with a corpulent greed. Eileen
agreed with him, but hushed him whenever a protest in his
mind rushed forward to the tip of his tongue. Many a time he
had sat at Eileen's bedside, fuming at the way things were
being done – the wobbling walk of the housemaids, the dirty
tray of slopped-over tea, the dirty window, the whole aspect of
continual carelessness; fuming so plainly that Eileen stretched
out a hand to touch his arm, and whispered – quiet, Sean, you
will only make bad things worse with a temper. Then he would
close his eyes, sever the tension by a great effort, and sigh for
the cowardice of his human heart. Children brought to birth in
a dust-bowl. The Little Johns and Maid Marions, whose people
had enough to pay for decent attention, were getting the worst
in the world. No complaints. The middle class would stick
anything to preserve the wan and wasteful manner of their
status, burying under it the best of their intelligence, energy,
and sense. They chloroform themselves with snobscent. The
moment a boy shapes himself into the world, while he is giving
his first cry, his parents dwell in Etonsville; if a girl and an
anglican, then Roedean – Roedean, oh, girl! If a roman
catholic, then a posh school of the Sacred Heart or the
Ursulines to learn all she needeth to know of how and when to
ape the gentility. Cease to be human, learn to be swell. They
shove aside even the sacred name of hospital and hang out
that of nursing-home, so that they may feel themselves of a
loftier mien than the mass of men, even in sickness and in
pain. Sheltering a stranger, entertaining a guest – so hangs the
holy name of hospital; and to the Christians all sick persons
should be guests of Jesus. He is on His way to visit a sick
woman – no, a lady. What hospital? No hospital, man; a
nursing-home. Does Jesus, then, turn his nose, too, up at a
hospital? Oh, no, not exactly that; but the sick lady's a lady
and thinks herself something of a nob snob, and must stretch
herself higher than the ordinary commonality of the country.

When I was a lady, a lady, a lady,
When I was a lady, a lady was I.

The sacrifice of children on the altars of Eton and Harrow
to a will-o'-the-wisp conception of grandeur is as superstitious
as, and sillier and much more subtly dangerous than, the sacri-
fices offered at Stonehenge to the Sun.

Eileen and he went for walks in the afternoon to give her
exercise, waiting, waiting for the event to happen; all along the
streets nearby, fearful to go too far lest the thing might come
upon them in the twinkling of an eye. Down and up a bit of
Knightsbridge, glimpsing Hyde Park, but never venturing in; in
and out by Lowndes Square, out on to Cadogan Square and
Cadogan Gardens, till they knew every number on every hall-
door. Round and round the village, round and round the village, as they had done before. Down the opposite way for a
change; slow march down Sloane Street and around Sloane
Square, and around again, bringing back to him memories of
his first fast days in London, his memory helped by the desire
to creep away from the fear that was with him now, walking
with Eileen. She was silent, dwelling in her condition, and so
helped him to slip away from the fear of a too-sudden birth.
Here, in her daughter-in-law's flat, he had met Lady Gregory,
and had set out with her to see T. P. O'Connor, MP, at
Morpeth Mansions, within the shadow of the roman catholic
cathedral; going to enlist his aid in the recovery of the Lane
Pictures; aid promised, but never given. Small blame to
O'Connor, for he was then three parts in the grave, and was
now being suckled from a bottle. No more chablis, no more
sauterne; no more running after a skirt; no more fiery words,
cheers, and the roll of drums, at the yearly Feast in Liverpool
in honour of St Patrick, Ireland's senior saint. Green grew the
rushes here no longer for T.P. After getting to know Sean, he
had appealed to him to go in his place to the feast in Liverpool, promising him 'lashin's of eating and drinking', and had
waxed very angry when Sean refused to go. Born in Athlone,
Ireland's centre, here he was now – a man who had healed
everything Irish in him, except his humbug. An abortioned soul
from the O'Connor clan. What a wild difference there was
between this Irishman and the other Irishman, Shaw!

They rang the bell of the flat's door, and O'Connor's nurse,
an elderly woman without a uniform, opened it and showed
him and Lady Gregory into the sitting-room; left them stand-

ing in the room's centre, pausing at the door to say, 'I'll wheel him in to you in a minute. Not any exciting talk, mind, to curdle his stomach – I don't want to be up half the night with him.'

After a swift look around, Lady Gregory and he subsided on to a crimson-coloured couch, sitting side by side, stunned when the look of the room had hammered itself into their eyes. It was ghasty and almost terrifying: red couch, red carpet, red curtains, red-seated chairs, and on the wall opposite, protected by a redder canopy, pulled to at night, looped back now, the picture of O'Connor himself, painted by John Lavery in his worst mood. The heavy, commonplace face, looking as if a dead hand had limned it, stared out with a simper at anyone daring to look at it. Me, the O'Connor, privy councillor and chief perennial of the Scotland Division of Liverpool. Flanking it on either side was a wooden corinthian pillar, heavily gilded; surmounting the picture was a gothic gilded roof, like a baldacchino; and underneath were four wide and shallow steps, covered with crimson carpet, leading the looker up to a platform from which to get a face-to-face view of the face in the painting. Around the fireplace was a thigh-high heavy brass fender, ledge upholstered in red leather. Lady Gregory, seeing the stunned aspect of Sean's face, laid a soothing hand on his arm.

—Don't look at id, she said. Tlose your eyes and dink only of the Lane Pictures.

So this room represents the boyo who yearly acts as Ireland's Ambassador, showing forth Ireland's culture and civilization throughout the centuries of her independence and the hard and bitter centuries of subjection to an alien power and still more alien culture; yearly shows forth the features of Ireland in Liverpool on St Patrick's Day!

—Tlose your eyes, Sean; dank Dod de curtains aren't green.

The truculent-looking nurse, her brawny body stiff, her face set firm, wheeled the hero in and placed him close to the carpeted steps going up to the picture: the real McCoy was now before them.

—Not too much talk from you, now, said the brawny one, bending down over the chaired giant, or I'll have to be stiffening your heart with tonics. At the door, before departing, she turned to say D'ye hear me – all of you?

It must have looked a comical sight – Lady Gregory and

Sean sitting on the crimson couch in the crimson room, their
eyes half shut, slanting down towards the red carpet, trying to
hide from the picture on the wall and shade their eyes from
the razzle-dazzle of the gilding; the over-blown body of the
privy councillor seeping over the framework of the chair, the
round head lolling on the bulging chest, the little eyes pushed
back into the head by fleshy folds, the big pudgy hands
clumped on the chair-arms, unable to grip them, the thick
voice, with the hint of a gasp in every sentence, telling them
that it would speak to this Minister and to that one, and that
the Lane Pictures would shortly be hanging on the wall of the
Dublin Gallery. A room in Huis-Clos, from which Sean, in his
mind's eye, could see the bulky steeple of Westminster Catholic Cathedral looming in the background, hearsed in this
pathetic figure and halting voice; Lady Gregory nodding her
sage old head at every promise of help trickling from the wide
and twitching mouth of this dying old humbug, able still to
convince far greater minds than his own of his amazing influence and the depth of his sincerity.

—A mistake, Lady Gregory, he was saying, his poor tongue
and shaky lips hesitating over the words; it will be rectified,
believe me.

—A lousy, rotten, god-damned robbery, if you ask me! burst
from Sean, and Lady Gregory's soothing hand was touching
his arm again.

He could scarcely contain himself listening to the blown-out
blather of this Irish leader who had always led everything from
behind, knowing that O'Connor was at his old game of hum-
bugging Lady Gregory as he had the Irish people who had sent
him, year after year, to the British Parliament to represent
himself. Now all this self-interest had shrunk down into the
recessiveness of a wheelchair. Here was the softwood face trying to be the same again, carrying the adulation of power to
the very verge of the grave. Here were the remains of one who
had declared during the Gladstonian and ecclesiastical opposition to the great Parnell that 'Parnell had done too much for
the Irish people to go back on him now. Ireland is socially,
enthusiastically, and fiercely on the side of the Irish leader';
and the very next day, the scut recanted with a shout, signing a
declaration that he was with the priests and against Parnell.
Well, today, none of the young Irish remember O'Connor;
most of the young Irish remember Parnell.

Sean's surmising was cut off by the entrance at the door of the old boy's caretaker. She stopped at the door for a few moments, looking in at them and listening to the talk; then she suddenly strode into the room's centre, and catching the hand-bar of the weal-chair, she whisked it round to face the door.

—You've talked enough for one day, she said, tartly. I don't want to be up half the night with you. Say goodbye now, and come along.

—Send me signed copies of your plays, Sean, he said, departing.

—He will, said the old Lady, swiftly, before Sean could reply, for de sake of de Lane Pictures; and the chair-imprisoned privy councillor, father of the House of Commons, vanished, and was never seen again by either of them.

He had signed the plays, and had sent them to the dying fossil; signed as if to a friend, for a scut who had helped to hound the noble Parnell to his grave. Oh, what a rogue and peasant slave he was to do it! One of the worst things his life had ever done. A tare in the tapestry. Right in the place, too, where he had woven the name of Parnell with reverence and with love.

—We'll go, said the old Lady, to the roman catholic cathedral, and look within id to forget de derrible room.

They had gone before to the Tate Gallery, had sat on a bench together, for she loved to look around wide, long, lofty, secular buildings, or those consecrated to what men called religion. Here they had sat for a long time, quiet, forgetting about the coloured misery of the dying pictures in the Turner Room; the hell of a golden glory. Here they were now, gazing into the womb of the Catholic cathedral, full of a flourishing dimness revelled in by thousands, with the lighted tops of candles twinkling patiently away in the far distance where the altar stood. Her old head was slightly thrust forward gazing towards where the Host must be resting somewhere between the twinkling lights of the altar. Sean guessed that she slyly welcomed into her mind a venturesome idea of the Real Presence, and that she might have been reconciling her own minor idea of the mystery with the major one of the roman catholic church, manifested by the exposition of the Sacrament in twice ten thousand churches. Here, then, according to the Christian Faith, Jesus was looking at the old Lady and she was looking at Him; very reverently she was looking, but calmly, for she was a venturesome and courageous woman, of good standing, combining the spirit of Martha with the spirit of Mary; the grace of useful common sense with the rarer grace of a gay and a vivid imagination. With these thoughts about her was mingled one of his own on the contrast between the seductive gloom of this big building and the glare of the little red room they had just left.

They came out, and waited for a suitable bus to carry her home. One came gracefully along and purred into a stop beside them. She gripped the handle, but the step was high and the ageing body was stiff; she stood rigid for a few moments, a hand gripping either handle, and Sean wondered if he should give her a handy hoosh up; but she tightened her lips, gave a pant, then a spring, and the stiff body lighted on the platform, her two feet landing together with a bang. She shot down into a seat, tucked in her black dress so that he could sit comfortably beside her, smiled and patted his hand, as if to say, Here we are, and we're bound for the Rio Grande.

Lady Gregory had married when he was being born, and it took many a long year before they met, before even he was prepared to meet her. Each had travelled his or her own different way, very different ways, yet, in the winter of her life, in the late summer of his, they had suddenly met, each facing towards the same direction. The pattern of life she was weaving, and the one he wove, mingled and stood out bravely in the tapestry of Irish life. The Lane Pictures should be facing out from the tapestry both had woven, but she is dead, and the pictures are as far away as ever. She can no longer trouble government officials, at home or abroad, with her vexatious babble about them. De Valera never thinks about them; Costello never bothers about them; neither does MacBride; nor do many at work or at rest in Kathleen ni Houlihan's Four Beautiful Fields. The younger ones growing up, one day, may, he hopes, stretch out a stronger arm, and take them back from the thieves.

Both gone now – the poor old parliamentary humbug and Lady Gregory herself. It was odd and a little sad that in the thousands of years that were in the future's flow, she would never be seen again, her charming lisp would never again mingle among the sounds of people speaking. Had she a place in the Universe now? In the memory of some, she had. A fleeting immortality; the leaves falling one by one from the tree

of remembrance till the tree is bare, and the tree is dead. What
is beyond us outside the world of what we see, hear, smell,
taste, and touch, we don't know. Not one of the philosophies
that has tried to hem us in or bring us out has told us, or can
tell us, anything outside of ourselves and our world. Science
has told us a lot, will tell us more, and we must wait for
science to tell us all. One philosopher has said that science,
having driven values from the universe, shows itself to be nor
good, nor beautiful, nor just, nor holy. To Sean, science was all
these things. It wasn't content with a guess, however good,
just, or holy the guess might be. A philosophy that set out to
solve a problem created another of its own. Whenever he had
read, or tried to read, a system of philosophy, he had always
heard the echo of a song, a song he had often chanted himself
when going round in a ring in a Dublin street:

> Oats and beans and barley grows,
> Oats and beans and barley grows,
> But you nor me nor nobody knows
> How oats and beans and barley grows.

The two of them, Eileen and he, now were concerned most
nearly with the strange energies of the body, and with the life a
body was soon to bring forth to the world they knew. More
children, with little thought for them, and less room. Round
and round the two of them travelled, past the Court Theatre,
where she had acted in a play of his, and where both of them
had first seen Shaw's *Back to Methuselah*; fainting memories
just now, for they had new events to record, bringing hope and
not a little fear. Up and down again, past a school where in a
tiny closed-up yard the children could but ape the action and
spirit of play; down and up, Eileen's steps growing slower, an
odd spasm of pain smiting her, sending them back at a quickened rate to the nursing-home. Halfway there, Eileen would
say with a laugh, False alarm, and round and round they
would go again.

One day in the hall of the home, about to go out, he saw a
look of disquiet on her face, and, answering an inquiry, she
said she didn't feel too good; then suddenly bent down in a
violent spasm of pain.

—I won't go out, she said; I feel it may come on me any
minute now.

I will greatly multiply thy sorrow and thy conception; in sorrow thou shalt bring forth children; thy desire shall be unto thy husband, and he shall rule over thee. A fine Dadlantic Charter! The king put into the parlour, the queen put into the kitchen. Woman has brought forth children with pain, and her husband has ruled over her for twice a thousand years; but things are changing, and, and now only, the church is busy bouncing this bonnie law about. The pain, subjection, and sorrow have declined with the years, and will be entirely banished in some year to come. The agony and sweat were still with the woman, but not so dangerously now, though shouts were still needed to prevent a woman being forced to go through this furnace of pain and danger too often. There must be a good rest between one ordeal and another. He for one would oppose the celebate clerics who frightened women into having a child year by year till she was battered into dumb agreement with her devitalized life and the ghastly problems of attending to a horde of children. One of the ghastliest pictures he ever saw was one in a roman catholic journal showing the Pope with a father and mother and their twenty children; and another of Cardinal Spellman, a grin on his face, standing before a kneeling Pole surrounded by his wife and fifteen children, who had travelled to New York by air, though the journal said they were utterly penniless. It was said that the Cardinal had emptied his wallet of a wad of notes, and had given them all to the old Polish ram; the journal adding that the Cardinal had entered New York without a make. Left himself without a dime! Your need is greater than mine. And how! Now what sarcastic voice whispers that it wouldn't be long till the Cardinal's wallet would be as full as ever with the finest and fairest of dollar notes? Since then the Cardinal has given ten thousand pounds to Ireland's St Vincent de Paul Society; Dublin's Archbishop has given a thousand; and Cardinal Griffin two thousand towards the rebuilding of Southwark Cathedral; three plates in the trim hands of three prelates, one carrying a thousand, the second, two thousand, and the third, ten thousand. Pie from the sky. God's Episcopate is doing very nicely, thank you. Gold and silver have I none – it's all in notes, crisp and fresh from the bankery. There's more, lads, where these came from. Do they work overtime?

Sean would like to see a celibate cleric stay with a pregnant woman day after day, hour after hour, during the last three

months of her trial; to try to help her along, entertain her with
chat, go for walks with her, bring change of thought through a
game of cards: it would learn the cleric a little; teach him that
birth wasn't just a thing to make a joke about from a pulpit.
It's easy for them to rant to women about their duties to their
husbands, or to praise the big families. Some day the clerics
will get their answer: like the woman coming out from a Mission to women, conducted by a friar of orders white boosting
bigger catholic familes, shouting at them to reproduce catholic
life quicker and oftener; the flushed and angry woman coming
out from it all with an angry ejaculation of – Jasus! I wish I
knew as little about it as he does!

A houseful of children! No glory left in that boast now. We
have begun to realize that children need not only life, but
liberty too. For too long the children have been buried alive in
church, in school, in the home. As Bernard Shaw has said,
'The most grotesque, wild, and costly absurdity in our social
order is the strictly enforced reservation of large tracts of
country as deer forests and breeding-grounds for pheasants
whilst there is so little provision of the kind made for children'. Sean knew himself of a discussion about a playing-field
for the young in a country town lasting for twenty-five years;
and, today, the field isn't yet ready for the newer young born
into the locality. The child is surrounded with enemies who
imprison it in a corner called a school, or a corner called a
church; it is a great concession when it is let loose on the
playing-field. One great blessing enjoyed by the kids of the
poor is that they spend a great part of their lives on the streets;
the parents have to let them, for there is no room in the house
for them. They get many a blow, but a blow is nothing to the
stealing of curiosity and conscience from the mind of the
child: those, says Shaw, 'who devote themselves to the very
mischievous and cruel sort of abortion which is called bringing
up a child in the way it should go; perverting that precious and
sacred thing the child's conscience into an instrument of our
own convenience, and to use that wonderful and terrible power
called Shame to grind our own axe'. How conceited we all are
to wish our children to be like ourselves! She's very like her
mother; he's the dead spit of his father! Put into the same
kind of schools, made to read the same kind of books, pray the
same way, think the same way, and make it a custom, instead
of a religion, to honour the God of Abraham, Isaac, and Jacob.

And such schools and such books! The books are getting better now, most of the schools getting worse. Hundreds and hundreds of them in Ireland and England, packed with children, though fit only as the dwelling-place of the rat, the cockroach, and the woodlouse. No; children, as Bernard Shaw says, 'should look up to their parents, not as an example, but as a warning'.

Childer, beware, childer, take care!
They're eager to make
You waddle through life like a duck, like a drake;
To turn each new soul to a shivering fake,
For ever too frail just to open its bake;
Quack-quacking consent to men and to movements well out
    on the make.

Bent down in a spasm of pain, Eileen stretched out a hand to touch Sean, and said, don't get frightened. It will be all right; don't worry.

He hurried back into the hall to shout up the stairs, Nurse, nurse! The only nurse there came slowly down the stairs, an impatient look on her face as she asked, Well, what's wrong now?

—The woman's in her labour! said he, fearfully; bring the matron.

—The matron's out, and won't be back till night-time.

—Phone her, then; phone her, woman!

—She didn't leave word where she was going; I don't know where to phone. You are both too anxious. Try to be a little braver. It won't happen today, or tomorrow either. She took Eileen by the arm. Go off, now, for a nice walk with your husband; and saying so, she turned back, and went up the stairs again.

They stood hesitant in the gloomy hall, then began to cross it to go out; but she bent again in a greater spasm of pain than before.

—Go home, she said to him, go home. Go home – I'll manage all right; and she ran from the hall and made for the room, with its dull bed, duller curtains, and dullest of carpets; while he, running up the stairs, caught the retreating nurse harshly by the arm.

—Get the doctor, woman, he said, fiercely, if you can't get

the matron; and go to her yourself till the careless and negligent bitch comes back!

A look of alarm flooded the nurse's face, and she rushed from him into the room of delivery. She was of little use, and Eileen had to bear the most of it alone; the frantic rush in the stripping of herself; the flinging of herself on the bed, the deep crescendo of ascending pain that seemed to be engendering death entering through a riving body, with ne'er a drop of chloroform to modify the biting torment of the struggle, and ne'er a voice near to say a word to cheer her on; for the air-tight box of bandages and drugs was away in a cupboard in the house-top, so that by the time it was hurried down and opened for use, by the time hot water and towels had been gathered, the courageous woman had delivered a boy herself. A young girl inexperienced, just beginning to realize and comprehend the seriousness of her own life and the lives budding from her; so sensitive that she shuddered at the thought of any child in pain; a lass who had had her first-born in her own home, a clever, sympathetic doctor beside her, a capable nurse at his right hand to help; now having her second one alone, surrounded by hasty confusion, with nothing ready, and with those who were, perhaps, competent to help, away in other places doing other things. Fortunately, she was vigorous and healthy, and had a curious quietness in serious circumstances and time of stress; so throughout all the pain that stormed over and through her, she kept her alert mind set on a determination to deliver the boy safely; a brave girl fought incompetence and carelessness to a standstill, and gave successful birth to a big and healthy boy.

Their one idea now was to get away from the nursing-home as soon as possible, for she had discovered that the babe, when taken from her after a feed, was often in the charge of a maid with a thickened mind, and that the child was set to sleep in the operating theatre, reeking with the smell of ether; added to the suspicion that the ether was helped by an opiate whenever the mite happened to be restless enough to disturb the nurses.

They fled from the curse-home on a cold, grey day in January, the strong tail of an east wind teasing their faces, tilting at the dust in the kennels, and chiding the scraps of paper thrown carelessly aside by passers-by; grey and cold, with a sky of a deeper and heavier grey hanging down overhead; no comfort without, but joy within that they were getting away from a place that was a menace to the health, and so to the life, of their child.

Some kids never escape – kids in orphanages, institutions, and foundling homes, not to mention those sent to industrial schools because, it is said, their parents are unable to control them. What a time the most of these must have! Never free for a second; always under discipline, for ever watched. He remembered visiting the home of a worker whose two boys had returned after serving their time in an institution. Every time a question was asked of them, they sprang to their feet with a yessir or nosir, waiting till they were told that they might sit down again, a voice behind Sean proclaiming that it had never met such good-mannered children before. When they got used to life outside their institution, however, they changed so as to become the most ill-mannered and ill-natured boys in the locality. There was the institutional school in Ireland, housing kids from five to ten, doddered by a group of nuns, kept in a gloomy building, well away from the convent where the nuns lived. At night the dormitories were locked and bolted, and all were in charge of an old woman who, herself, had been an inmate all her life. The building took fire; the kids were locked in; there was no light; and before the miserable help of the local fire-brigade came carrying ladders too short, thirty-three of the kids were burned to death in the dark. There was the gentle roman catholic Brother who caught hold of a child tricking at the gateway of a college and locked him up in the great hall, so that, when night came, the youngster in a frenzy of fright managed to climb up to a clerestory window, open it, and fling himself on to the pavement below, crippling himself for life; the gentle Brother pleading afterwards that all he meant to do was to frighten the boy, careless of knowing that to try to frighten a child is to try to injure it, not only in body, but in soul, too. A second gentle Brother, this an anglican one, who, helping to dish out dinners in Dartington Hall to the evacuees, demanded of a boy why he was a little late for the meal, and, on being told that the farmer kept him late helping on the farm, shouted that that was no excuse, and shouted louder that the boy would get no dinner that day; ignorant that the boy's explanation was no excuse, but a reason for his lateness. Still another gentle Brother, a roman catholic one again, who lugged a lad of fourteen – the working age – from an industrial school to a hotel that wanted a Boots, and asked the

Manager what were the hours the lad would work, and the pay
he would get; on being told that the hours were seven in the
morning till eleven at night, and the wages would be ten shillings a week, the Brother replied emphatically that ten shillings
were too much for a start, and ordered that the boy should be
given five shillings a week for a year or two to prevent him
from getting too hot in his leather. There was the widow who
couldn't keep her children properly on her widow's pension,
the Authorities said. She had kept them perfectly clean, fed
them as well as her means would allow, dressed them as best
she could: there was no complaint whatever against the
woman's efforts; yet in a frenzy of tearful protest by widow
and children, they were wrenched away, and handed over to
an Institution by the Irish Authorities, who paid the Institution
three times the amount received by the widow in the form of
her pension. Had she had so much herself, she could have kept
her little ones in clover. There was no yelp on the part of the
clerics against this interference of the State with the rights of
the parent. Indeed, they quietly commended it. The State can
do no wrong when it serves priest and prelate.

Oh, the sacredness of family life! So they say, so they sing,
so they even shout. Yet, as Shaw proves, most parents who can
afford it get their children away from them as far and as long
as possible. Tidy incomed protestants and catholics hasten
their kids off to boarding school, seeing them only for a few
weeks a year during the holidays. Oh, the tiresome holidays!
The famous Roman Catholic writer, Evelyn Waugh, has told
the world, over the wireless, that he 'sees his children only
during the holidays; that he never carries them on his shoulders, or plays ball with them; but that when they come to years
of coherent speech, he associates with them'. A very important
person, a model da. The higher schools, public and private, the
highschool convents of the Sacred Heart and the Ursulines,
are crammed with imprisoned kids; away from their people,
outside the family, living a community life, so dreaded and
damned by the clerics whenever they preach to the poor. The
domestic hearth has often been a cold one. Imposition on the
child, with God's bells ringing it in, from morn to night; from
cradle to maturity, till the newness and freshness of a young
life becomes a worn-out thing. Do what I have done; say as I
have said; think as I have thought; read what I have read; look
at what I have seen. Follow your leader. Example is a per-

petual buzz in the ear of a kid, loud as the buzz of a may-bug.
The last thing to be done is to let a child see for itself, hear for
itself, think for itself, and, when hands are old enough to be
used steadily, do for itself. Sean knew a father who, according
to his own tale, kept everything readable he thought to be
vulgar (even *Treasure Island*), and persistently read to the lad
Bible stories only. The result was that the lad, whenever possible, made a dive for a Comic. Now the Bible stories are fine,
however fantastic some of them may be, but, as Shaw points
out, the Bible is not enough.

The sage says, 'The real bible of modern Europe is the whole
body of great literature in which the inspiration and revelation
of Hebrew Scripture has been continued to the present day. It
cannot supply the need of such modern revelations as Shelley's
Prometheus or the 'Nibelung's Ring' of Wagner. There is nothing in the Bible greater in inspiration than Beethoven's ninth
symphony. Only a foolish one would substitute *The Imitation
of Christ* for *Treasure Island* as a present for a boy or a girl, or
for Byron's *Don Juan* as a present for a lover or his lass. And
the most dangerous art in the effort to help the young to dis-
cover a form of art that will delight them naturally, is the art
that presents itself as religious ecstasy. For religious purposes,
Ivanhoe and the Templar make a good enough saint and a
good enough devil.' Of course they do; and, when the boy and
the girl get a little older, there is the second Saint Bernard
waiting for them with wisdom, wit, and laughter; waiting, too,
to hear them take three solemn vows against poverty, obedience, and a chastity that belies life, forcing a woman to pose as
a portrait of good works and skin-deep satisfaction, and young
men to form a faction against the first clause of the creed of
life, and to hunger secretly and silently for a woman's favour,
for, as Langland tells us, 'There are no hardier, hungrier men
than men of Holy Church'.

Childermass – the Mass held in honour of the Holy Innocents, slain, according to the fable, by Herod in the year of
one. Time now to think about the unholy innocents born into
the world each day of a passing year; think more about them
than we do. There is more care given to hens, more diligence
in the gathering of their eggs, than there is in the care, and
gathering up, of our children. Rachel has now another crowd
of children, but she no longer weeps, though they are injured
and degraded in slum, school, and even, at an older age, in the

high-toned colleges of our land; till at the age of three score
and ten, they are still frightened children, afraid of the light
whereas once they shivered in the dark, thunderstruck now
that the old woman tossed up in a blanket ninety-nine times as
high as the moon, carrying a broom to brush the cobwebs from
the sky, has been replaced by the scientist who has brushed
away the cobwebs as well as the woman, and has shown us the
mighty nothingness of expanding space filled with a multitude
of blazing suns; or, in Ireland, its effect may be a simple and
consummate love of making money, for, as the poet, Kavanagh, tells us, 'In Ireland nothing else save money talks'. The
voice of God declares the rise of shares in the Stock Exchange,
and the price of fat cattle in the market.

Don't run off with the idea that this Childermess is celebrated here only and in Ireland, too. One of America's biggest
and best-known publishing firms has printed a folder telling us
that over two million of American children do not go to
school; that outmoded equipment and obsolete text-books are
in use in many schools; that many buildings are in sad dis-
repair, and that classrooms are overcrowded and teachers
underpaid and overworked. The folder further says that during
the last ten years, three hundred and fifty thousand teachers
left the public schools because of bad conditions, and that
fewer and fewer students are entering the teaching profession.
It says further that the USA spends one and a half per cent of
its National Income on education, while Britain spends over
twice as much and the Soviet Union more still. One father,
looking into a school attended by his son, found at the edge of
a fine residential district a school where the children had to go
down flights of stairs to the washroom which was without
flush toilet, soap or towels, and which served the whole building. There is more in the folder of the same sensible wail,
showing how governors, spiritual pastors, and masters value
the worth of the kids to the nation; though these very kids will
be the nation in another hour's time.

Millions will grow up to be unable to read *Moby Dick,
Treasure Island*, or *Little Boy Blue*. Won't know enough
arithmetic to be able to count their blessings. Won't dare to
have minds rising higher than the philosophy of donald duck,
or be warier in the ways of art than the words and music of
crooning swing king bing crosby.

We must think of the kiddies. We do, of course – at Christ-

mas especially. That's the kids' festival above all others; cakes
and wails. Christmas beer and bells, and the kids love bells.
Ring out, wild bells. Ring out the old, ring in the new; ring out
the false, ring in the true.

A lesson there for all of us, Mick. Yeah. Lay the red carpet
down for the Child and the children on the one day of the
year. Tinsel the stable couch with colours that fade when the
night must fall. The Crib. Oh, come, let us adore Him. Where
'r you pushing, you young scut? What are you pushing for?
You want to see the kings and the cow? Well, you'll wait till
your eldhers have had a look at them first. If you were my kid,
I'd learn you to respect your eldhers. I'd warm your little arse
for you! Where were you reared at all? Oh, come, let us adore
Him. Shout out your praise and your prayer, Mick; shout
them out to the little lay figure lying on the yellow straw filling
the manger in a lowly cattle-shed. Bring in the holly and the
ivy, the mistletoe, too; and line the walls, and hide the dirt
with the green leaf, the red berry of the holly, the white one of
the mistletoe. Blast you, you little pusher, where 'r you shoving? Want to see the cow? Didja never see a cow in your life
before? Don't you see hundreds of them walkin' the streets
every damned day? Doesn't it look grand, Mick? Yeah. Just
like what it musta looked like once in royal David's city, long
ago, wha'? Looks like it was all real. Yeah. Oh, man, looka
the shepherds in their velvets and their ermines. Them's the
kings, you thick! Of course; I know well, know well, no hell
no hell, now! Oh, boys, a stable for the King of Glory. Oh,
lowly Lord. Glory to God in the lowliest! It was a stable, you
thick, because there was nowhere else to go; there was no
room in the Inn. There are tens of thousands of kids born daily
in lowlier sheds than this one, and no kings either, nor a star
to light them up, or even a single shepherd bothering a head
about them; only a wail from a mother wondering what she
was going to do now. Nunna that kinda talk here, Mick. God
rest you merry, man. They are looking after the childer. This
very day, in churchtown, in churchtown, a handful of kiddies
are getting presented with half a dozen of newly minted pennies in remembrance of the gold presented to the little Jesus.
Shining like gold themselves, the pennies are. Lullay, lullay.
We must all cherish the childer. Suffer the little ones to come
to me – remember? We remember all right. They are the newly
lighted candles on the altar of the world. They are the nuts

gathered by the church in the month of May. Here we come
gathering scuts in May – remember? Precious jewels, precious
jewels, His loved and His own. Oh, yes, we must cherish the
childer, The kiddies' day, Mick, the kiddies' day. And why,
then, aren't your own kiddies here? They aren't here because
they were bold and misbehaving, that's why. They'll have to be
better childer if they want to have a gawk at the crib. They're
be themselves at home while the missus 's at Mass. Dtch dtch!
And you left the kids at home alone, with nothing but their
toys? No, no toys neither. No, no toys for them this Christmas
morning. No, not till they learn to behave themselves properly.
Deliberately sleeping it out this morning, and neglecting to
light the fire, get the breakfast, and bring up a cup of tea to the
missus and me to stave off some of the cold of the first taste of
the day. No, no toys for the like of them. I made them warm
with a fine hot larruping instead. I can tell you they're feeling
a sorry little pair today. If I teach them nothing else, I'll teach
them to think of others before themselves. I'll learn them reverence for their parents, for the Holy Child, and for the Holy
Child's day. They'll remember next year and be more careful.
Hard? How's it hard? 'A good larruping's better than a
cuddle', said an eminent judge t'other day. 'Snatch a doll from
the hand of a child of six', said Monsignor Wiseman, 'and at
thirty it'll know the greatness of self-denial.' I'm a catholic,
same as you, and I don't give a curse what the Monsignor said
– I wouldn't do it. I'd be damned rather than do it. Hush,
that's not the kind of talk for here. I won't listen, Mick; I
won't listen, I won't lis— Don't be 'Micking' me! I tell you the
one who'd jerk a toy from a child of six is nothing less 'n a
savage lowser. If I met such a one even up above, I'd give him
a hot one in the snot that would make heaven a place of pain
for the time being! Your talk's edging into blasphemy, Mick; I
won't listen. Young souls must be laundered into good beginnings. Original sin, remember! *Ad roddium salvationem
juvenilia est:* The rod is youth's salvation. Youth must be kept
under; corrected continually. Sin must be bet outa them. Original sin, remember! All God's chillun got stings.

    There is no end, no end to the jamboree of injustice to chil-
dren, the worst of them veiled in the pretence that all is
prompted by the love of God and the child. In a booklet about
Matt Talbot, one who called himself a 'slave to Mary', and to
prove it wore steel chains round his belly so that they rusted

into the flesh, we are told that this Matt said 'The kingdom of
heaven was promised not to the sensible and educated, but to
such as possessed the spirit of little children'. Put the kids in
irons, and make them more presentable to Jesus. Here's
another example of it culled from a Christian catholic journal: 'The mysteries of a complicated alphabet were expounded
to me by a black-robed ogre with the aid of a leathern instrument, applied to my palms from time to time. I dared make no
complaint to my father, who, strangely blind to the genius of
his lovely boy, would have belted me with a great black belt,
remarking with an utter lack of sympathy: "If you won't take
it in at one end, I'll wallop it in at the other".' So we see that
weals on the arse and weals on the hands of a little child are,
after all, but the small matter of a joke. Biff! Whoosh!
Wallop! Purify the kid's vile body with a wealth of weals.
Monsignor James Redmond, Liverpool Diocesan Chancellor,
warned his listeners that magistrates weren't empowered to
order punishment by the birch to boys who had turned fourteen, adding that if parents only gave the much-needed corporal punishment, he would guarantee that juvenile delin-
quency would end within a year. Another cleric tells us that
cruel children (ignorant, apparently, that all kids are thoughtlessly cruel) should be birched, for, he says, when they hurt
others, it is reasonable that they should be warmed up themselves. Exorcising cruelty with further cruelty. Why is that
little child screaming? Oh, they're only knocking hell out of
her under the mantle of Mary. The sign of the three kindles
of piety: the whip, the cane, the crozier.

So, well within the borders of Battersea, Eileen and he went
on with their life, now widening out into a family; receiving
friends from Ireland, from Manhattan, Massachusetts, Penn-
sylvania, Minnesota, and California farther away, to say a few
words, and to let the great Republic shake hands with the little
one, standing unsteady yet on one foot only; old comrades
from Dublin who had gone with him through the great Lock-
Out of nineteen hundred and thirteen, grey now, and wrinkled,
like himself, but eager to go over again the scenes of battles
long ago, filling the room with their husky laughter, mix-
ing with the slender, silvery laughs of Eileen, when they told
Dublin stories of man's ridiculous conceit, or woman's comic
frailty. Souls so different from the jodhpurred souls of Battersea's middle class, so different from the soul of Tay Pay

O'Connor, MP, yet no different from his own or Eileen's, and very little from the soul of Lady Gregory or the soul of W. B. Yeats.

All mingled with the growth of their two sons, Breon and Niall, Eileen smiling and delightful with all comers against the background of a vanishing bank account; and through all these friendly and human activities, the casting of bread upon the waters in the writing of a first biographical book – *I Knock at the Door*.* Those who came, came, and in their going, went not, but left impressions clinging to the life of those to whom they came; came, and went not, the time T. S. Eliot was passing through his *Ash Wednesday* in prayer and meditation within the desert in the garden and the garden in the desert, in and out between the blue rocks, going in white and blue, colours of Mary's mantle and Mary's frock, hoping to hear and hear not, to care and care not, to be still among a thousand whispers from a you tree; they came, and were distrained to waver between loss and gain, for this was God's disposal, saying, The land thou tillest shall be plundered with thistle and with thorn, and in the sweat of thy face shalt thou eat bread. Sweat-stained bread. Tommy Tucker must sing for his supper. The life God gave cannot be silent, cannot be still; it has too much to say, too much to do to live; and he who runs away to hide, deserts the life that God gave. God has decreed the whole earth to be a forced labour camp, and so we must work before we eat. He has put wings to time, and so we can build from toil and time but a little corner in a little room for a little thought. To sit still and care not, in desert or garden, is a vain thing, and may but ripen a soul into drying dust that cannot be spat out like withered apple seed. The blue isn't always bright, and the white must at times be blemished in the cares of life and the keeping of a household going; the slender hands grow rough in time with the washing and the work. In the voice of many speaking, in the whirl of the world's changing, the word is heard; and the whirl of the world's changing is the word, and the noise of men is the word growing louder. Among all who come and go, who is there fit to say that in men's anxiety, their bargaining, their lovemaking, their laughter, there is no sign of the blue of Mary's mantle, the white of Mary's frock, or the red-like crimson of Jesu's jacket?

Sweat-stained comrades of building-site, railway line, and

* Pan Books, London, 1971.

ship-lined dock, you did what you could to make oncoming
life safer and sounder, in bitter strike and vengeful lock-out.
Coarse you were, but never common. Yes, we have all done
something to change the childermess to a Childermass of
security, health, and a bonnie-looking life. You, Promethean
Jim Larkin, with the voice born of the bugle and the drum,
Barney Conway and Paddy Walsh of the docks, Paddy
Mooney of the horses, Shawn Shelly of the workshop,
O'Casey of the pick and shovel; you, W. B. Yeats of the lovely
lyrics, Augusta Gregory of the little, the larger, laughing plays
and the wisdom of guidance, Shaw of the drama and the pro-
phecies, and Joyce of the sad heart and the divine comic mind,
touselling and destroying our mean conceits and our meaner
vanities. We all ate of the great sacrament of life together.

> Yes, we had some bread and wine,
> We were the Rovers;
> Yes, we had some bread and wine,
> For we were the gallant Soldiers.

> What car'd we for the red-coat men?
> We were the Rovers;
> What car'd we for the blue-coat men?
> For we were the gallant Soldiers.

Nothing, comrades.

CAMBRIDGE

A LONG taxi-drive carried Sean to Liverpool Street Station to catch a train going to Cambridge Town; the town of the three ships passing under a castellated bridge, flanked on either side by a fleur de lys and a rose – the rose of sharon and the lily of the valley. From the station at Cambridge, another taxi would whip him off to the University. A Society of St Catharine's College has pressed him into coming to give a lecture to the Society's members and their friends. Dear God, now he was on his way there! He was no lecturer; the word itself frightened him. Lecture: connected with the reading of scripture in a church; a formal discussion on some special subject. He couldn't be formal; he hadn't the gift. He had no special subject on which to descant, unless he were to descant on his own deformity of ignorance in all things. All subjects relating in any way to life's thousand activities were special to him; but he knew damn all about any of them. Some society or another in almost every university in England had, at one time or another, asked him to lecture, but he had refused all requests, save one he gave in the London School of Economics and one at Harvard. Even this request from the Cambridge Society's invitation he had first refused; and swearing he would ne'er consent, consented. Oh, dear God, he was on his way there now; on his way to Cambridge to deliver a lecture; to deliver the goods; sitting in a third-class carriage, buzzing along to the College on the Cam; away to Grantabrigge, the old Saxon name of the town. Swing low, sweet chariot, carrying me away from home.

It was odd, he thought, the idea flooding so many minds that the writer of a novel, of a play, of a book of verse, must have a wide knowledge of all things, human and divine. The nearer he got to the town, the more uncomfortable he felt; like as one might feel who kept lurching like a drunken man, conscious of instability, in a church procession, headed by a bishop. Steady, lad! It seemed to him that the Lord had departed out of Shyloh. Even if a writer (as apart from a scholar)

did know a lot about some things, it was another matter to
expose his knowledge to assembled listeners in an interesting
way. That was a gift, often transcending the knowledge itself,
for most people came to lectures, if not to be taught, at least to
be interested. Chin up, man. Come, let's thump the world with
talk.

—Cambridge next stop, thank God; said a voice from the
opposite end of the carriage.

He didn't want to be reminded of it. It was all very near
now. He'd have to don a mask, like Yeats, the minute the train
stopped. Hello, lads! Glad to meet you, and honoured to be
within the University. A smile on the kisser, too, and a look of
confidence, as if he took lecturing in his stride. Years ago he
had stood in halls, on platforms, often made of planks across
beer-barrels, at times in the midst of strife, surrounded by
armed police, speaking for Ireland or for Labour, without
hushing a second for a word, full of his own importance; speaking, maybe, a million words, often with eloquence, as often
maybe, without thought. Idle words? At the judgement day
man is to give an account of every idle word he spake. Of
every idle word man shall speak, he shall give account thereof
in the day of judgement; so Christ said, according to St
Matthew. Every idle word; one by one, not in bunches, but in
ones. A terrible thought! It will be a long session for everyman; an all-night sitting in a wilderness of words. What a
frightful thing if politicians were sentenced to listen throughout eternity to their own speeches; forced to listen in silence to
the speeches of others and their own, without permission even
to rise on a point of order; or, indeed, if playwrights had to sit
watching the performance of their own plays throughout
eternity, or the comic broadcasters forced to sit and listen to
their own jokes. The most lamentable punishment of all would
be the compelling of the clerics to sit down and listen to their
own sermons. A tiresome time for all. Idle words, idly thought,
idly spoken, idly sent aroving. The engineers of the soul hoist
with their own regards. The wings they thought would fly were
only vanes to beat the air, shown to be so now in the infirm
glory of this positive hour. What must we do, what can we do?
Nothing, but like Shaw's Jack Tanner, go on talking.

The title Sean had chosen for his talk had startled the Committee of the Society. They had never heard anything like it
before. He was to speak under the heading of *The Holy Ghost*

Leaves England. It puzzled them and probed them with embarrassment. There was a taint of religion in the title, and religion
is usually embarrassing, outside of a church, to all except to
atheists. Even the clergy, protestant and catholic, feel self-
conscious when they pronounce the name of God without the
sacristy; as can be seen in the apologetic, self-conscious, tiny
homilies appearing, week by week, in *The Sunday Times*, written by this anglican cleric, by that roman catholic priest. The
name of God sounds safe now only in Latin. It doesn't quite
fit in with the humour of the age. The name seems to have
become one of the idle words; and the clerics are to blame, for
week in, week out, their thoughts do not touch anything living,
or even anything dead.

Hello, lads! Here they were – two officials of the Society
waiting for him; St Catharine's College, the reds and the
blacks, holding out their hands in welcome. They had written
to Sean saying he was to dine with the Dons, but he had stipu-
lated that he should be with the lads, for he wanted to get into
touch with them to hear what they had to say, and what they
would do when they bid the University goodbye. Sean had
dinner with a crowd of them, all sending over glances, probably wondering what such a curious-looking guy had to say to
them. After dinner, a Committeeman told Sean that a professor wanted a word with him. More idle words! Sean hadn't
a keen desire to meet one laurelled with scholarship. A poor
scholar himself, he could learn more from a student than he
could from a professor. He was half-afraid of professors. He
asked the Committeeman to call for him in less than ten
minutes' time, before he was overwhelmed; and then went
round the grass quadrangle to the other college where the Professor waited for him. He was ushered into the apartment, a
very comfortable one, with cushioned settee and armchairs,
and the floor well carpeted. Well-filled bookcases, tidily set
against the walls; everything solid, with a sense of dimness and
static confidence over all. Very different from the lousy lordli-
ness of a London or a Dublin pub; but its dimness was illu-
mined gaily by some fine pictures painted by a young Welsh
artist, a friend of the Professor's and of Sean's. That was a
bond tying them for a while together.

They looked at the pictures, and talked of the hope they had
in the future of the young artist, while they sipped port from
finely cut glasses. The professor was a young man of about

forty, athletic-looking, quick in his movements, and rapid in
his talk. He had the air about him of knowing that everything
he thought of must be right. There was no cadence of query in
anything he said, even when he asked a question; he had already answered it himself. A man whose every thought was a
stride.

—Look here, O'Casey, he said, I want to ask your opinion
on whether our universities should or should not have the
power to send representatives to Parliament. The Leftists are
trying to abolish the long-established practice, and I am one of
those appointed to defend it; to vindicate the old traditional
right of the universities to have separate representation in Parliament, though vindication is needed only for fools. I needn't
tell you that, O'Casey; you know it yourself. It isn't permis-
sible to allow violence to be done to such an important practice.

—Black and red facing each other, thought Sean. Aloud, he
said: The privilege will be taken away from you.

—Eh? said the professor, surprised. Nonsense, man! If it
happened, knowledge and culture would be isolated from the
people. It would be a disaster, and well you know it.

—The privilege will be taken away from you, repeated Sean.

—What, whether it's foolish or wise, right or wrong? You
know, O'Casey, that the privilege, as you call it, is one
founded on centuries of experience, on severe common-sense,
preventing knowledge and culture from falling into neglect or
disrepute; for both begin and end with what the universities
think and do.

—When you defend university representation, said Sean,
you think only of two, your own and Oxford's. The others
don't swim into your vision at all. These two, with all others
close behind, don't form the beginning or the end of culture or
knowledge, sir. You can't imprison any aspect of one or the
other of them in a chair. And, to me, culture and knowledge
begin with Baa baa, black sheep; with the song, prose, and
wisdom of the nursery rhyme.

—You're trying to be funny, O'Casey. A university is an
acknowledgement that knowledge and culture are the flower
and fruit of our civilization.

—The universities may be all that, but their representatives
aren't. They have been invariably Tories, and defend, not
culture or knowledge, but wealth and the power of privilege.

The nursery rhyme, the song of the street, the quips and quali-
ties of the circus, the country fair, the dancing of boy with girl
in the evening hours, are the main part of our culture, coming
before, remaining behind, and surrounding the university, forg-
ing the shape of future life while the university is talking about
it.

—Stop quibbling, O'Casey. Stick to the point. I am introducing you to the university.

—And I'm introducing you to life, Professor. This is the first
time I ever stood within or without your gates; some years
ago, in a runabout through Oxford, I stood there for a moment, going in through one gate and out by another. What is it
to me that some think you and Oxford should send special
representatives to Parliament? What use are you to me there?
University men in the Commons are as useful to culture and
knowledge as the Bishops are to God in the House of Lords.

—You don't understand, O'Casey, and, I'm afraid, you
don't wish to understand. We don't represent knowledge and
culture; we are those things; we bring them in among the
materialistic thoughts of men, who, if they weren't reminded
of them, would forget them altogether. We make their presence felt there.

—Just as the Bishops make the presence of God felt in the
House of Lords.

—You're not a bit funny, O'Casey. Cambridge is too big to
be impressed by Irish wit. The question I put to you is more
important than the turning of a phrase. You have a grudge
against us because you never had the good fortune to pass
through a university. We, by our membership of the House of
Commons, represent thousands of highly educated men and
women in art, science, and literature, among a world of men.
You represent only yourself and your opinion.

—On the contrary, sir, I represent millions of men and millions of women, less scholarly, indeed, than your thousands;
but highly important all the same.

The professor was shocked into silence for some moments.
A hand lifting a glass of port stopped halfway up, and he
stared at Sean for several seconds.

—Oh, come now, O'Casey, he said, rather sharply, don't let
conceit run away with you! Don't think the few plays you've
written entitle you to represent millions!

—Oh, said Sean, laughing, I wasn't thinking of what I'd

written. Therein, I represent no one. It is in myself that I represent millions, in my upbringing, in my work for bread, in my experience, in my outlook on life, in my education. I am one of the great crowd who know you not, and we must know those to whom we give the power to vote in Parliament. We do not know even that you exist. We don't know the names even of those who represent the universities in Parliament. To recognize your right to stay in Parliament, we must have had a hand in putting you there.

—A damned ignorant attitude to take! And you don't condemn it, O'Casey; you even approve of it.

—Yes, I even approve of it.

—Then you've no mind of your own. You are forced to believe as a Party line dictates.

—No, not by any Party line; by my upbringing, by my experiences; just as your upbringing dictates your particular point of view. You do your best to infuse your students with your own manner and method, and when you say goodbye to a departing student, you put a hood on his shoulders and a parchment in his hand, hoping that your ideas will be hopelessly embedded in his head. You applaud the continuance of the older law and the older prophets that have gone beyond ripeness, and are turning rotten. It has all lasted long enough. A song from God is meant to sound in every ear, and not merely to be an echo in a university. When a mind becomes great, it leaves the university behind it, and joins the company of man. Coloured hoods are very charming, but they fade if the mind of the wearer isn't broader and more colourable than the hood. Literature, art, and science represent themselves. Milton, Shelley, Constable, Darwin, and Rutherford can go about without their cloaks.

A gentle knock, and the young man whom Sean had asked to come to get him away appeared at the door. I stand at the door, and knock.

—Well? asked the professor, glass of port in hand; What is it? What do you want?

—Mr O'Casey, sir – the Committee has sent me to fetch him.

—Mr O'Casey will come to you in a minute, and as the young man hesitated at the door, the professor said sharply, Be off! Just a small glass of wine, O'Casey, before you go.

A tart reception to the gentle knock. Bad manners on the

part of the professor, thought Sean. Why didn't he ask the young lad in, set him on a seat, and make him take a glass of wine with the two of them? Sean felt ashamed of the professor's rude and abrupt order to the student to go. Contemptuous of one within the gates, what must the professor think of lesser ones without? But wasn't Sean himself far worse and far meaner? He let the lad be snubbed, let the lad go without saying a word. Hadn't the guts to say that the lad had come by a prearranged request by Sean himself to get him away from the don. Stayed silent as if he had known nothing about it. Afraid of the professor. A mean and lousy act of cowardice. Let the lad go without a word, without a word.

—Well, goodbye, O'Casey. Don't be so sure that the privilege — as you call it — will be taken away. Think the question over.

—Goodbye, sir. You see, the question doesn't call for much thought from us. We hardly know you exist, and we don't care if you do or you don't. We know as much about you as we do about the rarer fowl aswim on the waters of Victoria Park. You have had a long time of it because we didn't know you were there; but times change, and you are no longer safe in the holy quiets of the past.

—Think it all over, O'Casey. You'll find I'm right. You will have to get above your upbringing, if you're going to live easily with educated people. You must grow up. Goodbye.

—Well, professor, we're united in our liking for Evan Walters' pictures — that's something, anyway. Goodbye.

Led away with a member on either side of him, a prisoner, and others following, Sean was guided safely through a gentle jangle of colleges — Clare, Peterhouse, Magdalene, Pembroke, Christ's, Trinity, Emmanuel; one of his companions pointing to another, somewhat distant, saying, That's Jesus College, famous as the place where Cranmer studied and began his end by reading too much of the Bible. While he was musing the fire kindled. Over a bridge crossing the Cam, and right through the Backs, Sean covering the walls with as many glances as he could get in between the chat that went on and on as they strode forward. Old stones, old stones, where Cranmer got ready for what was coming to him. All old stones, still giving out the fading scent of an old religion; the time when men burned their comrades; sent friends atwist with torture down to hell or swift to heaven up, because they didn't think the right things about Jesus. Old stories, old stories from old stones – Bethlehem, Jerusalem, Damascus. Tell me the old, old story of unseen things above. Here still is the smell of an old theology of the middle-ages, consigning most of us to hell, even destining life to eternal fire from the moment of its conception; when a demon might be swallowed with a lettuce-leaf, incautiously eaten; or hidden in a bubble of the froth of beer (Oh, dockers of Dublin, do take care of yourselves!). Then only the chosen few could be saved and the many called plunged into inextinguishable flames for ever; a dreadful fear buzzing in the ears of man from St Gregory up to Newman, and echoed, when the buzz had died, into his ear again by General Booth. Here too are the lingering fabrics of the old fables, of Adam and Eve, the winding-sheet of original sin, which C. E. M. Joad found lying about, dollying himself up in it to go strutting along in it as if sheltered with a cloak of indurable delight. The universities, smothered so long by clerical power and discipline and the Latin language, are only now beginning to breathe. It took Government commission after commission to get rid of this smothering medieval stuff.

But the cassock rustled around yet. The ghosts of the leaves of centuries were thick under their passing feet. Behind these old stones, God had become old and conventional. Midnight oil was burned here, but rarely daylight. The sun seemed seldom to shine on the books; the wind rarely stirred their leaves. It was all so picturesque and all so dead. How many scholars had gone in behind these old walls, head first; and had come out, feet first, without becoming known to a single worker from one end of England to the other. Professor Coulton's *Four Score Years* brings us close to St John's and St Catharine's Colleges, mentions many names of dead and gone Fellows, Professors, Tutors, and Clerics, not one of them able to suggest an echo in the heart of any common man. They are to the plain people as if they had ne'er been born. Unknown to those who lived through the same years with them, in the same land, maybe, in the very same town. Imprisoned for life behind these old stones, away from their own people. Even Coulton himself, a great medievalist, a very fine writer, an extremely brave and honest man – who knows of him? It is a pity that the core of culture and of scholarship should be so safely hidden from the sight of the common man.

There was a blue sky overhead and a cold wind blowing,

nipping the ears and forcing hands into pockets of trousers or coat. Sean saw a few bunches of daffodil spears thrusting themselves up through the frosted ground, but no yellow bell yet shook in the wind to give a challenge to the swallow to come before a June sun warmed the withering walls. Through the Backs, over the Bridge of Sighs, a copy of an Italian one, if Sean remembered right. Like the Greek portals in front of English bank, hospital, and poor-house, it pustulated that even an English college had lost touch with English character, song, and building. Out by a gate, through the town to the Fitz-william Museum, still between Committee members, more following behind, now increased by some young women friends. A place too full of treasures to see in an hour when contemplation is split to pieces by the aggressive chat of many friends. The one thing he remembered well was a picture by Rembrandt of a young man wearing a plumed hat – probably a portrait of the painter himself.

Cambridge isn't a very distinguished-looking town, in spite of its gay arms of three ships sailing under a castellated bridge, with a fair fleur de lys blooming on one side and a sweet rose on the other. It seems to abide by the fame of its colleges. Here come the colleges! They made up for everything the town may lack. One would think that a town housing a university would be, if not stately, at least dignified. Cambridge is neither. It shows little sign that within it is one of the founts of creative literature, science, and scholarship. It sidles and lurches round the colleges, looking like a shabby fellow waiting for a job from a rich relative. Any free expression of life is muffled up and half smothered by a thick overcoat of colleges.

Professor Coulton, recounting his life, tells a lot about the colleges, but ne'er a thing about the town. A student there for years, then a Professor too, for years. A Fellow of two colleges, he never mentions the town. Am I nothing at all to ye, Professors, who pass me by? He never mentions the Church of the Holy Sepulchre or the Fitzwilliam Museum. When one says He's a Cambridge man, the University is meant, and not the town or county. Sean put several questions to the students about the town, but they weren't interested. They knew their way about it, and that seemed to be about all. Why doesn't the University get into closer touch with the town? Why don't they invite lads and lasses, joining in themselves, to shake their feet in joy, swinging about to the tune of *Haste to the Wedding* or *Greensleeves*, on the green of a quadrangle, the older Dons looking on, and wishing to God that they, too, were in the bloom and bluntness of youth? Had Oxford or Cambridge even any student songs? Sean had never heard of any, and these students walking beside him said they were too busy to sing. Ne'er a Villon here. There were even chapels within the colleges wherein God served the students. The god of the University couldn't well mix with the god of the town. The god of the colleges wore cap and gown and had to keep to the rules. A boat seemed to be their love. The score was made by one college-boat catching up another, and bumping it. He had heard of dear Sydney Morgan, wearing a suitably coloured tie, running along the towpath during a contest, and shouting Go on, Clare!

To secret himself away from the cold, Sean wore an overcoat and his thick red muffler, walking briskly through the streets sadly lighted by an ailing and a fainting sun, noticing that the students wore no overcoats, though gay scarves circled their necks. It was plain that they were far from warmth, and that most of them wore clothes that weren't good enough to keep away the nip of the air or the bite of the wind. The streets were busy with undergraduates wearing nothing warm but their gaily coloured scarves. Were they a hardy lot? Is the undergraduate a hefty fellow, readily resisting cold winds and frosty airs? Quite a lot of them didn't look it. Was it a universal university vanity to go about without an overcoat, however sharply the wind blew or the frost nipped the ear? A foolish vanity, lads, a foolish vanity.

Down to the Common Room where he was to give his talk – a big, rectangular apartment with a grand blazing fire at its upper end. A common room in every way, presenting to Sean – bar the fine fire – an appearance of drab discomfort. No carpet on the floor, the boards themselves looking as if they needed a scouring. No cosy armchairs or settees, no pictures on the walls; no sign of a musical instrument, even of a tin whistle; no attractive lights to make reading profitable and pleasant; no brightness at all, save for the big fire flaming away at the big room's end. A full house, crowded to the doors, instead of the quiet assembly of members promised by the Society. The Chairman introduced the speaker, and announced the title of the talk so softly and cautiously that even Sean, standing beside him, didn't hear the fullness of *The Holy*

Ghost Leaves England. Odd how hesitant we are about mentioning any title of the threefold deity we say we worship. With all their cardinals, bishops, priests, and parsons, churches and chapels, we are shamefacedly reluctant to mention the names of God the Father, God the Son, or God the Holy Ghost. We will readily speak about Buddha, Mahommed, Krishna, or any other deity or prophet; but strongly dislike to mention our own. In any casual conversation, in almost any secular discussion, not concerned as to whether the Christian belief be true or no, any mention of a member of the Trinity is received with embarrassment, and listened to in a strained hush hush. It was Nietzsche who said that God was dead, and the Christians, in spite of their hymns, churches, catholic heralds, universes, churchmans, and methodist monthlies, seem to be damned glad he is. He no longer gets in their way of making a dishonest living.

One don came to the meeting. He was a Mr Henn, a young attractive man, and, seemingly, very shy. Sean was beginning to learn that souls shaded by cap and gown differed from one another as much as those hidden under costly cloak or simply patterned bib and tucker. Sean enjoyed himself very much, talking, talking, for his audience were young, eager, and ready to laugh at any funny thing he said. Living lads all of them. He felt he was among friends, far younger than he was, of course, but by their lively participation in his informal talk they made him feel as young as themselves, and just as hearty. But all his words were idle; words, idle words; not a damn bit of use to anybody or to himself.

After questions had been asked and answered, in a way, he was invited to a student's room to meet personally some of those who had listened to him; and off he went, guided by two students, and followed by a crowd of student companions. They went up and up a long stone staircase, the ascension protected by an iron handrail, making Sean imagine he was in a Dublin dwelling-house built for the deserving poor. Up, up, they climbed, till debouching to the right from a lobby, they came to the room, as bleak as the Common Room, except that this one had a comfortable armchair in its centre. They led him to the chair and sat him down in it, as if they had enthroned him as the bishop of debate: more idle words. A Dublin kid grown into a figure set down in the midst of the Cambridge Colleges. The room was lighted by one bulb dangling from the ceiling's centre. There were no flowers anywhere (too early in the season, maybe), but a few pictures imposed a bit of beauty on the dull wall, though the light was too dim for Sean to see what they were like. He tried to get the students to talk about themselves and their colleges, but they shelved all his questions, insisting on talking of the drama, a bit of religion, and a lot about Socialism. Sean cast many seeds of thought, hasty and unimportant, into the stuffy air to die there. Perhaps they're echoing round the colleges yet; in the wind o' nights – that sound's the sound of O'Casey's voice, mumblin' in the empty air. Don't listen.

Then suddenly the light went out, and for some moments blotted out completely the dynasty on the armchair and those who sat cramped on the ground around him; then tiny beams from half a dozen hand-torches came into play, and relieved the room from its grimmer gloom. It seemed that the college lights went out at a certain hour, warning the students that the time for bed had come. No warning, no bugle-call or drum-tap; just a darkness saying, off to bed now!

—They go out together? What, all over the college? asked Sean, astonished. Yes, all over the college, as our light went out just now. And how do the later students manage in the dark? As best they can. But why do the students submit? It is the rule. We must obey the rules, or go. But this sort of thing treats you all like helpless children. Oh no; it's just the rule.

Sean said no more about the vanished light. It went out according to rule, and the students took it as a matter of course. They didn't seem inclined to question the rule. Sean thought he detected here the sly psychical corrosion of fear. The students were very much afraid of the Masters, and their dogs, the rules. Few here, thought Sean, would be leaders of men, worthy leaders; or leaders in thought; few here would come out to mix with comrades. Many would leave to commit to life the rules they themselves had obeyed as students; trying to force life to remain where it stood. Just to stand; not even to stand and give challenge. As you are. Try no step forward: it might be against the rules. Suffer no new idea to spring from a human head: it might be against the rules; the sacred rules. God Himself was the great Ruler. Was He, too, immersed in the sanctity of rules? He punishes his unruly children; punishes the children for their father's sin when the father has gone underground. So the clergy say. They have carried out the will o' God – on others. Put them in jail; burn them at the stake; exterminate them all rather than one poor rule should perish. It was the breaking of a rule of obedience, Christian teaching tells us, that brought all death, all woe, into the world. It planted deep in man's soul the deadly fungus of original sin. This idea, long an article of faith, has become a fashion, the cold-spur of despair, the *arrah-na-vogue* of death. Professor John Gassner of the United States Columbia College says, 'Contemporary reconstructed "liberals" who exert a literary influence have recently discovered "original sin" '. What the hell is it at all? In a booklet called *Christian Doctrine,* published by Vassalli and Sons, Bath, England, a few years ago, blessed by the signs of *Nihil Obstat* and *Imprimatur* of Westminster, we are told that 'Original sin is that guilt and stain of sin which we inherit from Adam who was the head and origin of all mankind'. The Gaelic catechism strengthens this with the phrase 'in which we were conceived, and born *children of wrath*' – italics theirs. The Gaelic term used for 'wrath' gives the idea of intense heat, of seething, boiling; of fiery rage. And going further into explanations, C. E. M. Joad tells us that original sin explains everything. It hardly explained anything to Dr McDonald, Theologian of Maynooth. Joad's new panacea; not one that cures everything evil, but one that damns everything good.

In spite of the church's statement that disobedience was the source of original sin, most ordinary catholics hold that original sin was created by Adam acting the goat with Eve, a belief that gives the priests the delight of having it both ways; for having the desires of sex within themselves, at times voraciously, they can, at the same time, lash out ignorantly and venomously at anyone else showing the slightest sign of it in conduct, book, or play; and this belief hands to the clerics the gift of giving the laity permission to indulge in it, after a few mumbled words have been spoken in a church; a gift that pours a handsome shower of fees into the wide-open pockets of the clerics. Oh, Adam, Adam, why couldn't you keep it down! Hold your hand out, naughty boy! Was it any wonder, now, that Joyce said of Adam,

He ought to blush for himself, the ould, hay-headed
    philodophr,
For to go and shove himself that way on top of her:
Begob, he's the crux of the catalogue
Of our antediluvial zoo.

The inner walls of Cambridge colleges must be smoky with the many marks and smudges of centuries of philosophy taught and argued about, day in and day out, written down in thesis after thesis, book after book; their inner airs must be heavy with the incense of centuries of theology taught here, set down in thesis after thesis, book after book; theology-pastoral, pastoral-comical, historical-pastoral, tragical-historical; before Cranmer and after him; yet here were a group of students from the various colleges who were doubtful as to what was the wisdom of life, of what life was; having left off even wondering where God could be; students gathered in a room full of themselves and of darkness, seeking explanations still, asking questions of life, and finding answers only in their own experience of it.

What had been called the Truth had often run in and out of the colleges here, ambled through the corridors, crossed the lawns, fed in the refectories, slept in the rooms; Truth carrying a cross in her hand one day, a Bible in her hand the next, abandoning both for the *Origin of Species*, which many tried to tear from the hands that held it tight, and hold it tight still. Truth of one kind fluttered in the minds of Latimer and Cranmer, of another kind in the mind of Gardiner, shaking many shoulders to rouse them into reading *The Explication and Assertion of the True Catholic Fayth*. Yet no mind in any of the bodies here crouching in the darkness thought of either Truth, but sought one of their own making. That's it, by God! Every man must fashion by thought and experience the truth that suits him, the truth he needs.

Universities, said someone, are places where pebbles are polished and diamonds are dimmed. Each lad here sought a proficiency of knowledge that would give him a licence to dangle what he thought he knew before younger minds in minor colleges and schools, and so earn a living. Surrounded by Socrates, Chaucer, and Shakespeare, and all, they were, all the time, fixed to the bread-line. The book of verse, the girl, even the flask of wine, would have to wait till they could easily handle a loaf. Find a job, find a job, was written under every line of Shakespeare, of Chaucer, under every line of poetry or prose the studiers read; under every line they read now as it had been under every line written by Shakespeare and Chaucer, and all the other writers of the time; though Chaucer was saved a lot of worry by burrowing a job out of the Civil

Service. All great questions about immortality, the nature of the soul, human destiny, and of God were hedged in by the necessity of satisfying animal life; the significance of human life was tangled up in the desire for a job. God's curse had driven all into a forced-labour camp. Each had to earn bread by sweat of face, or get others to do it for him. After having made life harder by way of a curse, it seems that the Christian God has made its end harder still. Sean wondered how many, if any, of these lads bothered about the *Quicunque Vult* of the Athanasian Creed? Miss Dorthoy Sayers emphasizes its swashing blow in her *The Mind of the Maker*. 'The proper question to put to any creed', she says, 'is not, Is it pleasant, but Is it true?' 'It isn't', she says, 'that God refuses to save unbelievers; it is the more alarming fact that unless a man believe it faithfully, he *cannot* be saved.' In other words, if he doesn't lap it clearly and faithfully into his nature, he's a gonner. Down, down to hell, say Miss Sayers and St Athanasius, and say we sent thee thither. Well does Emerson quote the churchman: 'This was Jehovah come down out of heaven. I will kill you, if you say he was a man.' Outside of the catholic church, of the faith, there is no redemption. But, oddly enough, the roman catholic church of America the other day silenced a Jesuit priest for teaching this doctrine. The ones episcopal told him to hold his tongue; he refused, so episcopal authority shoved poor Father Feeney out and slammed the door behind him. So, it seems, they shove out those who won't or can't accept the Athanasian Creed, and, when they've recovered their breath, hustle out those who can and do. Well, here in this room, by the light of the tiny hand torches, a lot was said about Socialism, and nothing whatever about dogma, protestant or roman catholic. Even the echoes of dogma no longer tinkled in their eager ears that had long ago opened to the hearing of other things. Not only here, in this room, in this college, but under the palm and the fig tree, in the snow-carpeted lands of the north, among the vines, and under the oak and the elm, the ears of man had opened to the hearing of other things.

It was an odd sight with the sitting figures bending towards Sean, those crouching on the floor tucking up their legs to make more room for those crouching beside them; the electric torches throwing out tiny beams of light, now showing a young face tense with thought, a pale hand clenched or resting easily on the back of a chair or a comrade's shoulder; a leg thrust forward along the floor, threading its way among those gathered up, hands clasping the knees to keep them steady; a young mouth opening and closing, busy with the spoken formation of a thought; voices agreeing and disagreeing floating out of darkness; Sean speaking towards that light now, this light then; all in the centre of a curious quietness, for all the colleges were still, and nothing active but the silent grandeur of the night. What did their talking try to do? Tried to untangle a chain or two of all that cling and clang around the heart's desire. He had taught nothing; he had learned something of the ways of a Don; more about the ways of a student; saw within their air of brittle confidence, under the gay colours of their scarves, that they knew as much about the morrow as he knew himself. One by one the torches gave out in the midst of the low voices, till but one remained to give a single glow, like a firefly that had strayed into the room, and had come to rest on the arm of a chair. On the discussion went till some chime or another told them it was two o'clock in the morning, and time to go for the one torch left would soon give out, and the world would be left to darkness and to them. They rose up unwillingly, for the morrow of life would put wide distances between them and him for ever.

Talking still, they wandered forth from the room, all shaking hands with Sean, each going his separate way, save two, who, linking him on either side, led him down the stone stairs, out of the college, around a quadrangle, over to St John's College, where a room had been set aside for him so that he could find refreshment in sleep after the labour of his lecture and his talk. They bid goodbye to him at the door, after switching on the light for him, a single, naked bulb hanging from the ceiling's centre again. He was so full of what he had seen and heard that he forgot to ask how was it that while all the lights were out elsewhere, one shone in the room lent to him. Never having asked, he never knew.

There he was, standing alone, in the middle of a February morning, in the middle of a room in St John's College. Jasus, what a room! A slum room, without a slum room's brightness, defiantly facing him in one of England's primate colleges! The floor was bare and dirty-looking; there was no fireplace, not even a mark where a fireplace might have been. One window, unclad even with the symbol of a rag, looked out on to the night. To the right of the door, a dangling piece of wooden

framework carried a cord from which hung a patterned curtain, the flower pattern soiled with the marks of dusty years:
this was meant to be the wardrobe, for, behind the curtain,
some hooks were driven into the wooden frame. A small cane-
bottomed chair sat itself by the staring window. Opposite the
door stretched the bed, an ordinary iron-framed one, painted
black, but with the paint peeling off in places, showing the rust
beneath; over it lay a bedspread, thin and abject, of a dirty
yellowish-grey colour, ornamented with a blue-grey pattern;
under this two thin blankets, and under these again, clean
sheets, once white, but now taking on the colour of fading
unbleached linen. There was an air of bruised poverty in the
place, more abject than some of the rooms he had entered
before, and sadder because of its emptiness. He himself had sat
for hours that had mounted into years, studying the beginnings
of knowledge, in a room as poor and as bleak as this one; but
behind its bitter bleakness had stretched the cosy pattern of a
room nearby, where a fire burned, its flames framing his
mother mending an old shirt or darning an old sock. If one
were a Christian, what would he pray for here? For a quiet
death on the pale, dejected bed, for if this room was the usual
habitat in a student's life, the best thing for a student to do
would be to die. Youth is here, but not youth with a red rose in
his breast. Most of the students he had met were too anxious
about their future; too strained in an effort to make both ends
meet; men of the world hurried by, intent on their business; the
world wasn't with them enough.

He peered tensely out of the window, but couldn't see a
thing; not a twinkle of a light or a star anywhere; must be
misty: just a dark void, and he in the midst of the silence.
Earth with her thousand voices is silent now. He shivered; it
was damnably cold, too, though he still wore his cap, muffler,
and thick blue top-coat. He opened the door, his hand resting
on its jamb, and peered out: a black void here, too, without
any rapture in it. The light in the room was too dim to go
beyond the doorway. He had no torch, but he struck a match,
and before it died out, he caught a glimpse of a corridor that
led God knew where. He took a step beyond the door, his hand
touched the switch, knocking it down and extinguishing the
light as he found himself plunging headlong forward to prevent himself from falling smash on his face. Fortunately his
outstretched hands struck a wall and not his head, and he

stood by it, panting, till he got a calm breath back again.
O'Casey wild and loose in St John's College, Cambridge, in the
dead of the morning. Like a thief in the night come to rifle,
rob, and plunder. He wondered how far he had shot forward,
and hoped there weren't many doors, for then he mightn't
know which one was his. Good thing he hadn't crashed against
some dignified don's door. Where the hell was his door? There
was a draught blowing through the corridor like a low wind in
Jamaica. There were but three matches left in the box. It
wouldn't be fun to have to spend the night in the corridor
waiting for the Blue of the night to meet the Gold of the Day;
an old song among old stones. How would it go, if he sang it
loudly here? Would it be against the rules? And Sean, leaning
against the wall, bubbled with laughter. A sound of revelry by
night. 'Tis now the witching hour of the morning. He wondered if Wordsworth's ghost had a beat here at times? His old
college. Too far away from where he lies now. Did the shadow
of him, who thought the bow and arrow more effective than
cannon, flit about anywhere here now? Roger Ascham, great
at least, as one of the first to coax English language out of its
dusty corner, and send it forth to say its own say and speak its
own grand message.

He carefully struck a match, and swiftly looked around. Ah,
there was the door of his room wide open in welcome. Won't
you come home, bill bailey, won't you come home! He will,
and cautiously stepping to the door, he wound his arm round
the jamb, and switched on the light. Peering down, he saw that
there were three narrow triangular steps leading up to the level
of the room's floor, so narrow that one would need to step
down them sideways. Led in by his friends, he hadn't noticed
them before, and so, unaware of them when he stepped bravely
out, he had plunged headlong into the corridor. He would
open the door softly again. Had he not had a few matches on
him, God knows where he might have wandered. Oh, where is
my wandering boy tonight! While the matches were giving
light, a swift glance around had shown him that there were no
pictures in the hall here; not even a poster from the Underground: all bare and drab. No connexion with any other firm.
The old ecclesiastical idea of seclusion: the students the elect
of God instead of the elect of the people. An idea dead that
won't lie down. No drums under the windows either; no band
ever played on any of the squares.

He closed the door and looked at his watch; on the border-
line of three o'clock. Time for bed, for the skip would be
knocking at his door at seven o'clock in the morning. The low
wind from Jamaica was whistling in under the door; God, he
was cold, so the sooner he got under the bedclothes, the better.
He hung his coat up on one of the nails behind the faded
chintz curtain, put his ordinary coat on top of it, with his
muffler hanging over both. He hurried off his jersey, boots, and
trousers, and pulled his pyjamas on, tucking his shirt into the
top of the trousers, for it was too damned cold to take that off;
turned the light out, groped his way across the room, and
climbed into bed, shivering. A friendly lot of lads, these
students, many of them in such poor circumstances that university life must be something of a torment to them. Poverty
was beginning to go a long way up as it went a long way down.
He was shivering now with great elation. Colder here in bed
than out on the bare floor. No heat in either blanket or cover-
let. There would be no sleep for him while he kept so cold. He
got hastily up, groped about in the dark, shoved on his trousers
and socks, and shot into bed again. Cold as death.

Full of eagerness, a lot of these lads, to meet and answer the
questions of life. Brave lads. If only the way was straight before them; if even they could think that their way was straight
before them. God, it's colder, colder than it was out in the
corridor; frost is flitting about the room. Sweeney, roosting on
the frosty fork of a naked tree, was no colder than he, here,
buckled up in this bed's centre. Shivering shamefully, he lepped
out of bed again, he groped a way across the room, thrust
himself into his smaller coat, wound the red muffler round his
neck, put out the light, groped back across the room, and shot
himself into bed again. But the frosty air nipped as strong as
ever, and the low wind of Jamaica sent chill currents down his
spine and around his shoulders. Twist about how he might, tug
as he would at the miserable bedclothes, it was beyond him to
coax a single sign of warmth into where he lay. Up he got once
again, groped about till he found the light-switch to turn on
the light – the only blessing he was to find beside him through
the bitter night. He donned his heavy overcoat, put on his
boots, fixed his cap on his head, and set himself down to spend
the rest of the night pacing the room. Up and down, down and
up the little room, muffled to the ears; up and down till the
damned doxy dawn came to his relief; under the silent bulb of

light pendant from the ceiling's centre: *per amica silentio lumine*. Was there ever anyone else like unto this one, perishing with cold at Cambridge, in the vast middle of the night! Up and down, down and up, hour after hour, quietly treading the floor for fear anyone in the college should be wakened, and wonder who was walking. Cold as death. Somewhere in the distance, a clock chimed the quarters, but, though he knew the time too well, Sean had never looked at his watch so often. At last, the dawn came to the coldest spot in England. First, he saw her fingertips shoving up the shutters of the night, delicate fingers, dimly seen through a curtain of mist, till the whole hand spread over the whole sky, and the night was over. Through the grey mist he saw the blurred outlines of the great colleges, grey walls, zig-zag roof-lines, pierced here and there by tall, austere chimneys, without a trace of smoke coming from one of them. Below the mist he saw that the ground was shrouded in the cold whiteness of a whore frost. Slowly the lazy sun rose higher, and the bright light adangle from the ceiling turned into a watery, ghastly gleam, making the poor room look as if there was about to be a sickly end of its life. Even the skip was late, but he came in the end, bearing a can of hot water, his mouth opening a little to say Good morning, sir; I hope you had a good night. Never mentioning the kind of night he had had, Sean took the water with thanks, leaving a little to use for shaving, and using the rest to bathe his swollen, aching eyes; for one of the irritations of life was that he had to bathe his eyes at least twice a day in water but a degree away from boiling, so that the lids, heavier than that weighing down over the one eye of Balor, might remain high enough to allow the eyes to look out on the world. He was in haste, hurrying over a wash and a shave that he might slide into his heavy clothes again, and save himself from frostbite.

Then another wait, and more pacing up and down the room, till the young guide of the night before came again, hoping, too, that Sean had had a pleasant night, and they sauntered through the frosty air to the lad's room, where the morning meal had been laid out for him. Here there was a generous fire, and with the chair drawn up beside it, the table pushing itself against the chair, Sean found comfort at last. The breakfast was a sound one of two eggs, a dish of porridge, a number of rashers, a heap of toast, a great pot of tea, and a jar of marmalade. At the opposite side of the table the student busied himself with his own breakfast, starting (as Sean thought) with a saucerful of filmy oats, ghosts of the true grain, dampened with milk poured cautiously from a tiny jug. When Sean had finished one of the eggs, with tea and toast, he noticed the student drawing away from the table as if satisfied, and he asked him if he wasn't going to have an egg and some of the porridge.

—Oh, they're for you, sir, the student said. I've had enough. I never eat more; I find I work well having eaten a light breakfast.

—Eat nothing, then, and you'll work better, said Sean explosively. Good God, man, a young lad like you needs a bigger meal than a saucerful of dried dust! That's no way for the College to feed you. If you go on that way, man, it soon won't be worth a bug's while to bite you!

—Oh, said the lad, with embarrassment, if I needed more, I could get it from the buttery.

—Here, said Sean, pushing them across the table, take the porridge, this egg, the rashers, and half the toast, and don't let me go thinking I've wasted good food.

—Sure you don't want them, sir? asked the student, shyly.

—Quite sure. I never eat bacon, and one egg's enough for one of my age. Muck into them, now, like a lad of mettle. Sean put it off jauntily, realizing it was poverty that kept the lad on a diet of dried dust.

The lad mucked into them all right, enjoying the first fair breakfast, probably, he had had for a long time; talking away of his study of English Literature from Chaucer to Shakespeare, so that he might win a Degree in Arts that would flit him out to teach children who had never read a line, and never would, probably, of either poet, and like it, in their life's short journey. It was likely that there were hundreds living here like this young chap, some of them even under harder conditions; for this room had, at least, a fire – though, maybe, it had been lit only to entertain a guest. A number of the rooms Sean had entered had been like his own, fireless and freezing. The poor scholars! Reading Chaucer, reading Shakespeare for a living! Land of warp and worry! Mooching curiously around, he had had a hunt for a bathroom. He found them preciously gathered together in a small group away from the buildings, serving several colleges; and not long there either. An after-thought.

Indeed, Dr Coulton in his *Four Score Years* tells us that in 1922 the Master of St John's College, speaking about a long-lived professor, told how he had lived to see the introduction of railways, electric telegraphs, motors, and aeroplanes, adding 'And we hope he will live to see baths in St John's College'. Anyhow, why worry, said someone, we're never in the college longer than eight weeks. The medieval ecclesiastical affiliation with dirt still lingering on lively in the colleges of Cambridge. Old walls, old walls, and old ways, too.

On the wall facing Sean an elegant, slim oar stretched itself along proudly, held up by brackets. Asking why it was there, Sean was told by the student that his boat had won a competition on the Cam, and that each student of the crew had been presented with the oar he had used; and the glow on the student's face showed he was glad that Sean had noticed the trophy, with the date of the race and the name of the competitor emblazoned on its slender blade. He gets more joy out of his oar than he does out of Chaucer or Shakespeare, thought Sean; and rightly so, for this is something he has done himself. This would be a memento to him all his life. If he married he would show it to his children: rowing on the Cam on such a day against a rival crew, we won, and this is one of the oars that pulled us home. A natural and a noble vanity. All the vanity in Vanity Fair isn't vain. Bunyan was wrong.

The taxi to bring him to the station would be here in a minute or two. Already a group was gathering to bid him goodbye. He had told some of them that he intended to write about the condition of the colleges, but they had begged him to wait a year or two; till they had taken their degrees or diplomas, and had gone for good; for they were fearful that what he might say should do them harm. He went back to his room to collect his grip, where he found the skip tidying the bed that had proved to be such a wretched refuge during the night.

—The college doesn't seem to be busy this term, he murmured to the skip.

—Not busy, sir? We're crammed out, we are; couldn't put up another soul.

—But how is this room empty, then?

—This one, sir? Oh, this was full, but the fellow, 'as were 'ere, 'e got took with pneumonia, an' 'ad to be taken 'ome.

Penumonia! In his mind's eye, Sean could see the poor figure on the bed, feeling first the heat of the blood and the

tenseness in the side; unsettling, but to be borne till they passed
away, and the body righted itself. My people have paid the
fees. Only a few days. Vain hope.

> Send speedy help, we pray,
> To him who ailing lies,
> That from his couch he may
> With thankful heart arise.

Soon be better, soon be better, have to be, for the pain became a
red pain pinching deep into the lung, pinching deeper, so that
he cried out, though no cry came, for it was stifled within the
gasping cough that tried to cast the biting lung out of the
frightened body, itself now developing a heat of its own, a dry
and crackling heat, contestant in its venom with the crackling
heat of the lung. Knight of the burning pestilence. Twist on the
old, ironic bed, and let your rasping coughs break through
whatever chimes may sound softly from the college buildings.
In the mean, lonely room, within the meaner bed, away from
home, in the midst of scholarly culture, a young lad was gasping out part of his life on a college pallet, silence praying for
help, and poverty bathing his brow.

—How is he now? asked Sean of the skip.

—'Ow's 'oo, sir?

—Young lad who had the pneumonia?

—Oh, 'im? 'Ee's dead, sir. 'Eard 'ee just died. 'Is mother
come, an' fetched 'im 'ome. 'Adn't the stamina, sir. Lot are
like 'im 'ere still. Poor fellas, y'know, sir; always on the scrape.
Not the class, really, for the colleges. Thank you, sir! he
added, as Sean slipped half a crown into his hand.

The rules! He had just obeyed a college rule himself! Condemning them scornfully among the lads, here in the silent,
miserable room, he had confirmed one. An unwritten one, but
a rule just the same. Curious conscious and unconscious emo-
tions of inconsistency in the heart of a man.

—Well, goodbye, sir, and the skip had gone, leaving Sean
with himself and the lonely room. A boy's lungs had hardened
here, sending flaming coughs quivering from a parched mouth.
Send some Lazarus that he may dip the tip of a finger in water,
and lay it on my burning tongue, for I am tormented in this
flame. I am fighting it out, fighting to avoid the cold clutch of
the tomb; fighting to get back to Shakespeare, to Chaucer, and

to Sidney; here, in this lean room, amid the faded chintz, the naked window, the bare floor, the meagre chair, the drab walls, the unholy bed; while outside stretches out the scholarly land of hope and glory. No more foraging for fees. I did my best, mother, but life was too much for life with me. Open the door, mother, and let me go from this lonely room. Come quick.

Here she is, lad; your mother. Woman, behold thy son. She is come to take you off from this dumb room, and to enfold you with her own cuddling talk. She is come to take away her dying boy to present him with the happiness of a far less lonely death, and a lonelier room at the end.

He went out, and climbed into the waiting taxi, waved a hand to the group of lads waving goodbye to him, and set off on his journey home.

DEEP IN DEVON

THERE is an immense amount of activity, of anxiety, of care, and of thought, in the bringing up of children. It is a harder job than that of any prime minister, of any archbishop, or any general on a horse, or any admiral on a quarterdeck. A mother is busy the livelong day and the deadlong night. She has been left alone too long at the wearing job, and now the man must join in with a sensible helping hand. In spite of all the scientific and mechanical equipment surrounding us, and the colleges and schools, we know next to nothing about the strangest equipment of all – the child, the greatest, the loveliest, and the most delicate equipment we have for the development of life's future. We know more about the child than we did even twenty-five years ago, yet there are still millions of ageing minds who think that the best way to fit a child for happiness and resolution in life to to stuff his delicate mind with a creed, Christian or Communist. For Christ's sake, let the child laugh, let the child play, let the child sing, let the child learn, let the child alone.

A deep talk about schools. Prospectuses fluttering in from various places, all very fine and large and damned expensive. Two boys to be educated now, and another child on the way. Eileen, asking all the questions and answering them herself, wanted a school where the boys would be welcomed as day-pupils, for G.B.S. had advised against boarding the children, saying that a mother's affectionate regard and care should remain breast to breast with children till they had reached an age that allowed them to go forward gay and strong without them. Eileen sought a school where a child's nature would be neither checked nor ridiculed by customs stale; one where no fantasia of pietistic chanting would deafen a child's mind away from its own thoughts; where a child would see trees, herbs, and animals living a natural life, and not as they appeared woven into a nursery-rug, or emblazoned on a nursery-plate or pie-dish.

—Dartington Hall is the place for your boys, said Shaw.

—It's going to cost a lot, murmured Sean, anxiously.

—No more than the others, said Shaw, shutting up Sean. Give the children the good things and the fine things, and, when they grow up, they'll refuse to do without them; and that is what we need, he added emphatically, the refusal to do without the finer things of life.

Eileen thought the world of Shaw, and loved his magnificent, laughing austerity; so it was decided that the two lads should go to Dartington Hall School. Another upheaval for Sean! A change from the city's busy life and colour to the wider and quieter ways of the green country. He feared the country, for it robbed him of much, his eyes there losing a lot of the little power they had. In a city the view was a short one, and his eyes hadn't to travel far to see things; all was at his elbow. The great sky was always a narrow strip, hugged by the city's skyline. In the country the way was wide open, and all around was a great carousel of sky, forcing him to keep his cap well down over his eyes so as to cut most of the sky away, and keep a workable focus in front of him. In a city, on a sunny day, one side of a street was usually shaded, so he could stride along in comfort; in the country, the sun spread everywhere, so he would have to march, head bent, and slowly. In a city, at night, the street-lamps and lighted shop windows were a wide lantern to his feet, so that he could go anywhere safely; but all through the winter, in the country, he would be blind at night, and every step he took from the house then would have to be arranged by some guiding hand. Night-time would take away his independence; and he hated any hand trying to guide him in the way he should go.

Down they went to Devon for the children's sake, carrying all their wealth of worldly goods with them, settling in the busy little town of Totnes, and, once more, going through the arduous orgy of fitting into a new home – a big, clumsy house, full of pretension only, the only one they could get; a one that even a miracle couldn't make comfortable. Totnes is set out so that its main street slinks slowly up a slender hill in the valley of the Dart, Devon's beautiful *Anna Livia Plurabelle*. Halfway up the hill of the main street stood the church, its spire rising over all, and higher up on a spur of the hill, on the church's flank, stood the circular stone keep of a Saxon castle. The castle and the church – the two *sine qua non*s of the long ago. The guardians of God's Truth in the town are plentiful, for we have in this town the anglican church of the priory and St

Mary, the roman catholic one of St George and St Mary, the
wesleyan church, the baptist church, the congregational
church, the gospel hall, with sundry amateur evangelists, a
couple of salvationists, and visits from jehovah's witnesses
knocking at our doors to hand in tracts, sell books, and give a
quick word or two about the surest way to get to God. A little
way off, if we happen to stray, in a beautiful part of the Dart's
flow, we knock up against the Benedictine monastery of Buck-
fastleigh, a simpering silhouette now of what it was in the
Middle Ages when the Abbey owned many fine fat smiles of
the shire. It has its languishing pipe-dream that England again
will be managed by monasteries and pickled in priorities. Help,
help! Help to build up Fountains Abbey! Help to build up
Prinknash Abbey! Names entered in the Golden Book of Remembrance for a guinea a time. Buy away, buy away, fond
hearts and true, and open up heaven for England, their England. A guinea for God. Guineas are good for us. Send them
twinkling in; invest in monahysterical consoles, Jerusalem the
golden with milk and money blest.

Here, in Devon, they were anchored on the real red earth,
rich earth, and very fruitful. Here, maybe, Adam was made,
for in a Bible Sean had had when a kid, he remembered a
marginal note telling the world that Adam meant red earth; so
here, maybe, Adam was needed into life. Adam filled a
vacuum. All he had to do was to keep his feet, and all would
have been well, and all would have gone on living. God, what a
grand world it would have been! The brontosaurus would have
been a pet, and pterodactyls would have been flying in and out
of our windows, chirruping just like robins! But the man had
to fall down. The woman done it, sir – pushed me down;
caught me off me guard. Couldn't keep his feet for all our
sakes; fell, and ruined the whole caboosh.

Here, now, in a house in Devon, he was looking over the
page-proofs of his first biographical book; for, while writing
plays and thinking about the theatre, his mind had become
flushed with the idea of setting down some of the things that
had happened to himself; the thoughts that had darkened or
lightened the roads along which he had travelled; the things
that had woven his life into strange patterns; with the words of
a song weaving a way through a ragged coat, or a shroud,
maybe, that had missed him and covered another. His own
beginning would be the first word, a little logos born into the

world to speak, sigh, laugh, dance, work, and sing his way
about for a day, for tomorrow he would die. First weave in a
sable tapestry would be the colourful form of her whose name
was Susan, ragged dame of dames, so quietly, so desperately
courageous. Life couldn't get rid of her till she died. She went
on going forward to the end, ignoring every jar, every misfor-
tune, looking ahead as if she saw a great hope in the distance.
A dame of dames, a patient, laughing stoic. Always forward,
with her gleaming black eyes, her set mouth, for ever smitten
with a smile; ragged and broken-booted, still looking forward
as if she saw freedom and everlasting truth beside her. A
dauntless feminine brennan on the moor of life. Thirteen children, and only five surviving. Next door to a Niobe. Apollo
shooting: bring me my bow of burnished gold; and he shot
eight of them. Whizz! Thinned out now; safe; go ahead. Eight
little O'Caseys planted safe in God's acre. *Confiteor meum.*
She never mentioned but three of them – Susan and the two
Johns. Maybe she had forgotten the others. Maybe she thought
there wouldn't have been room in the world for so many; or
room in her own deep heart for so many. She had certainly
fought death away from him. Here he was, deep in Devon,
surrounded by his wife and two children (soon to be three), and
the savage grace of a day that is dead cannot come back to
him. Only in sleep might he dream it back; never again, except
in sleep.

Here in his little garden, as the year branched into the
month of August, two rows of runner-beans were gaily climbing up their tapering bean-poles – called string-beans in
America, and scarlet runners in Ireland. The twining stems
have topped the poles, and hundreds of vivid scarlet flowers
hang pensively among their handsome greenery, like rubies
resting from their fuller glow. They bring to his mind the
scarlet runner, planted by his mother, that grew up around the
framework of the tenement window. Somewhere, from someone, she had got a bean, had shown it to him, remarking on its
odd colouring of blackish purple, mottled with pink blotches.
She had coaxed him into getting enough fresh clay from an old
dump-field to fill a small box, and had carefully sown the bean
in its centre, gently tickling it into exhilaration with some rotting dung gathered by her from the street outside. She had
watched the first leafing of the scarlet runner with delight,
feeling sure that a bright jewel would one day hang from it.

When she saw the twisting stem, she knew it was a climber, so she wove threads in and out along the window's side to help it up. Then came the crimson flower, just like the flower of a sweet pea, and all red, and she rejoiced with a quiet joy, her hand touching it gently; and, at times, Sean saw her pouring over the clay the sup of milk she needed for her own tea, flushed with the idea that since the milk nourished her, it would nourish the plant as well; and it seemed she was right, for when the plant was in its prime, the scarlet runner was hanging out its gently vivid, red flowers all around the side of the window's edge. In the later autumn the flowers shrivelled and fell off, the leafage grew dry and wrinkled, and long pods dangled down where the crimson flowers before had fashioned their own beauty. Waiting till the pods seemed to be ripe, she took a number of beans from the pods, and sowed them in the cold clay; but no leaf appeared when the summer came again, nor did any thrust itself up from the clay in the summer of the following year, though she watched it day by day, evening by evening, for the sign of a rising leaf. Her fuchsia, her musk, her geranium, came up steadily year after year, never failing her; but the scarlet runner never came again. Neither he nor she had known that the pods could be eaten, had ever tasted one. Though they had been put before him at dinner while staying at Coole Park with Lady Gregory, he had never connected the succulent green strips with the scarlet runner that had draped with red and green glory the framework around the tenement's miserable window-frame; and it wasn't till they had grown some themselves while they lived in Buckinghamshire, and he saw the blossoms, that he realized he was looking at the red flower which had delighted his mother, that had withered away in the autumn, and had never come again.

Now he was handling I Knock at the Door, his first biographical book, which would give her life for an hour again; but some other book soon would shut away the story of her days. The lover of the scarlet runner would be gone for ever; gone after her fuchsia, her musk, her geranium, and her scarlet flower. Fuchsias are still here, hedges of them; geraniums bloom again in countless gardens; musk grows in many places; and his own wee garden here, deep in Devon, is alight with the scarlet stitching of the runner-bean. But not hers. They are gone as she is gone. Thoughts in the memories of the living alone ruffle the dead into living again: the muffled drums of the dead beating a faint roll of remembrance; so faint that the memory ceases to hear it before it ends.

A surprisingly large number of educated Irish have a curious idea of what England is like, of what England is. As in an article called 'Joxer in Devon', appearing in number thirteen of the quarterly, *Irish Writing*, written by Denis Johnston, author of *The Moon in the Yellow River, A Bride for the Unicorn*, and other plays, who was a bright young thing for a time in Dublin, and who had the oh-inspiring experience of being educated in Dublin, Edinburgh, Cambridge, and Harvard. He musta missed Cardiff. Selected for one of a number of broadcasts on Living Writers, Denis Johnston came to Totnes to see and to build up what he would say about this living author and his work. He said curious things. Attention! Sit at ease! Sensitive of talking about himself, Sean chatted of many Dublin things, including the Gate Theatre, of which Denis Johnston had been a Director. Ah, the Gate Theatre? He seemed to be tired of the Gate, for he talked of it in a tired way, as if it were to him but the acrid dust of fireworks that had gone up the night before to make a dark sky falsely gorgeous, to spray the dark sky with fictitious gauds. Each production was as it were a trooping of the colours. They tired one in and tired one out. Most things were done in a tiring, caparisoned rush. MacLiamhoir was getting tiresome, too, in that he still wanted to do the parts of young and handsome laddies, though years had rubbed his bloom away, and a fattening chin had hidden the dear reflection of redolent youth that had stood before the back curtain of age when life was younger. Ah, me, we all diminish when the musk departs from the rose.

The visitor's eye-glance wandered round, and stopped to gaze at two pictures in the hallway, one a Giorgione, the other a Gauguin. He asked whose they were, who had painted them. A shock for Sean! He had thought that the visitor and his circle knew all there was to be known about painting; and as the picture, 'The Sleeping Venus', was one of Big George of Castlefranco's best-known paintings, it came as a swift surprise that the visitor neither knew the picture nor the name of the man who had painted it. The glance then moved to Gauguin's picture: from Gauguin to Giorgione, and back again to Gauguin. Where was that one done? Who did that? Gauguin? Oh, yes, of course – Gauguin. He had got it at last. A new discovery. No glance at the other pictures hanging on the same

or the opposite wall – Cézanne's 'Boy in the Red Waistcoat',
nor at the lovely golden browns and gentle greens of Simone
Martini's 'Angel of the Annunciation', nor at the lovely water-
colour by a young Welsh artist, 'Hydrangeas', before which
Augustus John himself had stood, looking long at it before he
murmured 'That is beautiful'; no glance at the striking portrait
of Sean himself by John, or the other John, 'Head of a
Gitana', an inch or two from the visitor's nose, a picture exquisite in its delicacy of colouring, its calmness of pose, its
quiet lyricism singing of the charm of a beautiful girl. He was
interested in art only for what a few pictures might give him to
say about his host. This picture by Giorgione, that by Gauguin,
fitted him out for the statement in his broadcast of O'Casey's
comical attachment to painting, and the epiphany of the man
within it. 'O'Casey', he said in his broadcast, 'declared himself
by living with these two pictures in the same room.' Denis
Johnston must have felt really ill by having to sit for hours in a
room where Giorgione and Gauguin almost shook hands with
each other. Sat there, pale and white and cold as snow.

Though silent about his own particular selection, the visitor
probably thought that it was Gauguin who should go.

It's Gauguin who should go; well, he's the one should know.
It's without grace, it's out of place –
It's Gauguin who should go.

Brightness and boldness frighten the souls of the precious
ponderers. The bright scarlet, the purple, the blue-black, the
lemon-yellow, and the grand green, afflict the suave-swooning
minds of the aesthetic toffs. The fervent way in which Gauguin shows the life of a primitive people in ceremonial form,
in impudent line, in vivid colour, irritates the lordly ones as if
sand had got into their souls. How beautiful they are, these
lordly ones; how beautiful! The swan is their one bird. All
other birds are crows to them.

Well, Denis Johnston came to Totnes to gather manna of
atmosphere for his talk, and, after staying in it as long as it
would take a swift bird to fly over the town, this is what he
says about it:

The little Devon town of Totnes is about as English as
they come. In decorous bus queues the gloomy housewives

stand with baskets on their arms. Odd spectacle of Ireland's
only living dramatist with an international repute buried in
one of the more arty-crafty corners of England. O'Casey
looks a little out of place in these surroundings, and the
housewives are inclined to stare after him as he walks by in
his cap and his jersey, with a Red Army badge displayed in
his buttonhole. The better-informed ones know that it is just
another inoffensive literary gent, and they pass the word
along – that's Sean O'Casey.

Now Devon is almost all a Keltic County, founded by a
Keltic tribe, which gave its name to the county, a tribe that
came over long before the gallant Gaels came sailing over the
sea to Eirinn, which can be confirmed if Denis Johnston reads
O'Rahilly's *Early Irish History and Mythology*. Another
branch of this tribe gave its name to Cornwall. In other ways,
Devon tells us the story of her Keltic origin. It is still tinted
with the tantalizing thoughts of fairy lore. The pishgies or
pixies of Devon are brothers to the Gaelic shidhe. They do the
same curious things – stealing babes from cradles and leaving
changelings in their place; misleading travellers in the dark;
galloping wildly about on the moorland ponies, a minor manner of the Irish pooka. At times they do good things, threshing
a farmer's corn for him; but they must be watched, and food,
fresh and tasty, must be left for them on the farmhouse floor.
A Devon dairy-farmer, well known to Sean, told him how he
had been spellbound one night to the floor of his cattle-shed;
how he was surrounded by the pressure of influences hateful
and mischievous. He couldn't see but he saw them; couldn't
feel, but he felt them; couldn't hear, but he heard them. The
flame of his lantern had flickered, gone out, and he stood, stiff
and motionless, mid the hot smell from his cattle, his body
shivering in the steady trickle of a chilling sweat, his mind
trying to move him to the door, his body refusing to stir, so
powerless that he couldn't even stretch forth a hand to touch
the homely, reassuring body of a cow for comfort, the spiteful
influence of some evil thing passing and repassing through him
as he stood terrified, body and spirit shaken by the evil influence befouling the byre.

Another farmer told Sean that he had been beset in a contrary way. He had worked in a field all day, and was leaving it
in the darkening dusk, but couldn't find the gate that led from

the field to the road. He searched where he knew it to be, but it wasn't there; he searched where it might be, but it wasn't there either; he quickened his steps to the quicker beat of his heart, and trotted round the wide field, but saw no sign of a gate, anywhere; anywhere; and the darkness deepened so that he ran round and round the field, probing the hedge here, probing the hedge there; but his fingers touched thorns, the needle-like points of holly leaves, and there was silence everywhere so that the panting of his breast was loud in his ears, coming slower and slower as his legs grew weary, sagging down towards the earth, till he fell down and lay there, fell down flat and lay there still; lay there till the morning came, and they found him senseless, lying stretched out beside the very gate he had sought for throughout the night, in the darkness, under the stars.

As Ireland isn't anything as Irish as some Gaels make her out to be, so England isn't so English as many Irish think her to be. Half of England, and maybe more, is as Keltic as Ireland herself. Let Denis Johnston listen to the pipe-playing and folk-singing of Northumberland, or to the Cumberland farmers still counting their sheep close to the way the people of Bally-vourney number their scanty flocks. Let him listen any night to 'Dance Them Around' (if folk-custom and folk-song be not too lowly for the beautiful and lordly ones); their band is as Irish as any Ceilidh band in any country town of Ireland. The old songs are neglected and half forgotten today, and are no longer commonly sung in cottage or farmhouse, just as they are neglected and half forgotten by Cahersiveen in Kerry and Cushendall in Antrim; though now there is a sleepy interest taken in holding fast to a folk-lore that had almost bidden a picturesque goodbye for even to the common song a people loves to sing. In listening one night to a gathering in a village hall, near Leamington, in Warwickshire, Sean heard an old woman of seventy-four, the traditional singer of the locality, giving the audience 'Johnny, My Own True Love', just as he had heard his own mother sing it in the days of long ago. It was H. G. Wells who, through *Mr Britling Sees It Through*, voiced delight in the fact that the bigger part of England's place-names had a Keltic origin; so, what with all this, with Wales by her side and Scotland over her head, adding the Irish and their descendants, England is really more Keltic than the kilt. The old name of London was Caer-Lud, city of Lugh of

the Long Hand, and the city's name today is said to mean Fort
of the Ships, as she, indeed, is to this day; Lydd in Kent re-
flects the name of the Irish Lugh, though the English of today
regard the myth with indifference, as do the spiritual and
imaginative Irish. Bud is the name now. Keltic echoes in myth
and story and belief linger on in the countryside throughout
Wiltshire, Somersetshire, Dorsetshire, Devon, and Gloucester-
shire, up as far as, and beyond, Northamptonshire, for

> If ever you at Bosworth would be found,
> Then turn your cloaks, for this is fairy ground.

Over the border, a few short miles away, is Cornwall, packed
with the Keltic daylight, with its Derrydown, its Kelly's
Round, its Doloe, meaning two lakes. Here are the Hurlers,
remains of stone circles, called this name because certain
Cornishmen persisted in hurling on Sunday; here are beehive
huts, holywells, and all the glamorous clutter left by a receding
past. It is recorded that a hundred years ago, West Ireland
(Ireland herself) used to play hurley yearly against East Ireland, comprising the counties of Devon and Cornwall. Even
the story in T. C. Murray's play, *The Wolf*, had its origin in a
Cornish town. Yet another link was that of wrestling, or wrast-
ling, as it was called in Dublin; left hand gripping the shoulder
of an opponent, right one gripping his hip. Cornishmen
wrestled in their socks, as did the Irish; the Devon men in their
boots, made as hard as craft could make them. The reward for
an Irish wrestling champion was a coloured garter worn round
the right leg below the knee. Each Sunday, a champion stood
out on a green sward in the Phoenix Park, his trouser-leg
tucked up to show the gaudy garter, and challenged any
among those who crowded round him. Sean's own brother,
Michael, wore a garter for a year. The Cornish and Devonian
prize was either a silver-plated belt or a gold-laced hat, either
of which, earlier on, exempted a wearer from being forced into
the Navy.

There are some curious remarks hung out to dry in Johnston's article. He says, 'One gathers from some of the sourer
pages that O'Casey never felt comfortable in Merrion Square,
especially when it was trying to be civil to him'. How nice!
Merrion Square, the GHQ of Irish civility. Stirring itself up to
be specially civil to him. Sit ye down, an' I'll thrate ye dacent;

dhrink up, boy, an' I'll fill your can. Oh, how nice! Well, the
fact is that O'Casey never had the chance of feeling comfortable or uncomfortable in the houses of Merrion Square. During his whole life in Dublin, he had been in only one house
there – the house of Yeats; and then felt uncomfortable but
once, when he talked to the great poet in a terribly overheated
room, while the songs of a hundred golden canaries in a
golden cage shattered the harmony of his hearing. Another
remark of Mr Johnston's: 'O'Casey has a profound and
deeply-rooted resentment for Yeats, in spite of the poet's
efforts to help him'. Really? Well, O'Casey has already written
of The Radical Club, formed to try to tumble Yeats off his
pedestal, a Club which O'Casey refused to join. But there is
more: The Gate Theatre for a long time had a hope that it
would scrape the gilt off the Abbey's fame, and, by so doing,
take a cubit or two from Yeats' stature. Yeats was too high for
the most of them to think of anything but a downfall. The two
theatres were rivals in the lights of night; the Gate stood envious of the other's fame.

Another attempt to hurt Yeats, touching Denis Johnston,
oddly enough, for he was a Director of the Gate, was that the
theatre, by Hilton Edwards, wrote to Sean, asking him to give
them *The Silver Tassie*, saying that 'While they thought the
play a bad one, it would do good business on account of the
row raging because of the Abbey's rejection of the play'. Oh
very nice nice oh yes indeed yes very nice indeed. Kill two
birds with the one stone – do good business and hurt the
Abbey. Though indeed the royalties, even from the Gate,
would have been something of a godsend at the time, the request was refused, Sean writing back to say that he was surprised that the Gate Theatre should wish to produce a play
they were sure was a bad one. Another incident touching
O'Casey's attitude towards Yeats nearer still occurred at the
first production of Mr Johnston's own *Bride for the Unicorn*
in the Gate Theatre: Yeats, who was present, rose from his
seat during the progress of the play, and walked out of the
theatre, part of the audience turning to boo him as he passed
them by. Various reasons were given for this action of Yeats,
and the poet told Sean himself, afterwards, that he had done
so because he thought the production an atrocious one. A few
days after the incident Sean got a letter from the lady editor of
the Gate Theatre's occasional magazine, an imitation of the

Abbey's earlier issues of *Bealtaine*. The letter called upon him, with an air of angry enthusiasm, to denounce as ridiculous the conduct of Yeats. O'Casey's reply must have been disappointing, for it was a loud and blunt refusal to do what was asked of him; so disappointing that the letter of refusal never got no answer; not a line, not a single word.

Mr Johnston seems disturbed because O'Casey got on with Lady Gregory. He didn't, apparently, and was more uncomfortable with her than O'Casey was in Merrion Square. He didn't catch on; the old tilted head always looked past him. She said no too often. Perhaps she didn't set herself out to be civil to him, even though he was so familiar, oh so familiar, with Merrion Square. The credential wasn't good enough. Oliver Gogarty was another that couldn't cotton on to the old lady for some reason. Even though he was a great friend of Yeats, the old lady's greeting to him was always a hail and farewell; and Gogarty often referred to her as 'that old hake'. Had he called her an old hawk, he would have been nearer the mark, for whenever a difficulty loomed up before her, or before the Abbey Theatre, she went towards it, head thrust out, beak thrust forwards, lips tight, in a quick pounce to set the difficulty aside, or knock it down, and pass over it; the head straight up now, the splendid old face smiling. And in it all, and through it all, she always chose her own wild swans.

The brother of good counsel. He tells O'Casey how he should feel – 'one wonders whether O'Casey hasn't lost the compassion he once had for his fellowmen' – what pictures to hang on the wall, and points out a place where he oughtn't to live. Totnes doesn't suit him, where the housewives stand to stare after him. Well, they don't stand to stare, but stand to talk, for he knows most of them well, and a lot of their children, too. Johnston knows a lot less about the town than he does about a Dainty Tea. Bad and all as Johnston thinks Totnes to be for O'Casey, it has allowed him to write five major plays, three one-act plays, and five volumes of biography. No, Mr Johnston isn't such a good brother of good counsel after all. The cuckoo's song and the rainbow sometimes come together.

There is nothing sham about Totnes. Next to London, it is the oldest borough in England. All its 'shoppes' are genuine examples of Tudor or Jacobean housing; not in any way so splendid as those found in Conway or Shrewsbury, but as genuine all the same. Neither is there anything 'arty-crafty' about from the bottom to the top of its hill. The housewives who stand in the queues are far from 'gloomy'; they haven't time to be, for they are too busy with the things of life. And there are many Irish incidentals about Totnes: the caretaker of the Drill Hall was a Tipperary woman; the owner of a café was another, but now has one in Stoke Gabriel, a few short miles away; the plasterer who pasted up new ceilings in the O'Casey house, brought down by bomb concussion, came from Roscommon; the parish priest and the O'Casey family doctor are Dublinmen. The one post-woman Totnes had, during the war, came from Tipperary, too. A few miles away, in Brixham, a statue of King Billy stands on the quay, and like Dublin's old figure, has twice been given a contemptuous coat of football-coloured paint. O'Casey is as relevant in Totnes as he would be in Navan or Kells, and more so than in Dublin now; and Johnston's article is pertly and partly proof of it.

Totnes is about the size of Mullingar, but busier, wealthier, and much more lively. Apart from the quiet hurry of market day, gentleness is the first quality to give to it; gentleness in its buildings, and in the coming and going of its people; and in the slow, winding, winding of the River Dart from the moor to the sea. Oh, lord, the natural lie of it is lovely. Except when visitors pour in during the brief summer, the town is so quiet that it looks like a grey-haired lady, with a young face, sitting calm, hands in lap, unmindful of time, in an orchard of ageing trees, drowsy with the scent of ripened apples about to fall, but which never do; hearing echoes of her own voice in the laughing play of children; or in the whispers of that lover and his lass seeking out some corner of the drowsing orchard that is free from any entanglement of time, care, thought, or casual interference.

Though getting some ready money from summer visitors, the town, like so many Irish ones, depends mainly on the farming communities surrounding it. So the eyes of all often scan the sky – not to see the reality of the sensuous enjoyment of its beauty shown by a Constable, a Ruisdael, or a Turner; but to judge the coming weather, for their livelihood depends on it. In a rainy season, they look for a sign of the sun; in times of undue heat, to catch sight of a hidden cloud. Cattle, sheep, poultry, and crops depend largely on what the sky gives; so, when the sun wears his welcome out, or the rain falls too fulsomely on the land, all eyes search the sky for the chance of a coming change.

An old town, stretching out from Lugh of the Long Hand to Winston Churchill and Clement Attlee, a coming together of a strange god and odd men. Years later, it is said, the Romans came clanking along with spear, short sword, and pilum, the time Julius Caesar was mapping out the way the world should go; but it is doubtful if the Romans pierced farther than Exeter, and, held back by the fighting Kelts, ever had a chance to cool their tired and sweating bodies in the waters of the Dart. Fact or fancy, Totnes is a very ancient borough, stuffed with potent parchments signed by kings and princes, giving it a gorgeous right to live. Ancient, too, are its narrow streets, once fitting well the knight's charger, the lady's palfrey, the abbot's mule, and the peasant's cart; now altogether too lean to enclose comfortably the fleet of horning motor-cars and the clattering lorries that shove and push a stammering way through them. Ancient, with its old butterwalk, its guildhall, its Saxon castle, its red-stone church, so commingling with the past that a reminiscent mind might see again an abbot on a mule, padding up the street to a priory, an armoured knight on his warhorse, followed by a squire, the knight carrying on his shield the red rose of Lancaster or the White Hart of the Hollands; or a velvet-skirted damsel or dame on a palfrey trotting through the old archway that was once a town-gate. But no more shall be seen the casqued horseman clattering up the slope to the mouldering castle, a blood-red cross on his surcoat, the head of a poor paynim at his saddle-bow, slain before the walls of Jerusalem the golden; the knight chaunting a merry strain in a merry-hearted mood:

> Where I did slay of Saracens
> And Haythin pagans many a man;
> And slewe the Souldan's cousin deere,
> Who had the name doughty Couldran.

The pageantry of banner, banneret, and trumpet, appears suddenly on occasions in a new way, as when band and banner heralded Victory Day, and at night, from the Market, began a torchlight procession of excited relief and thanks, a gathering of the Devon clans, and a truly moving picture as the procession wended a flaming way down the hill of the town to the level of a green field. In this array of light the O'Caseys' little girl of six carried a torch, innocently honouring the gallant dead who had died that she might live and sleep unharmed, and grow confidently into a fuller knowledge of life, with all her other thousand sisters and brothers of Devon's red soil and tor and moorland; the gallant dead who had put our feet into the way of peace again.

In Devon, many of the women and men never seem to grow old; they keep going till they skip off for ever. They skip through the hours till the very last hour of all; though in the hour of middle-age, they skip more cautiously. The West Country people are human, talkative, and tolerant; seeming slow to city people, but they work harder and quicker than any city artisan or labourer. Many work far too hard and far too long; for, like country people in Ireland, they are too anxious to lay up for themselves treasure, not in heaven, but, more safely, in the banks; reminding one of Joyce's sleepy remark in *Finnegans Wake*:

Anno Domini Nostri Sancti Jesu Christi.
Nine hundred and ninety-nine million pounds sterling in the blue-black bowels of the Bank of Ulster.

Standing on the top of the hill that carries Totnes so lightly on its back and shoulders, a lot of what is fine can be seen in the county of Devon. Overhead, often, a rich blue sky, touched with leisurely clouds reluctant to leave the silky splendour of their blue bed, though in winter that same sky can glower grey or glitter with the threat of a piercing frost. Occasionally, higher than the white clouds, the dark shadow of a buzzard sails across the sky on wings that never seem to fly, satisfied with his own rare company. Hidden to the east lies Torquay, stretching herself languorously, letting herself be fondled by a soothing sea; a dwelling-place where many who are old and well-off live, some sick and resentful, trying to imagine they hear in the sad notes of the Last Post the stirring call of a new Reveille. Away to the west is Plymouth, a fair part of it bloodily scooped away by war; but definite still and as alive as ever; where Drake set foot on his rocking ship to sail out to shatter the bombastic shadow and substance of Spain's Armada, and so disperse the glowing dream of John of Austria, after the Duke himself withdrew from the coloured shadow-play of life. Newly ploughed fields of red earth, spreading out in a view as wide as the eye can cover, aglow with their differing hues, from reddish-purple, reddish-brown, to what seems to be a vivid crimson, separated here and there by squares and diagonals of a green as rich and velvety as the red, a sight to be wondered at and loved. Oh, the Devon people have a beautiful carpet under their feet. Through the crimson, maroon, golden-brown, and green goes the River Dart, binding the colours together with a ribbon of silvery loveliness, awakening in the sightseer the desire to wait, to linger, and to look on the common clay, and feel how wonderful common things may be.

Though few of the farmers, shopkeeprs, or labourers bother about literature or art, rarely thinking of them, or even dreaming about them, Devon is never without a sign that the body and its needs are not all. The other day a farmer visited Sean; he was in a lather of sweat, for he had just helped a brother to gather in the hay from a ten-acre field while the sun shone hot; and, while he talked of the hay and its value, he also talked of his lovely rows of purple, yellow, white, and scarlet sweet peas that were worth nothing beyond the beauty of their bloom and fragrance of their perfume. Though every garden be set aside to grow the things the body needs, there is always a spot there dedicated to a creamy rose or a crimson one. There they are by the fence, beside the door, the creamy and the scarlet roses, showing that Devon, however mindful of the needs of the body, never forgets the beauty of the rose of sharon and the lilies of the valley.

THE DREE DAMES

It was a glorious afternoon of a day tinting a dying June with joy. He sat alone in what was called the sitting-room. The family had gone to swim and jump about in the kindly, sparkling waves of Torbay. He sat in the bulge of the bow-window, an elbow resting on a fumed-oak table that he had laid for tea while he waited for the kettle to boil. He sat sideways, one eye turned towards the garden, the other taking in the rest of the room containing, as Eileen so often said, all the family's respectable pieces, all hers; pieces she had brought from her flat to the new home they had sorted out after their marriage. Not much in it, indeed, but her hand and eye had made it graceful and pleasant to sit in. A deep, bright-brown carpet warmed the floor, stretching itself out with a strain, but failing to come within two feet of the surrounding walls. They hadn't had enough money to allow a carpet to touch the walls; but Eileen had herself darkened the intervening space with a rich walnut stain, and its dark, defiant glistening made the carpet feel richer than it was. A square-backed, square-sided couch and armchair, clad in deep-brown velvet corduroy, faced the hearth, which was brightened by a pale-brown rug, ornamented with geometrical patterns in darker brown, white, and black; all wearing the honest badge of age and use. On a round table, the top of one piece, silken-surfaced and rimmed with walnut, supported by diagonal panels filled with books, lay a wide, shallow bowl of deep yellow, gaily rimmed with coloured patterns resembling the spiral ornamentation of the older Kelts, a wedding-present from Doctor Cummins to Eileen; and on a rosewood china-cabinet stood the head and shoulders of a young and slender woman, deep in meditation, or breathless with adoration, done in grey-blue porcelain; a mantle covering the bending head and falling down over the shoulders so that the gentle face was half hidden in a niche of drapery: a graceful piece of work so serene, so wrapped in thought that catholic visitors always took the figure to be a symbol of the Blessed Virgin. The Lady of whom an old-time praiser has said that only once has she wrought a miracle of stern justice rather than an act of mercy, when she sent Saint Mercurius to pierce

Julian the Apostate with his lance. Pig sticking. But there were
other instances of stern justice recorded then, and more in
modern times, such as that meted out to three Communard
soldiers, who, in a burst of derision, according to a widely read
catholic journal, *The Messenger*, fired at a wooden statue of
hers, one shooting it through the head, another through the
belly, and a third through the heart. That same night, that very
same silent night, when all was hushed, a holy priest passing
by in the holy night underneath the gaslight glitter of the
moon, hurrying home after a quick one, like Chesterton,
found them, the three of them, stretched out dead to the living
world. And when he came close, through the holy night, and
looked closer, he saw, by the light of the loitering moon, that
one had a bullet-hole in his head, another, one in his belly, and
the third, a bullet-hole through his breast. A sudden flash of
lightning from Erewhon made the holy man shiver as it went
through him, in at his feet and out by his head, explaining all
that had happened as it whirled by, and causing the holy man
to murmur piously as he returned to the Everlasting Man for
another quick one, Good hunting, oh mighty peers of light
effulgent; damned good hunting!

On a higher level, flanking the quiet comeliness of the blue-
grey figure, its porcelain shining like watered silk subdued by
time, stood a deep-green glass vase filled with the gay loveliness of Cornish anemones. Facing the bow-window stood a
Bechstein piano, Eileen's pet property, for touching things
musical, Sean hadn't brought into the home as much as a
mouth-organ: all Eileen's, for even the table at which he
worked had been Eileen's before they were married. On the
walls were a Segonzac print, a tiny figure of a man walking
along a path through an avenue of towering trees; Van Gogh's
'White Roses' over the fireplace; a lovely water-colour of blue
hydrangeas by a young Welsh artist; a tenderly beautiful picture of a Gitana by John; and the same artist's portrait of
Sean, the mouth tight closed in a quiver, the face tense, and
the eyes seeming to shrink away back from what they may
have seen; the dim blues and grey-greens of the picture festi-
valled with a splash of orange from a handkerchief flowing
from the breast-pocket of the coat. A kingly present from a
kingly man.

So here Sean was sitting in the midst of good things, of
grace and quiet charm brought to him by the imagination and

sensible selection of his wife; here he sat in close touch with art, literature, and music encased in simple serenity of colour and line and form – as every human being ought to be in hours of leisure; for the young beginning life; for the old ending it. Though security for the future was no nearer to him, yet it would come, too, within the conquest of the people desiring and demanding it, till good things and serene security impregnated and sanctified the life of every human family.

He waited for the tea to brew strong. He sat down to conjure his thoughts into changing images and sprinkle a few glinting spangles on experiences; but he couldn't do it. His mind was vexed and wonderful with the thoughts of a poet, Hugh MacDiarmid, set down in *To Circumjack Cencrastus* and his *A Drunk Man Looks at the Thistle*, books of new thought, daring, and lyrical with fine songs. Lord God, this fellow is a poet, singing a song even when pain seizes him, or the woe of the world murmurs in his heart. Evidently a scholar, too, knowing Latin and languages, with philosophies from Christ's to that of Nietzsche housed comfortably in his head. He wrote in the Scottish manner, adding riches to the rich music of the Lallans. His verse tore along like a flood through a gorge, bubble, foam, and spray flying from the deep rushing stream. Or like a torch flaming many-coloured, red, purple, jet-black, and through each *a white light like a silence.*

The tea wasn't too good. He'd leave it a while longer to draw better. He hadn't much faith in cosies to give tea a bite. This one was plain brown with a stylized scarlet rose on one side of it so that it looked like a Franciscan friar saying an Ave Maria silently, with the impudent red of a rosette of Revolution impaled in the breast of his homely habit.

> *To think nae thocht that's e'er been thocht afore*
> *And nane, that's no' worth mair than a' that ha'e.*

MacDiarmid, you sling a tough task in the poet's way! However hard and long we think; however bold we be; however fine we write, it's hard to say more than a bare amen to all that's said afore. But you have tried, and, to me, have done it often and done it well; have scrawled many a phrase for Scotland *On the palimpsest o' th' Infinite.* Many a fine phrase. Well in the midst of men's life, of their endeavours, you have shown well that

> *Better's a'e gowden lyric*
> *Than Insurance, Bankin' an' Law.*
> *Better's a'e gowden lyric*
> *Than the Castle's soarin' wa';*
> *Better's a'e gowden lyric*
> *Than onything else ava!*

Than onything else ava. I'm at your side, a mhic o. A gowden lyric's near a thing eternal. Golden lads and girls all must, like chimney-sweepers, come to dust. Ay, indeed; and all the little things we cherish; all the ecstasies and tempests of the soul; all the high hammering out in our minds of wisdom's way; all the pearly prosody of love; in each man's soul, in each man's mind, in each man's way, must go; must die, and come to dust; even the maker himself slinks into dust; some woefu' day. All but the gowden lyric.

Then there's the Tamashanterian joy, wild, relentless, and gay, of his *A Drunk Man Looks at the Thistle*, a many-hued pavilion of verse. Here the gurly thistle is made to grow till it opens out into the gigantic chrysanthemum of Strindberg's play; its jaggy stems and splendid plume are made to grow bigger still and higher yet into a Scottish pine like unto an Yggdrassilian tree with its roots firm to the good earth's centre, and its higher branches tripping up the angels running about in heaven. And down, down we go in pride and purple postulation, dragging our feet, our souls full with fidgets of shame as we hear him sing out the bitter lonely lament for the failure of the General Strike:

> *I saw a rose come loupin' oot*
> *Frae a camsteerie plant ...*
> *A rose loupt oot and grew, until*
> *It was ten times the size*
> *O' ony rose the thistle afore*
> *Had heistit to the skies.*

It rose high, then came down 'like the stick from a spent rocket'. It fell here; it rises higher elsewhere. What an odd contrast, starry-wide, lies between T. S. Eliot and this Hugh MacDiarmid! Both are scholars, both are gowden poets; and there the likeness ends. One so cool, the other so passionate. The one, apparently, seeing little of God's countenance in

man's mind; the other seeing in man's mind the one way to get
to God. T. S. Eliot coasting through a mean or meaner street,
indifferently cynical, amenable only to thoughts outside a
figure in a doorway, or a face at a window: a poet apropos;
the other a part in sympathy even of the vennel's pokiness;
unafraid (feeling them even in his own) of the tired limbs and
hardened hands of the struggling people :

> *Whaur a' the white-weshed cottons lie;*
> *The Inn's sign blinters in the mochiness,*
> *And lood and shrill the bairnies cry.*

And for a' Eliot's fine philosophy, MacDiarmid's philosophy
goes deeper; is braver, and questions man and questions God;
challenging the licht said to licht every soul venturing into life;
challenging darkness, too.

> *'Let there be Licht', said God, and there was*
> *A little; but He lacked the poo'er*
> *To licht up mair than pairt of space at aince.*
> *And there is lots o' darkness that's the same*
> *As gin He'd never spoken.*

There is resentment in MacDiarmid's Gloria, Eliot's is always disconsolate and desolate; but in the poetry of the Scot,
even through its sadness, the shepherd's piping of terli terlow
is always clearly sounding.

Sean could easily see MacDiarmid in an evening suit, one or
two of the concise creases annulled, maybe, by carelessness; but
still trim in it, and handsome, too; and he could see him, as
well, in hodden grey, at home with those who have none else;
but never T. S. Eliot in the hodden grey. Pity at times the poet
does not wear the hodden grey and hob-nailed boot. When this
poet traverses *Streets that follow like a tedious argument*, and
*Watched the smoke that rises from the pipes of lonely men in
shirt sleeves, leaning out of windows,* he never stirs his sympathetic, supercilious mouth to call out even once, What cheer,
me buddies. Yet these may have been some of those who built
the home he lives in; carted the coal that gives the heat to
warm him; brought to his door the food that keeps him living.
And these same images of God, shirt-sleeved and smoking,
may, for all we know, be thinking of Shakespeare's native

wood-notes wild; or of a daughter freshly married; or of a son lost in a war; or may be solving the mathematical problem of a football pool; if it be the last, though we shrink from the lowly mathematical mind, let us not wander away from his usefulness to life. But few would refuse to be moved by the graceful choice of words by the poet, and the stabbing effect of his images. Would he could show favour to those grimy ones whose minds come no closer than the garment's hem!

Sean had no learning, no knowledge, no instinctive gift, to warrant him to place his hands on men, and say, This man to be a deaconis, this a presbytyr, this one to be an episcopus of poetry. What he set down were but his feelings moulded into words; there they were, and there they'd stay. For the one, whom he had met, as gurly, at times, as the thistle he sang of, he had a strong love; for the other, the elegant rose, whom he had never met, he had a sincere affection; for both, reverence.

In his play, *The Rock*, T. S. Eliot conjures up a church entirely built with hands, though set, quite snug, epergnel in an anglican heaven. Apart from his own chosen words and sparkling phrases, the church he builds is one of wickerwork and moth-eaten canvas. In sentiment and exhortation, the play is a religious dumpling. If ever there was a play about what is called 'religion', to prove that 'religion is the dope of the workers', this is the one; and not Eliot, but his helpers are largely to blame. It is odd that apart from shadowy bishops and an abbot chattering in Latin, there is but one clerical character in the play, a bishop who 'comes in briskly' like Blomfield Bonnington of Shaw's play; and smatters the readers with the dullest dialogue ever donated in poem, play, or novel to any cleric. Yet an odd admission is made by this blowzy bishop who thought of heaven in terms of stone slab, brick, and mortar. The spiritual tenor of the play is the necessity to preserve medieval manners against modern morals; yet, when the workmen complain about the severity of the work before them, he reminds them that 'Men have mechanical devices today that we never dreamed of'! Devices, mind you! Bishop Chasuble watches the bulldozer advancing the kingdom of God. Then Bishop Blomfield Bonnington adds the Crusaders as an example of what 'a few men of principle and conviction can accomplish!' Accomplish! When do would do. Men of principle and conviction! When Christian Venice was more anxious for the destruction of her Christian trade rival, Constantinople, than she was for the liberation of the Holy Places from the Infidels! What good did the Crusade do bar learn the holy Christians a little of the art of cleanliness from the Arabian Knights?

But worse goes before and far worse is to follow. In the preface to the play, Mr Eliot says 'The Rev. Vincent Howsom has so completely rewritten, amplified and condensed the dialogue between himself (Bert) and his mates that he deserves the title of joint author'. A rascally and conceited interjection. The characters to Ethelbert, Alfred, and Edwin, the workers, are so ridiculously done; are such fakes of pretence and pious poising that one can but throw back the head and give a long and loud guffaw. How sweet to, and familiar with, the workers is this fellow, Howsom! To the workers, of course, who are sweet to him. Here, let me do it, Sean can hear him saying to Eliot; I'll show you what the workers do, what they say, and how they say it. And How! Some dialogue! He even brings on an 'Agitator', and shows us how *he* goes on. Did poet or dialogian never meet and eat with an 'Agitator'? Did either never say 'hello' to Keir Hardie who brought coal-dust on his boots to the Commons' carpet; Tom Mann, Bob Smillie, Jim Larkin, Bill McKie, who organized the workers of Ford's Detroit, or Jim Connolly? Pity, pity, they never did. Though Eliot hasn't been chosen, maybe not even called, he would have led the workers in the play nearer God with a song anyway, and would have added dignity to the way the song was sung. Yet how could he sing such a song, when, seemingly, he senses death even in the birth of Bethlehem?

The whole play's about building, yet Sean would nearly swear that neither of them could tell the difference between a bricklayer's trowel and a mason's or a pavior's float; between a Flemish and an English bond; between even a header and a stretcher; or between a straight-edge and a template. He'd swear that neither of them ever saw slaked lime and sand banked together to make the common mortar, or putty run to make that for the finer plastering. He'd say that neither of them ever slung a shovelful of clay from a foundation trench; shouldered a pole for a standard or a ledger, tied a rope to fix one to the other, or to a putlock fixed into the wall; he'd say that neither of them ever sledged a stone to bring it within the compass of a mason's hammer. All these things wouldn't matter so much if the two creators of the play about building a church didn't set about to patronize the workers; to tell them what to say, how to act, and show them their duty to God, the higher clergy (the fisherman presenting a salmon to an Abbot – instead of snatching one from him), and the upper classes. The building of a church to the mason, bricklayer, carpenter, and labourer doesn't mean a chance to glorify God, but merely a chance to make a living; and the most of them today would rather be building a cinema. Under the way we live, all a building means to the builders is a job. Instead of singing a psalm, Sean could hear Ethelbert and his mates chorusing out

> Th' next who cam' in was a mason,
> A lad as strong as Jason;
> A lad as strong as Jason.
> To join our jolly crew.
> He rattled his trowel against th' wall,
> An' pray'd that churches an' chapels 'ud fall,
> For then there'd be work enough for all;
> When Bunker's Ale was new, me boys,
> When Bunker's Ale was new!

Bread and cheese was the goal of the workers in medieval times, as Geoffrey Coulton points out in his *Five Centuries of Religion*, and grub is the goal of the workers today; and no gem-stained thoughts about the Middle Ages can alter this fact. The right to work is the narrow gate through which alone the workers can enter the kingdom of earth. And who can claim a share in God who does not take the part of man? To Sean's mind, Hugh MacDiarmid makes far more of the Thistle as a symbol for God and man than T. S. Eliot does of the Rose of Sharon. MacDiarmid can rasp and tear the shams of life; but Eliot seems to rasp at life itself, looking at men as living only in so far as they have not yet been buried. Yet with all his well-fifed madrigals of death and desolation, Eliot longs after life. A glow from a warm heart takes the edge from the chilly, searching mind. He desires the people's redemption as we the commoners do: he through the Son of God; we through the sons of men. Let Lisbon-born Anthony of Padua thrill in his trance of self-adoration, kneeling in ecstasy. He has his reward, but not from men. They will hear and hearken and leap at the calling shout of a Garibaldi.

Sean struggled away from his contemplations, praying a

kindly curse o' God on Hugh MacDiarmid and T. S. Eliot for forcing him to dwell on their work rather than on his own. To help an escape, he turned his head to look out of the window: there was the limited lawn, more hospitable to plantain, daisy, and dandelion than to grass. It was odd how dandelions adapted themselves to the frequent mowing that cut them down in their infancy; or to the throng of struggling, weedy life beneath the hedges. On the lawn, the dandelions flowered almost level with the ground, or from a tiny stem scarce an inch and a half high; while in the rowdy life beneath the hedges, they pushed and probed their way up through surly bramble, crowding nettle, tough coils of grasses, and buxom docks till on stems a foot and half long, and more, they breathed air, found the sun, and flowered. Up and up and on and on, climbing more steadily than poor MacDonald. In a corner of the hedge, an elder bush spread about its frothy platter of waxy flowers. A sturdy plant, for hack it how you will, it grows again. One says this tree gave the wood to make the cross for Christ; another that Judas had his last look at the world from it when he dangled there to death. Strange uses for a single plant. In Ireland, Judas would have hanged himself from a sour apple tree. God's creation: without Him was th e nothing made that was made? The elder tree and its elderberry wine. The dandelion? Medicinal properties. The thistle? Oh, here he was letting the damned thistle into his mind again! He'd stifle thought, and take his tea in peace and gorgeous quietude. He turned away from the window to begin it.

Jasus! Three middle-aged women were standing in the middle of the room, staring at him. Two of them he knew – a middle-aged lass, Donah Warrington, a writer herself, plump and grey-headed; and Mrs Jen Jayes, a daring-say-nothing, sane secretary, a tall, gangly figure, with the best curve of the body as fluent as an arrow's head. Her head was fenced within a 'kerchief, worn peasant-wise; a face framed for frowning, though it could beam devotedly on anyone well in with the manor set on the hill. The stranger was tall, too, and gaunt; bonily built, the bony structure of the body showing itself more bonily off whenever the sweet lady moved a muscle. She wore no hat or 'kerchief, and the greying hair fell down to the shoulders in slender hanks, hanging untidily. Her face was pale, nay, very pale, and moist eyes peered out from behind

wide horn-rimmed lenses. The face, strained into resolution,
glared brazenly forward, straight at Sean. The middle-aged lass
was dressed in a homely way; the woman sane-secretary as
neatly as one would expect a secretary to be; and the figure
from God knows where hid some of her gauntiness beneath a
thick tweed dress; a sombre bodice filled itself with ripples as it
flowed over the bonifying body (no disrespect here: Sean was a
damned sight bonier himself); and a brown scarf knotted sideways round her neck gave the wearer half a bohemian, half a
hiker look.

—This is Creda Stern, Sean, said Jen Jayes, beaming with
grace, and indicating the gaunt lady. She has had a shocking
time, and is trying to find a little rest with us up in Dartington.
She insisted on coming down to see you before she left us. She
insists that you should know the truth.

Sean murmured a howdydo, shook the bony, unpromising
hand, while he wondered who was Creda Stern, and why the
hell she forced a visit; and what truth she bore as a present for
him. He fetched additional delf, poured out the tea, and
handed round bread, butter, and jam. He hated these unexpected visits. He wished to retain the privilege of deciding
who should come to see him and who should not. This
annunciation of an earthly angel wasn't to his liking at all.
Playing the hypocrite, he smiled and said it was a lovely day.
He talked a little of Dartington and Devon, got a few smiling
answers, though the visiting angel said never a word, contenting herself by glaring brazenly, straight at Sean.

—Creda has something important, very important, to say to
you, Sean, said Jen Jayes, suddenly. She has the truth for
you.

—Creda wants to tell you about her terrible experience, said
Donah Warrington.

—Creda has suffered a cruel loss, said Jen. She feels you
should know all about it.

—Irreparable, added Donah; and only because she stood for
socialism and freedom of thought. Only when she herself told
me could I believe it. It's a revelation.

—Creda has had to bear the loss of her husband; taken from
her suddenly, without a charge; gone in a moment; taken away
for ever, said Jen Jayes. Terrible!

—And where, and by whom! Creda startled Sean by spring-
ing up from her chair, and bending towards him, the bony

figure glaring down at him sitting at the other side of the table. She was shouting now. Your Soviet Union! By the Ogpu! What do you think of that? I'm a Socialist, and I know; I was there. I know! The truth!

—Creda knows, murmured Jen Jayes.

—Creda saw it happen, murmured Donah Warrington.

—I was there, went Creda on, breathlessly; I and my husband held important positions in the Commitern on the Commissariats of Foreign Trade and Light Industries. I believed in them then. I don't now. She bent over closer to him, squalling, It was all a false dream!

—We all believed, murmured Jen Jayes; but it was all a false dream – Creda knows.

—My husband was taken away without word or sign. He vanished. That's the way it is there: millions in concentration camps. Grey faces everywhere afraid to look left or right, or even behind to anticipate a blow. All hungry, all in tatters – that's the way it is there. She banged the table with a violent fist. A false dream! Now, what do you think of your Soviet Union?

—Take it quietly, lady, advised Sean.

—Oh, do you hear him asking me to take it quietly! she appealed to the others. She turned again to Sean. I'm told you are all for the Soviet Union; that you still dream it is a Socialist country. Do you believe it now? Can you believe it now? Can you? Answer, man!

—Hardly, now, Creda, came a murmur from Donah Warrington. He couldn't now. He knows the truth at last.

— Lady, said Sean, softly, I have been a comrade to the Soviet Union for twenty-three years, and all she stands for in the way of Socialism, and I don't intend to break that bond for a few hasty remarks made by one who obviously hates the very bones of the Soviet people. And the more you shout, lady, the less I hear.

—He couldn't have been listening to me! Creda squealed to the other two. She stood straight up, then bent down again over him. You must listen to me, you must listen to me! I know the truth! Her voice turned into the semblance of a howl. You can see, can't you, that my husband isn't here? Where is he then?

—That's the question, Sean, purred the voice of Jen Jayes: where's Creda's husband?

—I don't know the hell where he is! said Sean, sharply. He may be anywhere.

—I can't understand you, man! shouted Creda. No one knows where he is. All that's known is that he was taken by the Ogpu. Can't you understand that? The Ogpu knows. One day he was with me; the next, and nothing was with me but silence. What do you think of your Soviet Union now?

—Well, apparently, silence didn't stay long with you either, said Sean. I've no evidence that he was taken by the Ogpu, he said, beyond your word. That isn't enough for me. Even if he were taken, there's no counter-evidence to show why; for even the Ogpu don't arrest people for the pure fun of the thing. And, if he behaved there as you are behaving here, I don't wonder he was removed as a potential dictator.

—Do you hear what he says? Creda's voice was near a snarl now. He calls one a dictator who fought for freedom all her life, and is doing it now. What singular, inhuman minds the Irish seem to have! She drew back, still bending, her hands resting on the table. Aren't you able to see the truth when it's put straight and clear in front of you? The voice now flew into a fuller snarl. I tell you, Irishman, the Nazis are far superior, and more to be preferred, than your savage comrades in Moscow! Do you hear me?

—I've heard you, lady, said Sean, quietly. You've just told me that the Socialism of the Soviet Union is not only the hope of the workers, but, also, the hope of the world.

Creda was astounded. She stood spellbound and silent for a few moments. Then she moved a little away from the table to hiss out in bitter and steady tones – I confess I can't understand the Irish mind; it is a twisted mind, and utterly irresponsible.

—Aha, said Sean, quickly, there you show your elemental nature. He indicated Donah Warrington. The mind of Mrs Warrington is as Irish as mine, but to you it is a fine, straight, and honest mind, because that mind agrees with yours. Mine is a horrible mind because it doesn't.

Jasus, Creda was real angry now! She didn't like being caught. No one does. In her angry face, hatred for Sean was mingled with hatred for the Soviet Union. She started towards the door, and the two other dames rose slowly, and made to follow her. Creda pulled her 'kerchief roughly around her neck till the knot lay in the right place under her chin. She clenched her bony hands, and turned towards him again, halfway to the door. The truth was going away.

—If I stayed here any longer, she said, I'd stifle; I'd stifle. Someone told me you were an intelligent man. She let out a squealing laugh. Intelligent! The fellow's a fool! It is such as you that are the cause of Socialism's failure in the Soviet Union; such as you are responsible for fear, for slavery, and the concentration camps. But your Soviet Union will go rotten. At the first assault on it, it will fall asunder like the rotten thing it is! Oh, I'd stifle if I stayed here longer! She went out, followed by the other two, and Sean, from the window, watched the dree fearsome, fearless dames go down the garden path where the hollyhocks nodded to them, and red, cream, and mauve dahlias whispered a word for beauty to them, but the dree dames passed on sourly, giving no sign by any pause that they felt colour and line and form touching the hems of their garments.

—Strange shadows, thought Sean, sometimes slide in to mar the serenity of a sunny day! What an arrogant mind, what a blustering manner, that woman had! The truth is mine. Some seem to think that truth comes banging at everybody's door. A mind that flushes into a rage whenever another ventures to disagree with it. Out for free thought, yet dragging compulsion into every word she uttered! Only what I say, only in what I believe, is the Truth. An individual authoritarian. Only her truth contained divinity. The way some hurl the truth about: down a man with it! Odd how she believed that she could just rush in and take his own little kingdom of thought by storm. She hadn't given a tittle of evidence to show that what she had said happened was a fact. If the way she had behaved before him was her common manner and method in social life, even in argumentative intercourse, he couldn't wonder that her husband had disappeared. Sean wished he could have disappeared himself: away, away from this rowdy truth. Better the peaceful passion of a lie.

It was comic, in a way, to think how many thought they carried Truth fast in the hollow of their hands. Ready to sell it, too, for a shout. Shout my shout, and you shout the truth. Truth becomes a town-crier. What is Truth? asked jesting Pilate; what is Truth? asked serious Sean; and either was as near to the other in knowing. Truth was rarely a visitor: one had to trudge a long way to find her; and, even when you got

to where she was said to be, she was often not at home. She
had gone on a voyage of discovery to find herself. Law and
Order were out looking for her so that she might be put back
safely in her comfortable cage. She could be honoured there;
she could even be worshipped there; but there she would have
to stay, for it wasn't safe to let her roam at large. It was far
better that Truth should be cornered and kept safe from
spreading falsehood about in the receptive minds of men. In
her cage, she can look happily out on the world of men with
safety to herself and satisfaction to them. Here, she is dressed
up to the nines and introduced to the best people. At liberty,
she has a nasty habit of stripping and going about nude, disturbing peaceable persons, and making them feel self-conscious. It is by no means a pleasant thing to meet this naked
lady roamin' in the gloamin' where lay scribes and clerical
pharisees are having a respectable and a quiet rest.

Some said that Truth could always be produced out of
prayer. Prayer, before and after, could make everything done
and said, right and proper and fair and good. Aha, now we
have it: truth comes flying into the word said and into the
action done. Like the judge of the high court, mentioned in the
roman catholic *Universe*, who used to spend hours in prayer
before giving a judgement, and always wore a crucifix under
his robes. It's very simple, isn't it? The power of prayer. No
chance of any mistake. It would solve everything. Imagine all
the judges down on their knees a full hour before giving a
judgement! Oh, the sight entrancing! Better still, imagine all
the doctors down on their knees for an hour before prescrib-
ing; the proletariat down on their knees for an hour before
dawn to fit themselves for a fair day's work; the employers
down on their knees, at the same time, for an hour to fit
themselves for giving a fair day's pay. A beautiful arrangement
with a slow accompaniment on harps from high above, with
sounds of cymbals softened. There's only one foul snag in it –
it wouldn't work! The judges would go on giving judgement
within the limits of the law, however unjust and unrighteous
that law happened to be; the doctors would go on killing and
curing in their old-fashioned way; the employers would go on
believing they were giving too much; and the workers would
go on believing they were getting too little.

What is Truth? Man in his individual nature was still asking
the question, and man in the mass was answering it. Facts,

though true, were not Truth; they were but minor facets of it. Parts, but not the whole. The great achievements of the Soviet Union; touching material possessions, deprived of all by one war, and most by another, having to start afresh twice with little more than a few flint hammers and a gapped sickle or two. The inexhaustible energy, the irresistible enthusiasm of their socialistic efforts, were facts to Sean; grand facts, setting the people's feet firmly on the way to the whole truth, calling all men to a more secure destiny in which all heads shall be anointed with oil, and all cups shall be filled.

He looked at the garden's corner where the elder tree grew; the tree that gave the wood to make a cross for Christ. *Genus Sambucus*, meaning, we are told, a musical instrument. How odd! Wood that can make a musical instrument can make a cross, too. Fifing was going on round the cross today, with prelates conducting – one two three, one two three; one two three four. Happy thing that the tree was so widespread, for much wood had been needed for the martyrdom of man. Every exploitation by one man, or by a bunch of men, of other men was a crucifixion. It was still being done; to the sound of fife and drum when good dividends were declared. A man exploiting himself for the good, for the charm, for the safety of others was a noble thing; a man exploiting man for the grin of gain was an evil thing. But the people are ending the evil. In spite of cowardice and selfishness hidden away under chasuble, cassock, and geneva gown; in spite of a swarm of encyclicals wormy with counsels saying sweet is bitter and bitter is sweet; the people are ending the evil. In the uprising of the peoples, the Spirit of God is once more moving over the face of the waters. No cross on which to hang a man shall ever be made again from the trunk of the elder tree, or from any other wood. Neither shall a fire ever again be kindled against any man owning up to what fury calls a false religion. Adelphos, the brother; we are all from the same mother.

REBEL ORWELL

In the mist of bombfalls, blackouts, and all the thrust and overthrow of war, the biographical books appeared, the third one making a pert bow to the public some time before the curtain fell on the tableau of the Nazi collapse, and war-weapons began to be piled before and around the heaps of ruins giving Europe and many parts of England a new skyline that rasped the serenity of the sun and mocked the gentle rain that fell from heaven. The book was titled *Drums Under the Windows*,* and all the bum critics of Ireland filled the Irish air with hums, hems, and Hail Marys. Hugh Walpole once wrote that 'O'Casey is an uncomfortable writer', and the Irish critics gave the amen of He is So. So with fingers fidgeting with their beads some of them tried to do it grandly, bowler hat on head, kid glove on hand, elegant cane under an oxsther. Said one flushing critic: 'Honest indignation is one thing, and egotistical protestation another'. Another. Two things in fact. 'Egotistical protestation' is good. A swing of the cane and a touch to the bowler hat. Proceed, sir – we're all listening. 'This reader, approaching without any conscious prejudice, finds the mixture at times irritating, and, in the upshot, unremedial.' Mixture is bad; but still nice, and worthy of bowler hat and elegant cane. Upshot and downfall unremedial. That's sad. But the critic – there is nothing to show his identity – uses fine language, like a persilified white petticoat, dignified, and flavoured with lace. But he spoils it, spoils it, by rudely adding 'What is the point of punning, or rather "narking" about with the name of a cardinal whom Mr O'Casey thinks contemptible? Like abuse heard over the garden wall, one's natural impulse is to close the window so as to shut out the sound of it.' No, no; this is not so genteelly written as that which went before, the critic's frightened now. Shut the window! Keep out the sound and the sense! Shut the window! Bang! Gas-attack. Let the cry be heard only by the empty street; let the cry be heard only by the passing wind. Shut the window!

A grave and reverend critic, through an article in the *Even-*

*Pan Books, London, 1972.

ing Mail, a Dublin evening paper, came into Sean's presence, in a most masterly and magisterial manner, to say, 'If you, Mr O'Casey, could only grasp the fact that vulgarity does not always connote strength, and that for narrative style James Joyce is an insidious and also enervating model, you might, some day, give us a great book which we would read with some advantage to our social education and less of the repulsive-reflex which you excite in us by your rather unnecessary reconstruction of unimportant experiences'. How's that for a rattling fine sentence! The Master speaking seriously to the man. Bow the head. Quite a gent of diction. If O'Casey only would listen!

But these were but comic squeaks compared with the agonized yell George Orwell let out of him when he sat down to read the book, and then stood up to review it. Lots have been written about the honesty, the integrity, the fearlessness, of Orwell. But he had an odd glamour: the farther away he was, the more one liked him; or so Koestler says, adding, 'Thus the greater the distance from intimacy and the wider the radius of the circle, the more warming became the radiations of this lonely man's great power of love'. Keep off! The same writer says of him again, 'He was incapable of self-love or self-pity. His ruthlessness towards himself was the key to his personality.' Bannered balderdash, for no man can be without feeling for himself till he be dead. Self-preservation was a first law of nature to Orwell as well as to all the sorts of men. And Orwell had quite a lot of feeling for himself; so much, that, dying, he wanted the living world to die with him. When he saw, when he felt, that the world wouldn't die with him, he turned the world's people into beasts; Orwell's book of beasts. Since that didn't satisfy his yearning ego, he prophetically destroyed world and people in Nineteen hundred and eighty-four: Doomsday Book. The decay in himself was in his imagination, transmuted into the life of the whole world. Well, if that isn't self-pity, wrapped sourly up in yearned revenge, then nothing is. It seemed to comfort his ailing nature to believe that he was leaving a perishing world; a world that would soon ignobly and terribly die. He was a lordeen of Shalott who saw life in a mirror, not the lovely and coloured life the Lady saw, but the misshapen figures and manners born in his own ailing mind. He was wild that the world of men and women noticed him not, but went on fighting. They plunged forward into resolute hope, while he embedded himself deep in self-pitying despair; for Koestler himself tells us that 'Orwell's despair had a concrete, organized structure, as it were, and was projected from the individual to the social plane'. He yearned to drag all life down with himself into his own stony despair. Life dissolved, not even into amber, but into grey stone. Tried hard, too, to do it through the books he wrote; and he went wild to hear, in a muffled way, the sounds of life at work, and life's loud laughter a long way from it all. Koestler enthrones this poor wailer among the rebels, saying, 'His life was a consistent series of rebellions against the condition of society in general and his own predicament'. Rebel indeed! Rather a yielding blob that buried itself away from the problems of living that all life has to face and overcome. No fight in him; always a running away and a yielding. What did he rebel against? One can understand rebellion against his own predicament; but here even there was no resilient opposition to it; but rather a hugging of it and a hastening to places where it was bound to grow worse. As regards his rebellion against the condition of society, did he do a hand's turn to improve it? Rather, in desire and malignant prophecy, he tried to make it worse. The mass of the people never knew him while he lived; had never heard of him when his life had ended. He has been dumped beside Jonathan Swift, but Swift hasn't turned his head to look at him; for Swift was an intense star in Ireland's sky, while poor Orwell's pin-point of light hadn't even the power to point a way to where the greater star was blazing; Swift was known to all Dublin, and almost all of Dublin followed his body to the grave.

Koestler tells us that George Orwell was 'a dishwasher, a tramp, and a sergeant in the Burma police'. He was a dishwasher and a tramp and all! A pseudo-secular worker-priest. Probably never sang the bum-song in his life; the dishwashing tiring him in less than a week. One doesn't find experiences by seeking for them: they come naturally, according to the time, the place, and the conditions, or they don't come at all. He was a sergeant in the Burma police all right, for the sergeant's shout echoes strongly in a lot of his work; and, particularly, in the persistent egotism that all should think as he thought, or suffer for it. He was no rebel in his books, for in his ripest time there was a great mass of readers flourishing well within the context of despair, so that his thoughts floated far, and were

gathered into a warm reception room. Here, and in many
other places, there was a concourse of kafka-koestlerian souls
waiting to carry his books about on velvet cushions; so that,
instead of making souls uncomfortable, he filled them up with
gratification; all drooping in a sunny darkness of despair,
ready, to all appearances, to pop into the rotten mouth of
death. They were saying to the newly born, Abandon hope ye
who enter here; they were murdering life's little children in
their beds.

Orwell's *Animal Farm* hailed so heartily as a great original
work, isn't so original in form or substance as the heart hailers
thought it to be. A similar tale appears the time the English
language was beginning to be timidly lisped in a welter of
French and Latin. It appears in a poem called *Vox Clamantis*,
written by Gower when he was frightened near to death by the
rising of the peasants led by Wat Tyler and John Ball. Gower
tells of the crowd changed into beasts, asses fierce as lions, who
will bear no more burdens, oxen who refuse to draw the
plough, dogs who bark at huntsmen; all led by a Jay, represent-
ing Tyler, who harangues them, probing the air with shouts of
Down with the honourables, Down with the Law! The Jay is
killed, but the whole of life is left in disorder; there is a scene
of whole-hearted corruption, though there is a beat in the
poem of a hope higher than Orwell's despair; for Gower ends
by saying that the voice of the people is often the voice of
God. In Orwell's book, the voice of God is gone; no sound of
the people's voice; only the yell from Orwell. Gower is the
poet who is the measure of Orwell, and not Swift.
Someone has said that Gower is of value only as a measure
against the greatness of Chaucer; and, in the same way,
Orwell is of value only as a measure against the greatness of
Swift.

Loud cheers are given, wonderful claims are made for his
honesty : 'The most honest writer alive; his uncompromising
intellectual honesty was such that it made him appear almost
inhuman at times; his integrity was never touched'. Never?
Let this amazing integrity speak for itself, in one instance,
anyway, throughout his review of *Drums Under the Windows*,
in *The Observer*. He opens with, 'W. B. Yeats once said that a
dog does not praise his fleas, but this is somewhat contradicted
by the special status enjoyed in this country by Irish Nationalist writers'. Does he mean that Irish writers are fleas in the

hairs of the British bulldog? Is that honesty, is that integrity?
It is a curious connexion to give to a poem written by Yeats,
and dedicated to 'a poet, who would have me praise certain
bad (Irish) poets, imitators of his and mine'. Is Orwell, at an
opposite pole to Yeats, angry with Irish writers because they
don't imitate him? His manner, his mood? Is the use of the
plural but camouflage for an attack on the singular O'Casey,
who would have none of his mood, none of his manner?
Status! What status have Irish writers had in England? Shaw?
But Shaw was no Nationalist. Yeats then? But Yeats told Sean
himself that he was over forty before he handled a five-pound
note; and it was Sweden that gave him the Nobel Prize. James
Joyce? Read this great writer's Preface to the American edition of *Ulysses*, and learn of the wonderful status Joyce had
here. O'Casey? Ah, he, him, first and foremost. Well, we'll
see.

Orwell goes on, 'Considering the story of Anglo-Irish rela-
tions, it isn't surprising that there should be Irishmen whose
life-work is abusing England; what does call for remark is that
they should be able to look for support to the English people,
and in some cases should even, like Mr O'Casey himself, pre-
fer to live in the country which is the object of their hatred'.
Get outa me country! A curious cry from such a lover of
freedom and all humanity to yell. A jingo snarl – and from
Orwell; from the person who was stridently, or pretended to
be, out for universal freedom of thought, the fellow who, it is
said, fought against uniformity in life; now balling out a curse
on the head of a writer because he happened to be Irish.
Hadn't the savvy (had it all right, but had set it aside to suit his
malicious purpose) to realize that O'Casey could no more help
being an Irishman than Moses could help being a Jew.

Orwell knew that the support given to O'Casey by the English people wasn't amazing; knew it well. Let's get this clear;
put forth a few hot facts in this cold war. Two-thirds, and
more, of the support he got came from the United States; half
of the other third from his own country, the rest from Britain,
including an odd hand from the Scot and the Cymru. He lived
in England, but so far from living on her, he paid more in tax
to her revenue than he received from the south coast to the
banks of the Tweed. An uncle had fought and was wounded at
Balaclava, a brother had fought in the Boer War, another in
the First World War, a nephew in a submarine, a son of his

had served in the Royal Artillery, and another was serving in
the Artillery now. Wasn't this the record of as good a giver as
what was given by this yelling Orwell? Yelling out against
'abusing England', while he himself was abusing and cursing
the whole of life.

'England was the object of O'Casey's hatred.' To say simply
that this remark is a lie is but to give it a good name; it is
more, inasmuch as it throbs with malice, too. Certainly, he had
no liking for the England that was Orwell and his abune companions. But he had steeped himself in the culture and civilization of the broad, the vital, the everlasting England, not
through means provided by solicitous English Governments,
but by desperate, never-ceasing efforts of his own; half a life's
work which shows, not a hatred, but a great and a consuming
love for England's culture. He knew England's history better
than that of his own country, and that was saying a little;
knew it, probably, better than Orwell himself, for in his work
Orwell seemed to be strangely distant from it; ignoring the
great English souls of the past, ignoring those of his own time,
content to gratify his own tangled thoughts by shouting out rot
and rust to England's future.

This defender of England, lover of all her values, showed in
his review that he was ignorant of one of the best-known
pieces in the whole of English literature. His voice rises to a
special scream when he describes Cathleen ni Houlihan marching along singing what he thought to be an Irish 'Nationalist'
song:

> Singing of men that in battle array,
> Ready in heart and ready in hand,
> March with banner and bugle and fife
> To the death, for their native land.

Get outa me country! We won't let you sing these ballads,
breathless with hatred of England, here! But this ballad
breathed love for England, for it was written, not by an Irish
Nationalist, but by Tennyson. It is sung by Maud in the peom
of the same name, known to most, but unknown to England's
great defender, Orwell. One would imagine that an educated
Englishman like Orwell would have known it almost off by
heart; but Orwell had ever heard the Voice by the cedar tree,
in the meadow, under the Hall. Yet the wreathed garlands on

Tennyson's grave had hardly had time to wither when Orwell came into the world of England.

This logos of lamentation complains that the book is so written 'as to make it difficult to pin down the facts of chronology'. Facts of chronology is damn good. But there are quite a lot of facts of chronology that haven't been even pinned up yet. As a chronological fact, on what day of the year was Christ born? Mohammed? And what was the year, the month, and the day, on which Buddha first sat down under the Bo tree? He goes on, 'Sean did this and Sean did that, giving an unbearable effect of narcissism; the book is written in a sort of basic Joyce, sometimes effective in a humorous aside, but it is hopeless for narrative purposes'. Basic Joyce! Bad or good; right or wrong, O'Casey's always himself. Of course Sean did this and did that, because he was alive, and will go on doing this, doing that till something called death stops him. Everybody's doing it, doing it, doing it. The low note about cogging from Joyce is particularly ironical, seeing that in his first venture, sent to Sean for an opinion, Orwell himself tried to imitate Joyce, not here and there only, but in whole scenes as near to the genius of Joyce as Sean's few verses are near to the poetical genius of Shakespeare or Shelley. Orwell goes on, 'Literary judgement is perverted by political sympathies, and Mr O'Casey with others like him are able to remain almost immune from criticism. It seems time to revise our attitude, for there is no real reason why Cromwell's massacres should cause us to mistake a bad or indifferent book for a good one.' Well, that's a good one! Here's a lad indeed with honour set in one eye and death i' the other! Cromwell's massacre of Irish citizens is to be changed to a massacre of Irish writers by angry English reviewers. All nationalities are to be equal within the British Commonwealth, but some nationalities are to be more unequal than others.

—I wondher why the fellow showed such venom in a review, murmured Donal o' Murachoo, as he and Sean trudged through piercing points of sleet, a bitter red wind from the east numbing their backs; I wondher why?

—I imagine I know, responded Sean. Ten years ago, Gollancz, the publishers, sent me a book in proof-form, called *A Clergyman's Daughter*, written by Mr Orwell. In a letter they said they hoped I'd find time to read it, adding that though the firm didn't think the book maintained an even keel, they were

sure the scene in Trafalgar Square was one of the most imaginative pieces of writing they had ever read – equal to Joyce at
his best. They asked me if I had time to read it, and liked it, to
write them a line they could quote, with of course, permission
to use my name.

—Aha, the name, the name! ejaculated Donal. Not a
whisper of complaint from him then about an Irish Nationalist
writer's status. Oh, no, not when he was hot-foot after a puff
of praise behind him. The higher the status, the more he was
pleased.

—The name was all he was after, Donal, though the name
had no authority, either in training or experience, as a reviewer. Christ! This sleet's cutting the skin off my face! Let's
take shelter somewhere.

—That was his single-think; the double-think came afterwards, said Donal. Did you send the magic line that Orwell
wanted?

—No, then, I didn't, Donal.

—Then what did you do, love, and what did you say?
crooned Donal.

—I had my own integrity to guard. I returned the proof-
copy, saying I couldn't agree with the publisher's pinnacled
praise of it. I said that the scene in Trafalgar Square wasn't
even imitation Joyce, and curried the remarks with another
advising the publishers to suggest to the author to try to keep
'and so and so's and so forths, with etc, etc, etcs,' well out of
any future book he might write. Orwell had as much chance of
reaching the stature of Joyce as a tit has of reaching that of an
eagle.

—Good advice, son; but why didn't you reply to his review
of *Drums Under the Windows*?

—That I did, Donal, but the one reward I got was a civil
note from the Literary Editor of *The Observer* saying he had
sent on the comments to Mr Orwell. He answered never a
word, Donal. Like Dr Gogarty and Mr Louis McNeice, Orwell
shot silence at O'Casey, because either the comments were too
ridiculous to be noticed, or too difficult to answer.

—Let boyos like Orwell say what they like, said Donal, giving a higher hitch to his coat-collar, there will always be a spot
of green in an Irishman's eye. O'Casey's song and dance have
as much right on the stage of life as Orwell's bastard ballet of
lamentation. He stopped to look up at a sign that a lamp above

flooded with light, showing clearly a golden Crown and a crimson Rose. What about here? he queried; looks cosy, and the two of us near perished.

Shoving a glass-panelled door from him, Donal led the way into the lounge, into a glow, made brighter and cosier by the sound of the slashing sleet and bitter wind without. There was a fine sheen from many bottles, black and brown, green and golden; a gripping glitter from polished tankards, never used now, looking like sturdy old men watching with scornful wonder the more delicate ways of present-day drinking; a softer shine came from many glasses, and all were wrapped up in an enveloping warmth, from which crept the soft caress of a heady smell, vaporizing itself from the fumes of whiskey and of beer.

Donal got two whiskeys, hot, and he and Sean sat down on a leather-cushioned bench facing the bar; sipping their drinks with quiet delight, letting the soft, lazy comfort of the Rose and Crown seep through secular body and secular soul. Over at the far corner of the bar two men were seated on high stools, drinking iced beer, each with an eye on the crowd, though remaining intent on themselves.

—Wonder who are those two set-aside birds perched on the high stools at the far corner of the bar? Bedammit, he went on, answering himself, the lean one's Orwell; but who's the other with the cocky stance and stone stare, like an ageing owl, once wise, now witless?

—That one's a gossop-writer in an evening paper, one who, in his mind-nurtured column, said the British Prime Minister had allowed the British Council to send the Dublin Gate Theatre all over the Balkans as an advertisement for Britain, acting the plays of O'Casey, who laughs as loud at the British as he laughs at the Irish; though a little inquiry would have shown the blown-up duffer that the Gate Theatre never did an O'Casey play; so neither the Prime Minister nor the British Council had been guilty of misbehaviour in encouraging O'Casey 'to laugh at the British'. So, Donal, me man, it's out of the British book and off the British stage with the Irish O'Casey.

—God spoke first, said Donal. Looka, Sean, looka – towards the door! Is me eyesight going queer? Tell me if you see as well or as queer as meself.

Sean looked, and saw a bright young lady tripping into the

lounge. She was dollied up regardless, in a suit of steel-blue faille, gold-threaded, shimmering; with large stand-away pockets and narrow velvet belt. Over all, she wore a coat of smooth *velour de fouine*, lined with brilliantly blue silk, having a winged collar and voluminous sleeves. Handsome she looked, and handsome she knew she was, and, oh, the sight entrancing!

—It's Cathleen ni Houlihan! ejaculated Donal, fear in his eyes, and pride in his voice. As handsome a heifer as ever, though not quite as slender as she used to be. Look at her varnished nails, her clouded eyelashes – they don't fit in with her past manner of modesty. Among the English she shouldn't shape herself like that – nylons too! Doesn't look a bit like as if she came out of a cloud of disasther and woe!

—You don't expect her to come here dressed as she's shown on an Abbey Theatre poster, do you?

—Her get-up doesn't seem suitable, Sean, considering the way so many poets wrote about her; it does Ireland disservice. She looks too loud and gay to worry respect out of the English. Aw, she's seen us! She's making straight for us!

Over she came with a twittering run, a musical motion rippling her legs and hips, her fresh face flushed and smiling, her hands outstretched.

—I seen yous, the pair of yous, the minute I waltzed in; and glad I am that I won't be a bird alone here. I was lost alone in the hotel I'm in, and so I run down in a taxi to have a quick one here to warm me up a bit. Welcome to the Rose an' Crown, me rattlin' boys from Paddy's land. Well, how are yous? Why the silence? Aren't yous goin' to ask me to sit down?

—Sit down, do please, Cathleen, daughter of Houlihan, said Donal, made almost mute by the new look of his mystical love.

—Thanks, kindly, she murmured, sitting down facing them, stroking her skirt into attractive alignment with the contour of her shapely legs. Whisper, lads – don't call me Cathleen. I'm over here incognito, and known now as Lady Shan Van Vogue. Got a bit tired of being a tall, white candle before the Holy Rood. A real lady, mind you, and she slapped Donal on the shoulder. Isn't either of yous goin' to ask me if I have a mouth on me? Mother o' God, it's a cold welcome I'm gettin'.

—Your coming took us by surprise, said Donal, rising

slowly; would you like your lemonade warmed?

—For God's sake, man, I need something with a keener kick in it than lemonade – cold or hot!

—Shush! Careful! warned Donal. Not so loud. Those two boyos on the high stools have their ears cocked, and are watching you.

—Let them watch! said Cathleen, with a lovely toss of her head; they'll see something they'd like to have at home.

—Deh, deh, Donal clicked his tongue. Cathleen, please, remember where you are.

—Aw, for God's sake, man! I'm where I haven't to watch every step I take, or do reverence to ould rusty partialities. Looka, agra, she said to Sean, get me a tidy gin with a slim splash of lime in it, and let another nip of comfort go with it by yous tellin' me how're things with the pair o' yous.

—I'm not sure it was wise of you to come here to the Rose and Crown, said Donal.

—You don't say? said Cathleen, caustically, Ara, man, I had to come or go outa me mind, off me head – go demented, I mean. She gracefully sipped at the warm gin Sean had brought her. I come over here for a harmless flutter, for a little of what I fancy. The homeland's nuts on rushing towards the first house in heaven. A twice-nightly business now, and quite a few doin' well on it, thank God.

—Cautious, Cathleen, cautious, murmured Donal.

—Ah, you! retorted Cathleen. Every county's vying with the one next to it as to how many volleys of prayers they let fly into heaven; a continual *feau de miserére* of missions, retreats, an' novenas. All our poets, dramatists, an' story-tellers, are lyin' day an' night, flat on their bellies, just because a leadin' poet, Patrick Kavanagh, has declared that if only the poets an' writers fling themselves prostrate before God, an' admit their dire disthress, they may be admitted into a new dispunsensation; for, said he, all the great poets, says he, were, an' are, those who lie prostrate before God. Before God, it's terrible over there, over there, I'm tellin' yous, gentlemen.

—Still, I think you should have stayed at home to keep the old flag flying, said Donal.

—Oh, you do? Well, I don't. You go over, an' keep the old flag flyin', if you're that eager. You go over an' care for the poets lyin' prostrate. An' are they comfortable? They are not! An' do they want to lie prostrate? They do not! An' are they

spoutin' great poetry? They are not! It's just that they daren't
get up. The nation's watchin' them from window an' door.
Bendin' over one of them, with a sweet Tipperary lass be my
side, before I left to come here, I heard him mutter that the
longer he lay the worse he got; an' when I poked him in the
back with me snow-white wand, symbol of purity, telling' him
to get up, an' talk to the pretty lass beside me, an' be a man; he
only dug himself deeper, moanin', Oh, if it wasn't for the wife
an' kids!

—I don't know that you're going to be any better here,
murmured Donal.

—Don't you? I do. I'm betther already. Here a girl can show
the curve of a calf, of a bosom, even of a bottom, without
fearin' to have to face fury.

—Dtch, dtch, Donal clicked his tongue. You're sadly
changed, Cathleen. In front of the English too! We should
behave, while still showing we're Irish and proud of it.

—Aw, that boast's a batthered one now, Donal. There's
small use of bein' proud of what none of us can help.

—Looka! said Donal suddenly; looka, something's happening to the boyos on the stools! They're vaporizing into the
whisky-fumed air! Whisht, Orwell's saying something!

—Hear me, my people, said the voice from the top of the
vapoury column into which the figure was changing; why
should the Irish have a status in our comfort-mongering Rose
and Crown? Pack them back to their bracken-clad fields, their
stony roads, their tousled houses.

—Drive the Irish from our stages throughout the ages, tare
and ages, whispered the weakening voice of Gossup from the
vapoury wisps he was fast becoming.

—From our literature, too; away, away, whispered the voice
of Orwell; out of its pages throughout the ages, tare and ages;
let no Irish thought taint our English civilization! Away!

—For God's sake! ejaculated Donal, the mien of the secular
scholar rising up in him. There's no such thing as English
civilization – it's a mingling through the ages of many others –
Syrian, Jewish, Hellenistic, Roman, with the Scot, the Cymru,
and the Gael brightening it all up a bit. The very rosary beads
we twist through our fingers had their origin in Syria, and the
column keeping Nelson in the air has a Syrian root. If we all
haven't drunk from the well at the world's end, we've all had a
sip from the well at the world's beginning!

—Out of the books, off of the stage, went the dying whisper
out of the vapour dying down to silence as the two souls dissolved into the warmth of the whiskey-fumed air, and left
nothing but a slightly darker air hovering over where the two
souls had been sitting. The dour departed.

—Never mind them, buddies, called out a voice from the
lounge's centre; me own father's mother was an Irishman.

—Same here, called another voice from the far end; sure,
me own mother's father was an Irishwoman. Sing us an Irish
song, and forget them. A chorus of easy-going English voices
murmured approval, and gentle knockings of the tables gave
encouragement to the call for a song. Sing us one of your Irish
songs, one of your heart's desire; sing us one that you used to
sing around the cabin fire.

—Go on, Donal, me son, pleaded Sean; sing from our hearts
out.

—Do, Donal, pleaded Cathleen, laying a white, coaxing
hand on Donal's knee; sing, an' show we're Irish without
shame to ourselves, or danger to anyone else.

So Donald leaned back in his seat, and sang:

All round me hat I wear a band of green ribbon O,
Careless of what any lofty mind may say;
If anyone should ask me why, I'll tell them Eire wove it
All round me hat, an' there it's destin'd for to stay.

All that she is or was is woven in that ribbon O,
Her chieftains lyin' low in cloister'd Clonmacnoise today;
Th' bugle-call of Finn that shook the mountain high, the
    valley low,
Cuchullian's chariot-rush that took th' foemen's breath
    away.

All that her saints have done, her sinners' gay mortality,
Th' time they stood undaunted up, th' time they slipp'd an'
    fell;
Th' beauty of the oldher books an' all th' songs her poets
    sung,
Are woven in this ribbon green, an' woven fair an' well.

All th' Ulsther chiefs defendin' Eire from the Norman Law;
Tone tossin' on the sea, an' damnin' all its din;

Emmet takin' Ireland's hope down with him to a grave un-
    known,
When people had no peace without or gleam of hope within.

Th' rout of priests who ordhered Irish souls away to hell,
Who saw a Chieftain sent from God in Charles Stewart
    Parnell;
Larkin's apostolic voice that rang the workers out of sleep,
An' made undaunted fighters from a flock of baain' sheep.

An' them comin' lather when daffodils danc'd in th' sun,
When many were th' whispers that poor Ireland's days were
    done;
When Pearse an' all his comrades beat a roll upon an Irish
    drum,
A roll that's beatin' still to bring a rally yet to come.

So all round me hat, I wear a band of green ribbon O,
Zone of our faults, our fights, our love an' laughter gay;
All that Eire is or was is woven in that ribbon O,
An' there it stops till life is dead an' time has ebb'd away.

HEAVILY HANGS THE BROAD SUNFLOWER

THE first book of biography came before the eyes of those whose ears were listening to the stuttering, muttering rumble of war. Everyone was becoming tense; the nation was beginning to rise up on its toes. A great part of the world was about to do a ballet battle-dance in ruin: a slow movement to muted violins, tuneless; the conductor's baton a beat behind the rhythm; the music dwindling low at times to a querulous lullaby, always asking, never answering; till of a sudden the crescendo came, deafening the very sounds the music gave itself, shrieking a fierce overture for the tens of thousands of British men, women, and children, who, in a day or two, would be flung from the uproar into the odd stillness of a land of shadows. Neither England nor France had had the foresight to make an ally of the Soviet Union before, and they couldn't screw their courage to the sticking-place to make an ally of her now. England's Prime Minister, Chamberlain, had so many children that he didn't know what to do, and he had no Ma to advise him. He crept out at night to the building of the Soviet Embassy, and looked up at the lighted windows, murmuring, Shilli go in or shalli stay out? He had courage only to look through a window to see the time by the shadow of the Kremlin clock, watching the hands creeping towards the time when churchyards yawn; thought the clock was fast, and hurried back to Downing Street, where the cautious clock was comfortably slow.

See him standing up at the Lord Mayor's Banquet to speak, in the midst of the smell of food, the odour of wines, the rustle of silks, the glitter of jewellery. Hear him speak the word: We stand where we stood, we stand where we are, where we stood before, we stand still, and we refuse to sit down. Hear, hear. We shall stand fast, stand steady, stand forth. All listening? Yes, all listening. Gog and Magog agog with interest. What is the wild wave saying? No one there, no one anywhere, knew anything about the shape of things to come. No one knew that the daft god of the Nazis would soon be flinging down fire and

brimstone on England's pleasant land, or that the smoke of the
city would soon go up as the smoke of a furnace, nor did the
daft god know that the very fire he created would one day
make a cinder of himself. Gog and Magog are with us: no one
can harm us. A confident fellow is speaking. I warn Herr Hitler! A great clap-clapping of hands. A very confident fellow. I
warn Herr Hitler that we shall stand by Czecho-Slovakia; I
warn Herr Hitler that if he attacks Poland, England will read
the riot act; throw all she has on the side of right and justice,
and the British Army will march, tramp, tramp, tramp; and
show the world that Europe is still a Continent fit for zeros to
live in; if Germany attacks Poland, England will immediately
go to her aid! How? March across the Continent? Through
Germany to get to Poland? A short cut. Too dangerous for
ships to sail through the Skagerrak, so fill up small boats with
men, and let them pull to the port of Gdynia. With a long, long
pull, and a strong, strong pull, gaily, lads, make them go! If
neither way be possible, then tunnel a way to Warsaw! The
Lord Mayor felt he'd like to conk Hitler with the mace; but it
might have been better had he conked Chamberlain. Britannia
had changed her trident for an umbrella. Let us under outa the
rain. Attention! Umbrella down. It ain't gonna rain no more.
Poor man! He gave England all that was in him to give; but
national tension tightened the life out of him; and events beyond were far beyond the stretch of his terminal mind.

No one wanted war in England, and poor Chamberlain had
a distressing time fitting in the possibility of war with the mood
of the people. The effort hastened his end. There was none of
the excitement among the people which had emblazoned the
passions of the previous one. People were guessing what it
might be like, and they didn't relish what they saw in their
mind's eye. Thousands and thousands of disabled veterans of
the last war were dragging themselves about still; the Cenotaph
stood to remind them of the million of young Englishmen who
had gone from life a few years before, and the young men of
the day had no wish to follow them down to earth. Crêped
thoughts still lingered in English souls today. All were sullenly
silent, and all waited. Look, it's bending a little – the broad
sunflower. Ah, the first of wintry fear on the sunflower's stem.
Germany and Italy alone of Europe were ready to go out to
cheer on every public pathway and bid the nations bid themselves goodbye. Hitler had his banner hanging from every
German window, had turned every road into a route-marching

avenue, every square in every town into a parade-ground.
Mussolini had the ledges of every window of Rome worn away
leaning out to tell the people that Hitler was the new *lux
mundi* and he the *lux mundi secunda*, godsent, godborn, goose-
gospelled.

The one bright thing in England's pleasant land was the
British Blackshirts, headed by Oswald Mosley, a chromium-
plated tapper-tit, trotting through the London streets, trumpet-
ing *De Profundis Britannicum*, like toy soldiers embowed with
what looked like life for a brief spell, self-ridicule investing
them with its honour as they chalked their symbol, the Flash
within the Circle, on the road wherever two streets crossed.
The string in the egg; the egg and I. Mosley thought he was
leading a crewsade, but he but led a wandering to and fro. He
had one thing in common with Hitler – no sense of humour.
Mussolini was funny in himself, Hitler was sinister, Mosley
ridiculous. Some big-business men applauded him and supported his movement for a time because they thought he would
prove to be the Deliverer of the Goods; a deliverer who would
flatten the organized workers into a thin tail that would wag
delightedly for whatever might be kindly given to the dog. We
Want Mosley, chanted the Blackshirts, but no one else took up
the cry, and the winds of life blew even its echoes away before
many had time to hear it. Once, in the Albert Hall, Mosley,
after a funfare, came forward in a tremendous pool of electric
light to tell the English people how to live, how to die, and
how to do their shopping. Stood out in the fierce white light
that beats upon the drone. Stood there talking. Bands playing
and audience chanting Mosley's the Only Boy in the World,
and England's his Only Girl. England's Pick-me-up. The Duce
Anglicanem. The living Song of the Shirt. Shirts were in de-
mand everywhere. Men on the make were everywhere seeking
fresh gods and postures new, and the symbol was a shirt. Even
Ireland started to wear them; but to give her her due, those
who bought them soon sold them to be used as football jerseys.
It was a Shift that caused the great commotion in Ireland; a
Shirt everywhere else: Song of a Shift in Eirinn, song of a
Shirt in Sasana. Mosley led the stuffed shirts in England. He
caused quite a sensation of fear among some of our Communists, who didn't know a bumbell from a Jo Anderson, me
Jo John. The Blackshirts couldn't get going. They were heard
in silence, and, after a meeting, seemed to slink away, rather
than to depart; fold their taunts like the Scarabs, and silently

steal away. They never seemed to be at ease in their shirts; not
in any way at ease like a Scot in his kilt; not even like a would-
be saint wearing a hairy one. Mosley, seemingly, hadn't it in
him to go far. His vision seemed to be limited to what he saw
in the looking-glass. Malice through the looking-glass. Not a
tap came from Drake's Drum, though some Communists
thought they heard it thundering. Hitler's and Mussolini's sad
success had added cubits to Mosley's stature. Yet the apathy
shown to his cause by the English people and the ring of
clenched fists around him kept him in a corner. It was mad-
dening.

Far away in Berchtesgaden, the umbrella and the axe sat
together in the best room there, sipping tea and talking.
Chamberlain listening, nodding his head, and occasionally asking Hitler what time o' day it was; Hitler outstaring him, the
madman's glare already lighting up the bulging eyes; Ribbentrop beside him, smiling covert encouragement over to the
British Prime Minister: Now, Mister Prime Minister, you can
really see what a really charming laddie he is; the English
Ambassador, Nevile Henderson, hanging his head in embarrassment, knowing well that the Prime Minister Chamberlain's
talk was convincing Hitler that England's shoulders could no
longer carry a coat of mail.

—Well, we've had an interesting and a profitable talk, said
Chamberlain, rising to go. He gently touched the swastikaed
arm of the Furor: Don't forget, son, that you have promised
me to be a good boy. Now, you won't go too far?

—I promise, said the Furor, the lidless eyes staring and
fascinating the Prime Minister; all I want are the Sudeten hills
and the villages at their feet: when they are mine, I shall be
satisfied.

—Fair enough! said Chamberlain, ignoring a warning nod
from the head of his Ambassador, whose keener mind possibly
foresaw that Britain's life stood breathless in the middle of her
autumn, to be followed by a frost that would never soften.
Heavily hangs the broad sunflower over its grave i' th' earth so
chilly.

All through the ferment, the ebb, and the flow Sean worked
at the second volume of his biographical book, calling it *Pictures in the Hallway*,* and a play which he called *Purple Dust*,
the play coming into the world before the book. Soon in many
places, there would be no pictures in the hallway, no hallways

* Pan Books, London, 1971.

in which to hang any, no homes even for hallways. Soon umbrella-carrying Britannia's set and serious face would be ripped open, the slashed cheeks would be blood-dripping, with no time to stitch the gashes close. Let the blood drip and splash pitiful patterns on the pavement; no time to sew up the wound; no time: it will mean disfigurement, but life is at the last, long hazard now.

George Jean Nathan, the famous American critic, had welcomed the play, and had promised to do all he could to bring about a production in New York; and Sean was content to wait for one. Then a curious thing happened: he got an unsigned letter from a London Theatre Club asking an option on the play. A woman's name printed on the top of the letter indicated her to be the Secretary, and he wrote to her, politely saying that he was expecting an American production, and couldn't give permission. After some delay, a letter, signed by the producer, came along to say that the play had been in rehearsal for some time, and would O'Casey kindly give formal permission to the production by the theatre. No, O'Casey couldn't, and wrote to say so, adding that he didn't like the procedure of a group putting a play into rehearsal before getting permission from the author. Then a third letter from the producer told a strange tale: not only had the play been fully rehearsed without first even hinting to Sean that they were thinking of doing it, but Mr James Agate had been invited to see the play and give his views on it in the coming issue of *The Sunday Times*. Agate came, watched the rehearsal through, and, on the following Sunday, denounced the play as a worthless one; more, that it was an attack on England when England was helpless and unable to reply! Lil'Allegro to the watch-tower came, and tranceposed himself into the custodian of the British Commonwealth. He wroped himself in the Union Jack and over England's head his arm he flung against O'Casey. God, he was fierce! The world could hear him snorting!

> Hold thou my casque, and furl my pennon up
> Close to the staff. I will not show my crest,
> Nor standard, till the common foe shall challenge them.

Was it dislike of the author and the play, or love of England that made the Ego strike? This critic had great influence, and Sean did himself harm by not sending him a monthly bouquet of flowers. Sparse as the response to the play in a book or on the stage might be, the response was likely to die altogether now that a war was about to begin. Yet, to bring a play through to a full rehearsal, without telling the author anything about it, till a prominent critic had come to see it and to write about it in his next review; and to expect that the author would not object to all that, was, indeed, a very strange thing to think, and a stranger thing to do.

Mr Chamberlain came home waving the talismanic umbrella. Is it peace, Jehu? It is peace. Herr Hitler has met an old man in the halfway house, and has promised to be good; has promised to go over the hills only. He will go for the Reds, thought many, maybe Chamberlain, too. We need have no fear. He will level Moscow. He won't harm us. He as much as told Mr Chamberlain so. He calls the Russians sub-humans, and, maybe, he's right. I, for one, could never cotton to them. They are too vital for words. They think far too much about life, and all that life can do, as George Borrow saw and said during the black and frosty drip of the Crimean War. They should be stopped, and Hitler may be the man to do it. Pray God he may think quick about it. The Brown Shirts will soon be over the border! What border? Whose border? The Soviet Union's border. Do you tell me that? That I do. Huraah!

No hurry; no necessity to hurry with that job, said Hitler: that can wait. It will be no more when it comes than a jolly garden-party where a few shots are fired. I'll tame the fiercer first. Show France and England who's who there, here, and everywhere. The Russian venture won't be more than a rather long hunt; the chase will be half blinded by banners, ears will buzz with gay bugle-blowing, and, of course, a few will be hurt to take monotony out of the march. Heil Hitler! Sieg Heil! would soon be shouted in the Kremlin. It will be fascinating to spend a fortnight there, looking around, and bring a few souvenirs back to Berlin. The Bolsheviks must be in a sweat – that is if there be any of them intelligent enough to realize that their days are numbered by me. Our Nazi Army will go through the Red one like a hot knife through butter; even the English generals, admirals, and prime politicians know that well. The Red Army is but a moving heap of shreds and patches. My army will pave the way to Moscow with rusting Russian faces. Moscow will become a shooting-lodge for the Junkers and the generals. It will be an amiable and a thrusting day when the Nazi tanks thunder through the Red Square, and the Volga becomes the eastern Rhine. And Hitler combed his hair.

But the infatuated bastard didn't do that; he did this: on a fine September morning, he sent his thanks thundering over Poland's border straight for Warsaw. What the hell was the fellow doing? You've disappointed us all; you've taken the wrong turning, you fool! So Chamberlain took off his gloves and, uniting with France, declared war on Nazi Germany, but his bold words went up and up and over, only to be lost amid the smoke and fire of blasted Poland. Not even a war correspondent could be sent to help the Poles. France's time was coming soon, and England's too, for sparks from Poland's fires would shortly set brave London burning.

The Nazis got a shock when they came to the river Bug, for there, on the opposite bank, stood battalions of Red Army men watching them; cannons pointed, if you please, across the river towards the Wehrmacht men.

—Christ is risen! shouted the Nazis over to the Reds, knowing that this was a Russian exclamation common on Christmas or Easter Day – they couldn't remember which.

—He is risen, indeed! shouted back the Reds; and you're to come no farther – we'll take care of what's behind us.

The Furor wasn't pleased; indeed, the Furor was furious. This wasn't the act of a pal. Here were Stalin's Reds lined up on the bank of the Bug, with artillery and tanks facing his invincible Wehrmacht, and telling them, impudently, to stay where they were; to come no farther. Stalin must have a bad mind. After all, Hitler's word was Hitler's word. Aha, Stalin, my boy, you wait! Oh, when he did thump down on these Reds, his fist would thump them like the hammer of Thor! Better and wiser if they took what was coming to them lying down. Whom the gods would destroy, they first make mad. He'd leave this line of least resistance to the last; but when he got going, he'd leave nothing of these Bolsheviks but bundles of rags and bones blowing aimlessly about their own snowy steppes.

Bang! Jasus, what was that! Was it a car rattling o'er the stony street, or was it the cannon's opening roar? No, no; sit down; it's all right. Just Eire banging her big front door shut on I Knock at the Door. Hear the holy Confraternities shouting from behind it:

—Get away, old man; get away from here! The very mention of the book leaves a fume behind. Oh, do get off the doorstep. Go where you can't be seen or heard. The bad drop's in you. Vatican's raidar renders news that St Patrick's rending his whiskers, threatening to rip the shamrocks off his stole, if you is let inside the house. It's not silk you have in your wallet, nor apples for ladies to eat of. You, Joyce, Shaw, and George Moore, are the remaining echoes of the Lamentation of Aughrim. You're shut out!

Sean guessed that his books must prove very embarrassing to any intelligent mind reviewing for the Irish papers. However a reviewer may jib or fidget, he must always express opinions with a big X in front of his eyes. Once, Sean got a letter from M. J. McManus, then Literary Editor of De Valera's daily, *The Irish Press*. He wouldn't have written at all, Sean thought, if he hadn't had a reason, for a tailpiece to the letter said that a book of his own would shortly be published. This is a bit of what he says (he is dead now, so this enunciation can't make him lose his job): 'I enclose a review of your book which you may not have seen, and which, I think, is the first to appear in an Irish newspaper. I liked the book immensely, and only regretted that owing to circumstances which prevail in this country – and of which I am sure you are not unaware, – I could not give my appreciation an altogether free vein. The Literary Editor of a paper which has a large sprinkling of clerical shareholders cannot always say what he wants to!'

Bang! went the door against *Purple Dust*, too, against *The Star Turns Red*; sent to go as exiles, along with the outcast *Within the Gates, The Silver Tassie*, and *I Knock at the Door*; followed by lesser bangs of library doors shutting to keep the books out in the street. Ireland was hardly any longer worthy of the name. McManus dismisses her with the contemptible title of 'this country'; a country where so many were never afraid to die is now a country where so many are afraid to live. The clerical shareholders are listening. The writers of Ireland must get instinctively to know just what not to say. One may argue with Micky Muldoon, but not when Mickey becomes the Reverend Michael Muldoon, or, worse still, the Right Reverend Michael Monsignor Muldoon; unless one is brave enough to suffer loss. The slogan of Ireland's writers and thinkers now, according to Mr Sean O'Faolain, is 'If It Wasn't For The Wife And Kids'. Ireland's a decaying ark anchored in western

waters, windows bolted, doors shut tight, afraid of the falling
rain of the world's thought. All to give God a quiet life, and
keep Irish souls safe, so that the heads in Ireland are dwindling
down to knobs.

Out of hearing of the guns, stretching away from the threat
of them, Ireland busied herself shutting everything up. She had
shut out all mention and meddle with the USSR, shut out
Joyce, O'Casey, and allowed Shaw only to look over the garden wall; and now she set about shutting out the war: but, in
the end, she had shut out little. Shaw was jauntily climbing
over the wall, Joyce and O'Casey had a foot in, preventing the
tight shutting of the door, and her sons and daughters were
pouring out over to England through the upper exit of protestant Ulster; pouring out in such numbers and in such excitement that Ireland won far more honours in the war, in propor-
tion to her twenty-six-county population, than any other member of the British Commonwealth; and Stalin's name, if not
loved, was better known all over Ireland than any of her best
bishops, protestant or catholic, sitting snug on a carved ecclesiastical bench.

Lower and lower, in England, the broad sunflower was bending; lower and lower the hollyhock and the tiger-lily. Hitler,
abroad in the night, had suddenly laid violent hands on Den-
mark and Norway; the Furor was among the fiords, so large
detachments of British had been landed to link up with the
Norwegian fighters, and drive the Nazis away; detachments of
men, Mr Churchill said, who not only had never experienced
such shape of country or condition of weather in winter, but
had never even imagined them. Their experience of snow had
been of a few flying snowballs thrown in fun, quick, before the
snow had melted, or of some makeshift snowman in some
backyard; and whose highest hill was Primrose Hill in the
north-west, or Lavender Hill in the south-west of London.
Now they were up to their waists in snow, piled about towering
mountains, whose paths they couldn't see, whose ways they
didn't know; men who had never laid eyes on a pair of skis,
even in a shop window. Even had they known how to use
them, there were none here to use. Nor artillery either. How
could they have got guns here; and what good would they be,
were they here, for there was nothing to fire at, except the
mountains. The guns were down at the jetty, bereft of ammunition, standing idle, up to their arses in snow. Mountains

towering over the beset soldiers, frightening them with their nightmare gleaming, enclosing them silently round about, so that they knew not where to go; men murmuring at one another, Don't lie down in it; keep moving; keep moving for God's sake; I can't, for if we move we may tumble down into snow, deep as a sea. Brave men, they had turned from pushing the Nazis out into pulling themselves, pulling, pulling themselves out of the snow. Falling snow, falling, falling to deepen itself under us. No vision now farther than what we feel. Touch him, touch me, keep together; nothing around us now for miles but tangles of falling snow, weaving a winding-sheet for us. Don't say that; for you, and not for me. The quiet, still fall of it over us, all around, everywhere. The snow shall be their winding-sheet. Cold here is the snow of all the years, and falling still. Look, the shadows in the snow are blue like the Virgin's cloak. Where is Our Lady of the Snows that she cannot stop its fall on poor and patient men?

And those at home in England waited for news, news of victory that came this way and then went that way and was lost. Then rumours came creeping to them of deepening snow still falling, and of men stumbling about in it; men chittering with cold, faces pricked to bleeding by the sting of the icy flakes; men with frostbitten feet; men whose hearts were aching, hearts were hopeless, seeking a way back through the piled-up snow beneath them and the snow falling on the fallen snow, jacketing them with its clinging coldness. To the people waiting, news came later, mentioning casually, through the news of exciting movement, that many sons of anxious mothers, husbands of anxious wives, lovers of waiting sweethearts, had disappeared under the deepening snow for ever. The silent weeping behind closed doors was beginning in English homes; many rachels were weeping for their children, because they were not. Soon they would hardly have the time to weep, or the heart either.

Then, suddenly, like a thief in the day, the good catholic, Hitler, struck deep in the month dedicated to the Blessed Virgin:

> Oh! by Gabriel's Ave,
> Utter'd long ago,
> Eva's name reversing,
> 'Stablish peace below.

Passing through the silvery gateway of summer, Hitler's hosts swept into Holland, and ere the clock could strike ten strokes, Rotterdam was less than half itself, the poor half still left was trembling, and looking as if about to fall. In less than a week's time the Nazis held Holland, and were sweeping with a laugh over Belgium, tossing town after town behind them in the manner of light-hearted gifts to Nazi Germany, till the King of the Belgians, sprinkled with the flowery dust of May, slid from his horse, tired, to seek a rest in the lap of Hitler; and British tank and armoured-car, decorated on either side with battalions of dubious infantry, plodded over the magic imagined imaginot line to drive the Nazis out of Belgium, and prevent them from crossing into France; the time-burrowing Frenchmen polished the buttons of their half-buried guns, voiceless now, and for ever to remain so; while the Nazi Panzers shot over the line, merrily, merrily all the way, darting in and out through British and French divisions, till, giddy with turning and twisting, the British and the French made for the sea, leaving all they had behind them, an amaze of guns, tanks, and equipment, and leaving to others the task of digging up the red poppies of Flanders to make fresh room for the additional dead.

> Ho! Stand to your glasses steady!
> 'Tis all we have left to prize.
> A cup to the dead already –
> Hurrah for the next that dies!

The twilight war was over; the real tension had begun, and the first wrinkle of war-care began to seam England's face. As Sean listened in fancy to the booming of the guns in Belgium and France and heard, between the booms, the steely rush-along of the Panzers (wondering how near these would come to them in time), he had to get on with the labour of living, and run after the best way to bring a new life into the world, for Eileen was far gone towards the birth of her third baby – one of the thousands of babes born in the blackout; hidden away from the lights of the world. Within the glare of guns firing, within the tale of ten cities crumbling into dusty rubble, heaping themselves over buried men and women; within the chorused cry of scorched humanity, left bare of all but bare life, bewildered women bore children about within them, and were busy laying restless hands on calico and wool to knit and stitch together things protective for the infant entrants to a shattered world. Even in this, sewing up some of the coming wounds of war.

Hitler's roar of Fiat Tenebray had set all England snatching light away from life, in lane, road, street, and byway. Nowhere must a rayeen of light be seen once the sun yawned out a dismal cheerio to the declining day. Even the flame from a farthing candle demanded a curtain on a window. Angrily-moving hands and cursing lips each evening pushed frames of cloth or thick black paper against the windows, tight up, tighter, tighter, ere a candle could be lit. Black cloth and black paper got hard to get, and increased their price, and many a family in many a room, for many a night, had to sit in darkness, while the shadow of death crept nearer, before they could make a screen to hide themselves from the stars. Many an ankle was twisted, many a wrist strained, many a spine ricked, putting up the blackout curtains for the night. In the O'Casey house, the windows in four of the rooms were bow-shaped, big bullies, stretching from floor to ceiling, and weary was the way of life before these could be screened to the satisfaction of the peering, prodding eyes of some special constable. There were more than twenty windows in the rambling house, each to be darkened every evening, uncovered every morning, an irritation so penetrating that seven of them were permanently blackened out, leaving half of the house in perpetual twilight – the twilight of the cods. No light could hang in the hall, for that would have meant a curtain within behind the door to prevent light showing when the door was opened; so for six long years, Sean had to feel his way up and down the stairs, through the hall; a good practice, for England was becoming the kingdom of the blind. Outside, save when the moon shone, the deep darkness separated town and district from their own existence. Every city, town, and village had darkened itself out of visible existence. All over England tens of millions of hands blacked out their homes every evening at the same moment of time. An example, most noble, of expendable and expandable energy. Up arms, and at 'em! Oh! the bleak bother of the blackout, the funereal piecing away of the windows, with Peace a disheartened fugitive, hiding somewhere in the outer darkness – no one knew where!

Sometimes, at night, Sean wandered a little way down the

road, while Eileen was having her baby in Torbay Hospital,
whose walls were now bolstered up with sand-bags, the latest
unornamented cushions feverish hands were making everywhere, idly thinking to coax the hurt out of a bomb exploding:
hands trying to shove a hurricane aside. So, sometimes, when
all the darkness was there, Sean, armed with a walking-stick,
went out by the garden gate, and tapped a way along the path
beside the Plymouth road, looking forward, looking back, but
seeing nothing. There were houses all round, but they remained invisible and silent; hushed and waiting. There were
people here, there, but they were not seen, and rarely heard in
the darkness that pressed against the breast, the back, and
down on the head oppressively; so silent that even the cocks
seemed to have forgotten to crow. Occasionally, a figure, sil-
houetted by the hushed footfall, would go by silently on the
other side of the road, or, more occasionally still, one would
steal by on the path beside him, mentioning his passing presence by a hushed Goodnight, as if a word, too, as well as a
gleam of light, might soar upwards, and tell a hovering enemy
something. Once or twice a bus passed, no longer so swift, but
rather searching a way along from Plymouth to Torquay, or
Torquay to Plymouth, a pin-point of light from a headlamp
giving a sluggish safety to the way onwards; its lights
shrouded, the window-panes purple-blue, so that, in the dusk
or the darkness, it moved like a thick shadow along the silent
road, stealthily steering through the night to its journey's end;
as if it were the ghost of a brighter bus stealing one more visit
from the route it had so often travelled through before. When
meetings were held in the town, and those who had attended
set out for home, they went silently, walking carefully as if
their footsteps might, if let down loud, give an enemy an idea
that a town was near; no gossiping along the way, but a steady,
cautious wending of the way back; an unhurried quickness in
the movement homewards; a quiet opening of a gate, a pause,
the quiet opening and quieter shutting of a door, then silence,
complete and brooding, came again, leaving the night to darkness and to him. No gun had yet been heard, no hostile
aeroplane had yet purred shrilly overhead; but everything and everyone were waiting to see and hear them soon.
Heavily hangs the hollyhock, heavily hangs the tiger-
lily.

Fear was here already; hunger was coming too. Ship after

ship bearing corn and oil to England was going down, slowly or suddenly, in this sea's side, in that sea's centre, and England was threatened with a lean and hungry look. Feed us, heavenly Father, feed us! Feed us with a shepherd's care! Produce more food! Rip up the garden, the public park, the playing-field, and lawn, and sow! Dig up the pleasant places, abolishing colour and perfume. Dig, dig, dig for victory. A potato a day'll keep Hitler away.

There may be gas, poison-gas, too! Gas that blinds, gas that chokes, gas that turns a lung to a rotting cinder! Oh, what a tide of woes! Make millions of gas-masks and make millions of money. It's an ill wind! Call them respirators, and it will sound nicer. Get them from your Warden. Attention! Gas-mask drill! One, two, three – Thumbs under the band; chin thrust firmly into the sack; over the head – so! One, two, three! Practise wearing them. Make them comfortable by getting used to them. Put the baby into the bag-respirator, and see that whosoever pumps air into the bag doesn't stop for a second or the babe may suffocate. Don't forget to remember. Put the baby in daily, and get it used to the horror. Blow the kid up. Carry your gas-mask everywhere with you – to theatre, to shop, to church, to bed with you, even on first night of honeymoon. Flimsy things of rubber and tin, with a pad of cotton, but guaranteed to keep you alive, gasping for an hour or two during a gas-attack. So now you know. Carry it always. Churchill does, so he does, carries it about with him everywhere, slung around his shoulder like a tiny, brand-new accordion. A Service one, better nor yours, but, still, a gas-mask. A goggle-eyed and snouted nation. Handsome days.

Gas-masks weren't enough. Thousands harried about, and busied themselves turning out cubby-holes, larders, and little rooms, to turn them into protective chambers against gas, storing in them a tin or two of food, a box of biscuits, a can of water, a bottle of rum, and a Bible. They pasted strips of paper by the sides of windows and along the sides of doors, covering every crack they could see in window, door, and wall; over cracks in the ceiling, too, and cracks in the floor. They must paste. I paste, I paste! When the alarm goes, don't get excited – excitement hinders breathing – don't rush. Put on your gas-mask quietly and firmly, walk with dignity into your gas-chamber, without any fuss; close the door, seal it up, and sit down to wait patiently till the decontaminating officer knocks

to say hello. Sing a hymn to yourself, if you feel the least bit
nervous.

> Oh God, our help in ages past,
> Our hope for years to come,
> Be thou our guide while troubles last—

Oh, God, I'm stifling! There's no air! I stifle! Keep calm,
you fool! Stifle, if you want to stifle! What if you do itself?
Hundreds of thousands are in a worse plight than you are,
woman!

The Nazis held Europe, now – save where lines of red flags
from the Black Sea to the ice-floes of the Arctic held them
back from owning it all; and over on the beaches of France
were thousands of planes with wings swept back, ready for
flight, and thousands of Panzers, too, the snouts of their guns
stretching out, stretching over, stretching out towards England.
Invasion!

> Heavily hangs the broad sunflower,
> Over its grave i' the earth so chilly;
> Heavily hangs the hollyhock,
> Heavily hangs the tiger-lily.

ORPHANS OF THE STORM

(Not a drum was heard, though something like a funeral note
was sounding.)

No drum, no drum, the orphans come; thousands of them,
phalanx after phalanx of them, row after row of them; down
to Totnes on the River Dart, down to the apple trees in bloom
rosy umbrellas to shade them from the sun, sweet-smelling,
and promising fine fruit. They were coming to a blossomy
welcome, the time the gnarled branches were hidden under
sprays of fragrant silken beauty. But the winter would come,
and the trees would have to fight the frost and the chill irony
of the wintry winds, making them wince and wonder. The
pines seemed to enjoy the push of the fiercer winds, tossing
their branches gaily, this way and that; the oak stood spread
out, facing them, indifferent to where the winds came from, or
how fierce they blew; the elm stood straight, like a guardsman,
unyielding, as if it murmured, If I fall, I fall; the beech swayed
gently to and fro, not indifferent, but as if resigned till the time
came for the winds to go; the apple tree alone seemed to
resent the change, to complain, and to sigh for the time of its
blossoming again.

But now the winter's away, so come, kids, to the gathering
of clusters of the rosy-red buds, soon to open wide to the sun
and the searching bees. God's will is wending with ye. He
maketh me to lie down in green pastures. Don't be afraid – the
bosom of the West Country's a warm one. Come along, boys
and girls of London, and hide among the apple-blossoms from
the bombs. But the small faces, staring from the carriage windows as the train drew into the station, had no elation in them;
no shine of hope. They were unexcited faces, silent, looking
quietly out on what was passing, seeming to sense that this was
no excursion for them; that this visit wouldn't be a race
around and home again, but one that would keep them away
from all they knew for a long, long time. The little sweeneys in
the apple trees. Coming to purgatory to escape from hell. A
hades without the asphodel. Down to the populous solitude of
bees and birds. Away, away from the bright lights, the throngs,

the homely thunder of the buses, the shows crowding around
one; away from all the glitter, fume, and dirt of London;
away, away; to a land that would tilt them into a quietness
more than halfway to the quietness of death.

Silently they came, for no fife shrilled a tune, no drum beat
out the step: along in column of companies, teachers beside
them to see them safely deposited; no sound save the simple
patter of their feet along the hardened road, many carrying
millboard suitcases, some bearing parcels who couldn't afford
more, armed with a day's ration of biscuit, tin of condensed
milk, bar of chocolate, and an apple. Gas-mask slung round
each slender shoulder. The musk had gone from the rose. Gas-
masks among the apple trees. A new fruit growing on the
human body. A growth, a tumour, a welt. Hang up your gas-
mask on a weeping willow tree. On they marched so slowly,
ticketed by name of parent and name of school so that they
shouldn't be lost who were half lost already. Don't diddle and
fiddle with your gas-mask so, Neddie. It's government property, and may creep between you and death one day. One day.
I crept between death and Ned o' the hill. The Devon children
stared at these new lives marching from the wrath to come.
Some of the Devon women were weeping quietly as they
watched the buds of London humanity go by, while the apple
trees, doing their best, nodded their budding fruitfulness to
these young strangers, seeming to say in the confidence of
their gentle movements through sun and breeze that the juice
of the apple was as good any day as the juice of the pampered
grape.

Every kindly home in Devon was searching among racks, in
presses, and in boxes, to find something to give them; or preparing a refuge for these little spare parts of life receding from
the busy banks of the Thames to sit down on the quiet banks of
the Dart, and, maybe, weep there; for many there were who
would never see their home again; many whose fathers and
mothers would soon be lying still under cairns of brick and
stone; many, oh, so many. Help the kids! And badly many of
them needed help, for they were miserably clad, and had been
miserably fed over many years. The three who came the
O'Casey way – Doris, aged ten, Zoë, aged six, and Bobbie, aged
four, were in a woeful state. What they had on had declined
into rags that fairly stank; they were stunted and thin. In some
way, they had evaded examination, and so it was found that

their hair was a garden of lice and bonnie bunches of nits, so
providing Eileen with the shock of her life. She had never seen
the like, though Sean had seen it, and felt it too; for the grey
repulsive louse with its dirty lustre of clustering nits is the dull
tiara the crowded tenement puts on the heads of the children.
They had never sniffed the savour of cleanliness, so they did
everything they had to do wherever they happened to be at the
time, leaving whatever they had done behind them for others
to plant their feet in it, and cry out curses on their lice-ridden
heads.

These kids had been nourished when England's wealth stood
undisturbed: they weren't the result of plague, pestilence,
famine, or war; they were the result of poverty forced upon
them by a rotten life foisted on man by rotten masters, Bald-
win's Best. And master missionaries, hundreds of them, protestant and roman catholic, were out in afric's sunny fountains
and on greenland's icy mountains, trying to force worse conditions into the life of little Asians and Africans; conditions
that had made the life of their own little ones as unlike life as
life could be.

Speaking in a lecture entitled *Missions Under Judgement*,
given in Dublin University in February 1952, the Rev D. M.
Paton, MA, is reported in *The Irish Times* as saying, 'The
Christians and the churches they support are as reactionary as
part of the whole Western Imperialistic conception; and the
actual policy of the Missions tends to preclude, and not to
foster, a dynamically self-supporting church in China. I blame
the whole church structure in China for maintaining an atmosphere of western civilization, a policy that made the Mission,
both socially and religiously, a failure.' Look you, young Afri-
can and Asian people, you won't get to see even the hinder-
parts of God, if you don't learn to strut through this life in the
best western manner. Father Geraghty, a roman catholic missionary, writing in the February No., 1952, of *The Far East*, a
missionary journal, reports, 'I have just concluded a tour of
our territory in part of Northern Korea, and found destruction
everywhere. Chunchon, the provincial, and three other towns
have been levelled to the ground.' Probably, thousands of men,
women, and children levelled with them. But not a whisper of
denunciation from this kindly father of God; not a breath of
blame for the rough and savage work done by shaggy hands, by
the shag-haired villainy of war. The priests, Father Geraghty

said, were just waiting round for peace to come. They're still
waiting. Waiting for a chance to teach the Koreans the love of
Christ in the midst of the ruins of their little homes and the
ruins of their dead; with the incense of napalm bombs rising
round the throne of God. Time for a Tea Deum.

Is it any wonder that things are as they are with our children
at home here, and abroad among those termed heathen, when
we peep into the kind of schools and colleges set apart for
them who are chosen to lead life at home, and who go over the
seas to bring the dusky-skinned ones and golden-skinned ones
to the knowledge of what is termed truth, and into the wonderful way of Western Culture? Send out the manna and the
manacles. Three articles, published in the magazine of a famous roman catholic college for training men for the priesthood,
tell us something about the way of seminarian life with these
biretta barons. The ex-seminarians who wrote the articles knew
they would be overlooked by Collegian Censors, so they larded
their criticisms with professions of love for their Alma Matter,
who had been more than something of a bitch to them. Says
One, 'I grieve against you because you didn't teach me manners. This I learned in a thousand ways – when I sat for inter-
views, and didn't *know* how to behave; didn't know how to
speak properly, didn't know what to do with my hands.' Not
even manners! Says Two, 'The newcomer found the first term
as hard as did Tom Brown the first year of his schooldays. The
newcomer was the perpetual butt of the bully, the cynic, the
wisecracker. His duties were multitudinous, ranging from fetch-
ing handballs that had crossed the ball-alleys to polishing the
seniors' boots.' The fag! Fag in a fog of duties. Again, 'Class
was a big problem, with a liberal use of the cane to encourage
the flagging mind. We may smile now, but our hearts came as
near to bursting as ever they will that morning the gates
opened to release us for our first Christmas holidays!' Out
into the holy night, silent night at last. We may smile now;
smile, smile, smile. Open the gates, and let us through. Says
Three – from an ex-student of a famous English roman catholic college – 'New arrivals are the occasion of the ceremony of
bushing, conducted by the older students. This is a form of
baptism in a gorse bush – an experience one either enjoys or
does not enjoy, according whether one was an older student or
a newcomer.' And the holy, civilized fathers, so close to culture and Christ, keep their eyes shut. Says Four, 'Seminaries

have always had a bad name: A jumble of memories of things cold, things unpleasant, things miserable – cold, wet days spent walking up and down, up and down a corridor or a shed, cold, badly-prepared quality meals, cold (poor) dormitories, cold classrooms. When thrust out into life, many of the neglected matters are set right or short-circuited. The rest of the Seminary's mistakes are thrust on to a world which already has enough of its own. The students' immaturity in face of their new-found freedom at university or in a job is responsible for "berserk bend" and failed examinations which are so often the seminary student's initiation rite into adult life. Mediocrity characterizes our educational system at every level.' Cold comfort to prepare for leadership. Says Five, after giving similar details, 'If I have exaggerated, I ask forgiveness, and I repeat that I love you. Having gone so far I am tempted to say one more hard thing, that if I had a son, I doubt I should send him to you.' We hear you. Food, clothing, shelter, the trinity of need worshipped by all life; in the secular seminary, in the ecclesiastical seminary as well as in the mind of the atheist and in all the homes of the working class. What on earth do the saints think of all this? But these same souls, ripe for glory, have been nourished on bread and cheese and meat, washed down, probably, with a tot of wine. Oh, no, no! Oh, yes, yes, yes! The *Confessions* of St Augustine, the *Meditations* of St Alphonso de' Liguori, the poems of St John o' the Cross, all had their roots in bread and meat and cheese. Who provided for these chaps? Did they do for themselves? Did they buy their food, carry it home, cook it, before they golloped it down? Did they wash up the dirty dishes, carry the coal from cellar to fireplace, and kindle the fire that warmed them? Of a winter's morning, with their fingers nipped with frost, did they empty the ashes before they set a fire to make their coffee, toast their bread, to strengthen them for another day's worship? Were all these things, and more, done for them so that they might have a good time in writing a poem, inditing a confession, making a meditation? It is said that it takes ten men to keep one soldier in the field; how many, more or less, does it take to keep a saint on his knees? If they didn't do any of these things, having things done for them, then what the hell did they know about life? Leave it all to the drudge, the lay brother!

Hidgiology doesn't say much about these common things.

Puts them behind a sacred curtain, leaving hoy polloy to believe that the holy ones live on sweet airs from heaven; or, at
the worst, on watercress, spring onions, and water from a well.
Ketch them doing it, doing it. Even St Bernard found he had
to eat well, for we are told 'He had lived on common food for
a long time, but even this great man, in his later years, garn-
ished his table with tenderly done capons, fine muttons, and
fair wines, to balance his belly back to order. Almost all the
other monks had begun living on the best long before, waxing
furiously fat in eating, idleness, and sloth; as the great Abelard
tells us, saying, "Every lean fellow, when he reacheth the stew-
pond of the cloister, soon waxeth as fat and well-liking, that
seeing him again after a brief period, thou shalt scarcely know
him for what he was!"' But these things lie hidden behind a
rood screen. Men like to feel like gods, but the body's needs
stand obstinate in the way. The never-resting body has a lot to
do to keep the soul alive – the poor, despised lay brother of the
spiritual man.

The educational way of life, where the dear little shamrock
grows wild, is little worse, but no better, than that where the
ladylike rose is bedded out to bloom away its beauty. The
protestant secondary schools, the grammar schools, are equal,
or almost so, with the roman catholic seminaries in their rush-
hours after results, their overcrowding, their poverty in ameni-
ties, their coldness, physical and spiritual, and the mediocre
mutter of their education: consolidated decadence over and
under and in them all. The pupils are orphans in the storm of
dusty questions, dusty answers, dogma, traditional definitions,
with most heads empty of any thoughts of their own.

Then there's the curious servility and rigid idea of obedience
in conduct, question, answer, that attaches pupil to teacher,
the dangerous lack of friendship between the two. In every one
of these schools, church and state, there is a never-ending buzz
of Sirs among the desks; yessir, nosir, I willsir, I won'tsir. The
teacher has to handle far too many to be able to be friendly
with any of them. He has to rule, not with a kindly hand on a
shoulder, but with a box and a shout. He has to carry the buzz
of yessir and nosir with him even to the playing-fields and
running-track. No teaching-dick calls a pupil Harry, and no
pupil would dare call a teaching-mister Dick. The young are
fed with information as cattle are fed with hay and mangels.

Here, the children of the crowded cities, of the little houses, the human sparrows of London, come in a sad parade, to the loneliness of beech, ash, elm, and oak, to shelter among the apple trees from the bomb, from the bite and the blight of its blasting; down to Devon bearing the banners of their enormous tribe, their lack of harmonious insight, their narrow visions, their lassitude towards creativeness, and, some of them, their lice; not yet knowing how to ask, not yet knowing how to seek, not yet knowing how to knock at the door of life; each with his tin of condensed milk, his apple, his biscuit, and his gas-mask.

For a time, Devon forgot about its bulls, cattle, and sheep, to think out how best to show affection to these dear little souls, only a few of which came in nice clean faces and nice clean stoles; so deferential, so demure, that the sound of birdsong seemed an intrusion; but when this big wave of young life broke up and splashed itself abroad, the Devon folk were bewildered at the destructive fluttering of uprooted infancy. They told to all who would listen that Us be near driven mad with them evacuees, all muckin' up house an' home till us be near an end. I says to schoolmaister, I says, Us'll be left naked if they don't quieten quick; but 'ee shook 'ead, an' says, Frank, says 'ee, there's a wor on; an' I says to 'ee, says I, Ay, says I, an' us is in they middle of it now.

But many changed after a year's stay, recognizing order and the special aspects of the country; helping where they'd hindered; planting where before they had rooted things out of life. A friend who, in his youth, had been a champion sheep-shearer, with his wife, took two lads into his cottage. The garden, pride of the couple, became a waste; a great armchair, bought for comfort during leisure hours, had its lovely chintz cover ripped off, its stuffing pulled out; yet in less than a year's time, the garden looked as good as ever, the chair, renewed, was never harmed again. The lads had changed, and when the time came for them to return home, the old couple bade them farewell on the station platform amid many tears and kisses from the lads to the old couple, from the old couple to the young lads.

Eileen was shocked by the difference in the interest shown to the poorer children and that shown to those who came from well-off schools. It was made positive and particular; the richer ones never even saw the others. They were safely hidden behind their own apple trees. Never saw a kid rougher than themselves. If they did, it was from a distance, and in the company of a smart teacher or a cautious nun. One rich convent school settled itself snugly in Sharpham, a lovely place a few miles up the River Dart from Totnes, surrounded by lawns and deep woods that were garlanded with heronries, so that the lives of the children were pushed away from all untowardness in a lovely and dignified seclusion, for they were somebodies, so they were. These indeed were they who had dear little souls, nice clean faces, and nice white stoles. The parish priest often visited them, and as often came back with a beaming face.

—Such lovely children – delightful! he would say; so well mannered, such a credit to the nuns. All so charmingly dressed, with nice clean faces and nice white stoles. It is always a pleasure to visit Sharpham House.

These little ladies were not for burning. Precious jewels, precious jewels, Christ's robe adorning, rich gems for his crown. If only one could see clearer than through a glass darkly, it would surely be seen that the Guardian Angels watching over these little ladies, in nice clean faces and nice clean stoles, were better dressed, shone more brightly, looked far more respectable, than the Guardian Angels set to hover over the common kids. All England's; the tattered and the tidy; the one in the nice clean face, the one with the snotty nose and the finger poking at the lice in the hair; all England's, though, as Disraeli saw, one would think that they belonged to different nations.

A few of the young exiles were different – almost too quiet to be mortal. They ate sparingly and in silence, as if it was all bitter bread. They grew thin, pushing aside the affectionate anxiety of a foster-mother; going silent to school, coming sullenly back again to wait for night and loneliness so that they might weep in peace; weeping beside the waters of Devon for the lost bright lights, for the stimulating thunder of the passing red buses, for the crowded streets, for a home they had loved; and, later, maybe, for a kind mother now sinking deeper into the ground, the bond between them broken for ever. Oh, we who pass these things by, even go through them as hurrying helpers, and then forget them – we, too, are destitute, and sit in the deep valley of the shadow of death.

RED LAUGH OF WAR

THE shout of war had become more than an echo; it was close to every ear now, a bellow. Hitler's heil was hurrying for honour everywhere. Soon the battle would close in, thick and bloody. The waste land wondered at its own scurrying to defend itself. Everyone was out preparing; all were one. Corporal Nym lived by Pistol, telling winds and walls what he would not do if the Nazis came his way; and Pistol lived by Nym. Pickwick side by side with a Weller learned to hold a hose; and Prufrock was fitting on a steel helmet, reconciling himself to a sharp and stinging death in the midst of what he called his duty. The threat of death was bringing the waste land to life again. Oh, Mr Prufrock, what shall I do? Our home's become my husband's grave, and my babes are buried, too. The Englishman, so clever in his foolishness, was fighting for his life, and the Irishman, so foolish in his cleverness, was fighting with him. It was more than touch and go now; it was all touch and little go, for England was nearly naked. Not much else save the symbolic trident remained in her hand. A few lonely-looking tanks, a few guns, and a few ageing aeroplanes were all she had to call her own. Oh, Mr Prufrock, what shall we do? God has turn'd away, and left the most of it to you. We have a few guns, a few tanks, a few old aeroplanes, and we have the spirit of a brave people. All of what she once had had been left scattered along the way to the coast of Dunkirk. All her treasures of destruction had been abandoned to the Nazis. Prufrock and his friends could be armed only with a pike and the courage to use it. He had a splitting headache from the pressure of the steel helmet on his head; his legs ached in every joint from the dint of drill; his hands were torn by barbed wire learning how to make a prickly barricade. The ageing Churchill stood by the wireless to promise the British people a succession of gala years of toil, sweat, and tears; Prufrock beside him, murmuring Get us the tools, sir, and we'll do the job. Prufrock, you have busy days before you. He took off his collar and tie, put a muffler round his thin neck, raw with the sun, the wind, and the rain; he covered his thinning hair, thin legs, thin arms with steel helmet and battledress. More clearly than ever before, he saw the Eternal Footman holding his coat, heard him snicker, and was not afraid. Things were too active, too terrible, to let fear get in the way. Home they brought her warrior dead. Who is it? Some bloke named Prufrock.

Lonely men, leaning out of windows, in their shirt-sleeves, were lonely no longer; things were too terrible, too active, for them to be lonely. In carpeted rooms, with pictured walls, and cushions on the settee, women no longer came and went, talking of Michael Angelo. They were buzzy fixing helmets on curls, natural or permed, cutting them down a lot to let the helmet cover the nape of the neck; flitting out of their rooms to join the Waacs, the Wrens, or to fix Red Cross armlets on a sleeve of their coats. Men and women were measuring out life now, not with coffee spoons, but with rifle, tommy-gun, sling, splint, and bandage. A bitter change, but not all evil. Common life had to go on, but with a very different rhythm. Things were changed, changed utterly. Church worship in any sense of thought towards a Prince of Peace or a Father of Love was demolished in the fire and detonation of the struggle. All political diversions ran from the stage as the curtain rose upon war. Fee fum family reunion. A whole people massed communistically for such a war as had never been known before; no peace, no sign of peace, till one side or the other lay dead. The chastisement of Hitler was upon us all. Invasion! Well, fight! Than to be subjects of Hitler's herrenfolk, better to be

> *A pair of ragged claws,*
> *Scuttling across the floors of silent seas.*

The gentle town of Totnes, cuddling itself in its quietness, jumped out of its gentleness, and jumped into action. All classes strained themselves into activity, ready to fight in the streets, in the fields, on the hills, against the Nazis. Invasion! They meant it, too, nearly killing themselves with preparation. Fellows of well over fifty ran and jumped about, climbed walls, and flung themselves down to the field on the opposite side, unmindful of a broken leg or a cracked skull; old codgers did bayonet drill and turned somersaults till one's eyes grew blurred and one's head grew dizzy looking at them. Sprained arms and ankles, pulled muscles, and black eyes sprouted out

everywhere. In every corner, one heard the crack crack of
rifles going and the explosions of hand-grenades, till it seemed
that England was blowing herself to pieces. Busy people were
getting ready for their own burial. For a long time, the Home
Guards were very excited, and did everything at a bound. A
driver of a car, or a passenger in one, had to be wary, and keep
an open ear for the cry of Halt! A heedless driver, or a scornful one, would hear a bullet whistling past an ear, or, maybe,
feel one tearing through his back. All were on the watch, for
no one knew how soon, or where, the Nazis might show themselves in the London thoroughfares or in the Devon lanes. That
they would come, and soon, was certain. Hitler had set the
whole world the job of wasting energy, time, and thought.

Eileen was never so busy in her life. Minding the latest infant, she forced time to let her gain a first-class certificate in the
science of first-aid; she practised how to deal with an incendiary bomb, creeping, done out in dungarees, on her belly
into a hut filled with old furniture, set ablaze with magnesium.
Within smoke and fume, and heat of the blaze, she worked the
hose of a stirrup-pump – first the spray to gradually coax the
flaming venom from the home-made bomb, the spray from the
nozzle was turned to the jet till the flames died, and curling
smoke round the charred furniture showed that danger was
over. Then, each day, she hurried up to Dartington to help
with the midday meal for the refugee children, watching
warily and brightly over her own flock in her spare time; for
she and he often spent anxious times till their two lads were
safely home from school, having passed through the sullen
blackout of the bitter wintry evening. So many women had
been called to the colours that housewives with children had
now more work than three of them would be expected to do
normally. Then there were the lectures given to teach us all
how to deal with injury from poison-gas, that turned the flesh
into a green cindery rot; how to deal with burns from an incendiary bomb, or from fire caused by one; how to deal with
shock, with splintered bones, with severed arteries: Everyone
was learning anew and in a fresh way that God was Love.

All road signposts were swiftly taken down, all names of
places blotted out from railway stations, so that all England
quick became a land without a name. The district was seg-
mented by geometrical design into sections, sub-sections, and
semi-sub-sections, each having its own letter and number as

well as its warden, sub-warden, and semi-sub-warden, with messengers, callers, and couriers added to them, topped by a head-warden over all. There were those who wore khaki-coloured helmets, those who wore black ones, those who wore white ones; first-aid wardens, ambulance wardens, rescue-squad wardens, and churchwardens – the land bristled with wardens. No one was left out, grandsires and old women forming part of England's guard. The men pulled up their socks, the women their skirts. Cut your here up to your ere, your kirtle to the knee. Barriers were put up to check tanks at various parts of the roads, and one stood on the road directly in front of the O'Casey garden gate – thick portly pillars of concrete so placed that passing cars had to wriggle in and out through them. But convoys of heavy guns and tanks couldn't go through, so the portly ones had to come down, to be replaced by V-shaped angle irons, set into sockets of concrete, which were left on the sides of the road, ready to be thrust into the concrete sockets as soon as the rumble of the Nazi tanks shook the English roads, and tightened the hearts of the Devon people; the military experts seemingly unaware that the invading tanks had but to sidestep the barriers to make their way through the gardens fronting the houses, and go on their way, gay with the prospect of goring out England's vitals, belching fire and smoke, as if the dragon, killed by George, had come to life, had bred a host of his kind, and had gathered them together to destroy altogether the cocky consequence of the tarnishing legend.

One day, suddenly, the local park, the town, and the district flooded up with American troops, white, chocolate, and black. Men from almost all the States were represented by those who sat, who sang, and slept in the tents that formed line after line in the grounds; men from the borders of the Great Lakes, men from the West, from New York, and from Texas, too. All in for fight. Sean often sauntered round the camp, for there were few restrictions, and the Americans were comradely, and ready to talk. Even the lonelier sentries meandering around the fringe of the camp were glad to halt for a few moments to say Hallo, guy. How different these sentries from those around Buckingham Palace or those who had once kept watch over Dublin's Bank of Ireland! The American sentry had his rifle right enough, so many rounds of ammunition, and his greyish-green helmet was pressed down on his head, but there the military formality ended. No sane person would think of entering into conversation with a sentry around Buckingham Palace; it would be low treason. He has ceased to be a human being for the time being, and must comport himself as if he were a changed man. Puppet passes; major movements by strings.

The American sentry carried his rifle sloping across his arm, the barrel resting in the socket of an elbow. He sauntered round, stopping, maybe, to look at the scratch baseball match his comrades were playing; or gazed after a girl that happened to pass by, calling to a comrade within earshot that that was a good-looking dame. One of them Sean spoke to was from Kansas City, a lorry-driver in a store there, he told Sean. He wasn't a big fellow; rather one of the smaller men of the detachment; thin, too, but wiry and firm in his stand. His face was thin, made to look thinner by the enveloping steel helmet. His nose stretched down, thin and long, coming down more than halfway over his upper lip. The biggest mark in his face were the big, brown, wide-open eyes that gently and quietly stared out from the long thin face; eyes that saw little outside what they had already seen at home. The big, brown, wide-open eyes always carried about in them an image of Kansas City. Back in Kansas, he would forget the faint impressions, not only of Totnes, but of England. The Yeomen of the Guard in their scarlet and gold, the Horse Guards Blue, on their nobly-formed horses, found no nest in his thoughts: Kansas men, Kansas women, and Kansas town were all the world to him. He was satisfied with the streets of his city, its life, and the roads of Kansas and Missouri.

—Don't get this place, he said to Sean. Wha's its name?

—Totnes, the oldest town in England, bar London, and it's near the coast of a county called Devon.

—Ay, Devon, he echoed tonelessly. A long way from my home town, he added, after a pause; a long way; yessir.

—You'd like to be back in Kansas City? Sean queried.

—I sure would! he said quickly, a gleam of interest coming into the big, brown, wide-open eyes. Kansas suits me, suits me fine. Yessir, I'd like to be back in Kansas. Guess I will, one day.

—Devon's a very lovely county, said Sean, hoping to interest him into asking questions.

—It sure is, buddy, he responded, again tonelessly. Kansas

suits me better. I'm Kansas born an' Kansas bred, an' I jus'
can't get goin' anywhere else; I really can't.

—Well, I hope Kansas City will like Totnes Town, murmured Sean.

—It sure will, murmured the sentry; it sure does. It's a small
hangout, though, ain't it, buddy? Guess it could be dumped
down in Kansas City's smallest street, and not be in the way.
You could carry all that's goin' round here under one arm. But
the people are swell; gotta give them their due; swell, yessir.

—Where do you go from here? asked Sean.

—Dunno, buddy. That's only our second hop. Wonder what
the next hop's gonna be like? The eyes went dead again, hiding
any sign of an image of Kansas. Well, so long; be seeing you.
Gotta get goin' the round; and he turned away to continue his
sauntering parade, slow and mechanical, round the camp
seeking silence and solitude to bring the image of Kansas into
the big, brown, wide-open eyes again; and a red laugh of war
stung the ear of Sean.

Each was homeless near a thousand homes. Oh, to be home
again, home again, home again, under the apple-boughs down
by the mill. Throughout the camp there was an air of gay,
almost reckless, bewilderment, mild, but bitter, as if the GIs
silently thought it unwise to be here, The innocents abroad.
Far away from Jelly Roll and from Lead Belly, from their
racing simple songs, their wisecracks. Where is now the merry
party I remember long ago! Laughing round the Christmas
fire, laden by its ruddy glow. Or in summer's balmy evenings,
in the fields among the hay? They have all dispersed and
wandered far away, far away. Some have gone from us for
ever; longer here they could not stay – Oh, change it, buddy;
don't make gloom gloomier. Who was it, what bastard laughed
in that harsh, red way?

One or two of the tents had a ukelele-player, who could be
heard strumming out lively notes, with, maybe, some comrade
singing some jazz-song or hot ditty: singing sorrow and fear
away. Away, away! A hard thing to do, buddies. It didn't
sound merry. If one came from Chicago, another from Texas,
they were all, all lonely and all far from home; from things
familiar, from a sweetheart's kiss, from a mother's fussy care,
from a wife's companionship, from all things settled. They had
been hunted from the serene monotony of peace to the savage,
purposeless monotony of war. Privacy was gone, and all lived

an alice-in-blunderland life, with death, maybe, round the corner of the next hop. Some of these men, many of them, perhaps, may be phantoms already, gay as so many of them pretend to be. The Spirit of Pity no longer hovers over, no longer probes, the heart of war; the Spirit of Irony only gets where war is waged.

The Stars and Stripes flying from a tall pole at the camp's entrance made the place American territory, but it refused to make the place a home. The kindly and talkative Devon folk made things as easy and as natural as they could for the soldiers, but the Americans, white and black, carried but an image of home in all their eyes. The life in camp was dirty, dull, and boring. Besides, the guns were being stuffed now with something more than wadding and powder. There was more of death than of pageantry in their booming. None here sought death at the cannon's mouth. The next camp might be a camp of a dead brigade, and far away from Brooklyn. Gay as they might be, they all knew that they faced towards the front where the graveyards were. Many comrades were already under ground in the Philippines and other isles of the Pacific, never again to return to Dixie Land, to the cornfields of Kansas, or hear the patter of their own feet on the pavements of Broadway. It was all dreadful; yet here in the recreation-grounds of the little town of Totnes, hundreds more were waiting to join the dead. However they might hang out the colours of motley, however they might play their ukeleles, however they might shout their wisecracking comments on an improvised baseball game, the camp had around it a deep black border.

The Panzers were racing over Russia! Totnes was busy presenting things, making toys, holding concerts and dances to provide funds for Mrs Churchill's Russian Red Cross Fund. In the window of the Anglo-Soviet Headquarters stood three huge photographs, four feet tall and three feet wide, of Churchill to the right, Stalin to the left, with Franklin D. Roosevelt in the centre. The Soviet Flag was seen for the first time in Totnes, and hundreds wore a little Red Star in the breasts of blouses or in the lapels of their coats; for the fight of the Red Army had modified the fear, and had removed the very present danger of invasion; while through all the hurrying activities moved the American soldiers, attending concert and dance, their convoys of great guns and tanks rumbling along the street of the town, often to the gentle accompaniment of a tinkle

tinkle from a ukelele playing somewhere from a tent in the camp.

The Panzers were racing over Russia! We're owre the border, and awa'! Russia first; England next, and within a year the Wehrmacht will be doing the Lambeth Walk along Piccadilly and the Mile End Road. Race on, my brave warriors, invincible and hitlarious! Let the united drums of a united herrenfolk beat a united roll when Hitler enters Moscow! Henceforth, the world would form its life to the beat of Hitler's heart. Race on, my men! This is the way that Hitler rides, a gallop, a gallop, a gallop! Another day or two will see the Russians parking their cannon, garaging their tanks, and the Red Army dropping their rifles to lift their hands, and cry for peace. But the cannons went on blazing, the Russian tanks split the German tanks in two; and at Stalingrad, Germany's woe began. Oh, weep for the German dead; the young and sprightly ones lie still for ever! Red laughter of war echoing over the graves. And Hitler heard it; yes, Hitler heard it. It would soon be louder.

The work for England and for the Soviet Union went forward in the little town of Totnes. The rose and crown looked fine beside the hammer and the sickle. Sean helped as well as he could, addressing envelopes and delivering circulars, for one thing. He tapped at the door of a Totnes bungalow to deliver a circular notifying a meeting. The door half opened, and he saw half of a middle-aged woman standing there, crying silently, crying deeply. Mechanically, Sean extended the letter; she made no movement to take it; she didn't look at it; just looked aimlessly before her, crying silently.

—Notice of a meeting, he mumbled, trying to think how he could get away quietly.

—I don't want it, she said, tonelessly; don't want anything now. Just got a telegram telling me son's killed; killed, an' us doesn't know how or where. No grave of his own even, for us heard they are buryin' 'em in bundles now, an' us doesn't know where; doesn't know where. Crying silently and deeply, she slowly and silently shut the door.

She hadn't had the comfort of hearing her son's last moan, hadn't had the joy of committing his body to the grave. She had been denied the mystery of sorrow in stroking her loved one's body for the last time, like Gilderoy's sweetheart, who, at least, had had that gaunt privilege:

> Wi' tears, that trickled for his death,
> I washt his comely clay;
> An' siker in a grave sae deep
> I laid the dear-lued boy.

Not even that; not even that much elation for the mother.

It was everywhere: it followed Hitler about; it sounded soft, ironic, murderous, in the ears of the Nazis racing across Russia; it trickled through the fancies of the Americans digging trenches by the side of their camp, offset by deep pits for ack-ack guns; it circled round the British depriving England of a name, the hurried medical inspection of youth, the drill-donned gas-masks, the call for identity-cards, heard in the sound of the siren's wail, gurgled through the curses misspent fixing blackouts over the windows, its derision blurred blasphemously the gasps of a deep-wounded, dying lad, and here a gust of it had swept through a humble Devon bungalow, soft, ironic, murderous – the red laugh of war.

IN CELLAR COOL

D A U B the name of Dunkirk in black and gold on our banners. Forget the place, and for ever remember the time. An ugly smudge, gold-circled, in the people's fight for freedom. Hitler comes with tanks descending upon us. Backward to the beaches! The sea must save us. Between the devil and the deep blue sea. The Nazi Army is but a mile behind. Hitler's chosen people are on top. Forward to the beaches! Left right, left right, left right, left right. We are very tired, oh, kings and captains. Forward to the beaches! Tramp, tramp, tramp, the boys are marching. Hundreds of thousands of British troops and tens of thousands of Frenchmen are marching to the beaches, and the tramp of their marching feet becomes the pulse of England's heart; the pulse of Irish hearts in England, too. From every road, north, south, and east, press on to the beaches. Pile your rifles by the hedgerows, for they are useless now, useless now. They can kill no longer. Rank your tanks, your guns, across the wider roads to check the Panzers, for guns and tanks are useless now, useless now. Let the spirit drag the legs, let the legs drag the bodies along: we must get to the beaches. Can you hear the sea? Not yet, not yet. Left right, left right.

What was that flame ahead of us on the road. God damn it, the Nazi guns are firing on us! Right incline; don't look to the left; never mind them; pass them by; close your ears to the squealing. Let the wounded attend to the wounded; let the dead bury the dead. Start a song, lads; someone start a song. We thank with brief thanksgiving whatever gods may be that no life lives for ever, that dead men rise up never, that even the weariest river winds somewhere safe to sea. God, that's a meek, mournful ditty. That won't help, help us along, Long river of wearied men mus' just keep rolling along. A long journey through long days without end, seeing the day rise and the night fall. Don't stagger; keep straight, keep right on left right to the end of the road. Jesus! the Stukas are over us and the flames are pillaring the way forward and the ground is twisting under us. Looka, the trees are on fire, and the grass so green is brown and black and burning. Right incline! Eyes right! Close all ears to the squealing: let the wounded attend to the wounded, the dead bury the dead. What sounds are those? The scream of the seagulls, the cry of the curlews. The beaches are before us! Pass the word behind to halt. Halt? Why are we halting? What are them in front doing; what are they thinking of? Why the hell are we halting? For Christ's sake, push on! The Stukas will be here again in a moment. Bad enough to feel sick when a bomb falls and we on the move; how'll we feel when a bomb falls on us standing still! Forward to the beaches! Halt; the beach has as many men as a beach can hold. Oh, when will my head rest on the pillow at home while the vacant midnight passes? The boats and ships are loaded and gone; we must wait for another embarking before we move again. Halt! Stand at ease!

How far are the beaches now? two miles; five miles; ten miles. How long till we get there, get there? We're too tired to stay still. If we rest, we rust, and joints will bend no more. We are all crooked men already. The burdens are heavy; burden of sweat under arms, between the thighs, running down breast and back; burden of aching limbs, and the tightening pain in the head. Why do the damned seagull and curlew come in so far, deceiving us, deceiving us into thinking the beaches are but a few steps more? Many steps more; many, many: oh, the beaches, the beaches! Burden of fear in the heart. England's armed pride, armed no longer, bent and broken, stumbling along to the beaches, the road swaying under them, the Stukas over them, the cheers of the conquering Wehrmacht behind them; and the wayside full of the wayside flowers, wild flowers, gaily yellow, brilliantly blue, flaming red, safe in the sunlight, and silently shaming us; over the blossoms the birds everywhere, no tightness in the head, no ache under the wing; birds everywhere, yellow-backed, red-breasted, blue-tailed; busy nesting, shaming us in their song. Oh, the foxes have holes and the birds of the air have nests. We're all very tired. Who's that murmuring ahead? What's he muttering? Our Father which art in heaven, hallowed, hallowed, hall. No use, buddy; waste of time, waste of breath. The Stukas are between your words and the place where they've got to go if an answer is to come. May be a dead man before the words can dodge the Stukas, and go on to the top. The aches of hell are all on this one road.

The head is drooping, drooping, drooping down. Must be sleep. Forgot about sleep; had to keep moving. Drive the thought of sleep from the seeking mind. What's that gentle humming? Such gentle humming never came from distant Stukas. Bees! Odd things in the air. Bees flying about like the birds and the Stukas. If only the Stukas would go, and leave the birds, the bees, and the men alone. The road has become a corridor towards sleep: more – towards life. Why don't we go on? What the hell are we waiting for? Keep the head up. I hate sleep, I hate it! We're moving again! You in front – for Christ's sake, lift your feet! On to the beaches, the beaches. Through the sunshine, with the birds and the bees, move the men. Oh, when shall my head rest on a pillow at home while the vacant midnight passes!

Dunkirk was one of England's darkest victories. Having nothing left, she gained all back in time. Near four hundred thousand men, sound in wind and limb, were sailed, steamed, ferried and dragged over the waves from Dunkirk to Dover. It was as if the whole army had swum the Channel. My old Kentucky home, good morning! England, who had traduced herself with gloom, now took hold of hope, and confidence had become a great golden chip on her shoulder. But very few had much time to rest their heads on a pillow at home, for all were now ordered into the fury of regrouping and re-training to be ready for the coming fight in the coming invasion. Some even saw the parked barges of joking Germans racing over the sea to Dover and Dungeness; even over the sea to Skye.

A halt of a few seconds came after the exodus from Dunkirk, a heated halt. All in England were waiting for something to happen, something worse than the worst they expected. Send us the tools, America. They're a long time acoming. Hardly a gun in the house. We can't fight with umbrellas. Send them soon; send them quick; send them now. The bombers will come splitting palace and slum, and what shall we English do then, poor things! They were waiting with long-handled shovels to be used to scoop up incendiary bombs, nice and calmly, and carry them, blazing, out to garden, yard, or street; waiting with stirrup-pumps and to put out any fire started by any incendiary bomb that had evaded the prod of the shovel; waiting with their heaps of sand lying outside of front or back doors to be sprinkled over a big flame caused by a bunch of bombs, too many to be carried out by the scoop of a shovel; the

Home Guard waiting for the enemy with long-handled pikes
to thrust and thrust, parry and thrust, advance and thrust, till
their shirts were red, and the Nazis fled like a cowardly cara-
van. Full of fear and anxiety, but their hearts were strong; the
British were at their best; their hearts sang; sang

> *That song, whose breath*
> *Might lead to death,*
> *But never to retreating.*

But all got ready to crouch. They knew not yet how they
would have to go through the earthquake, the great wind, and
the fire. There had been straight talks and roundabout arguments as to where lay the best place to crouch should an air-
raid come. A safe, strong hiding-hole. No use to go into a
church, for sanctuary had lost its meaning: altar rails or altar
horns were no damned good now. Even the bird sanctuaries
might suffer. Some said the coal-cellar, some said under the
stairs, a few poor minds said under a table. Hoosh the cat from
under the table. One thing was laid down as a law – always be
behind a wall and always keep away from the windows, for
they had become mad, magic casements, opening out on to a
terrible death. Some built Hans Anderson shelters at the ends
of their little gardens, damp, unhealthy holes, more dangerous
than the bombs themselves. Under the kitchen in the O'Casey
house was a cellar about as big as a double and a single bed,
laid side by side. The floor was of earth, moist and maggoty,
giving out a musty smell. This they tried to strengthen by a few
uprights and struts; covered the floor with straw and the straw
with canvas; added a few kitchen chairs, cushions; set up a
shelf on the wall for a jug of water, biscuits and some sweets
for the children, with a pack of cards for a possible game. This
cellar was reached from the outside by a number of steep,
slippery steps of firebrick, requiring great caution and some
gift of balancing when descending them; but to get to these it
would be necessary to circle half the house. Experience told
them that in the haste of an air-raid, it would be quite easy to
break a neck. It wouldn't do; Sean had a lame leg for a week
after trying a quick descent. So a trap-door was cut out of the
kitchen floor, and a roughly-made step-ladder brought them
down from the kitchen into the mouldy and miserable place
that wouldn't make a decent tomb. There, then, was this handsome zone of security waiting for them when the tense mo-

ments of a bomb-raid came flooding over them. Safety right
beneath their feet. Now thank we all our God with hearts and
hands and voices!

Everything was ready: the long-handled shovel rested beside
the heap of sand outside the front door; the scullery window
had been gummed over so as to prevent it splintering in a blast,
though, of course, a blast not only took away the windows, but
the doors and walls as well. The box of first-aid equipment was
ready to hand; a large clothes-basket in which to carry down
the baby girl, and with Eileen's knowledge of how to deal with
almost anything except death, they waited, as all others waited,
for the terror to come. The heavens were hung with black.

Then, one night (one night of love), at eleven o'clock, pip
emma, the three children in bed, Eileen getting ready to go into
hers, and Sean working away at the biographical book, *Drums
Under The Windows* and the play, *Red Roses For Me,* the
Siren sounded – a series of rising, descending, wavering wails,
sending a shiver through all who heard it. The bomber is
acomin' in. Get going! Hurry, hurry! Get the children up;
carry the baby down; hurry, man, hurry, woman! Where's the
first-aid box Where in th' name o' God's the first-aid box!
Oh, do hurry, or the bombs may be down on us before we get
to the cellar. The blankets, the blankets – don't forget the
blankets! And down they climbed, down to the mouldy, maggoty cellar, meagre candlelight showing them in a wavering
way how to settle down, maybe for the rest of the night; perhaps, for ever. Now, overhead, they could hear the whirring
burr burr of the aeroplane engines; over the roofs of Totnes,
over this very house; no one speaking; all listening, bar the
babe in the basket; all knowing that a direct hit would make a
united bloody blot of them all. Sean's stomach was so tense
that it seemed the skin holding it could stretch no farther. They
seemed to be lower now – the engines were louder. His nerves
vibrated busily, making the heart give a quicker beat. Eileen
looked quite calm, showing no signs of tenseness; cool customer.
Both had to look unconcerned so as not to agitate the children,
though the elder boy seemed to be as calm as his mother. Sean
and the younger lad of six years were the only two who shook.
Sean died several times that night, though no bombs fell; not
on Totnes, but they were falling thick and fast a little distance
away. The minutes filling into hours were dotted with the sharp
snarling rumble of exploding bombs, and the sudden tremors
the explosions gave to the house made them all crouch closer,

tightening the nerves to throw the tremor off. It was a queer
thought that the ragged, runabout guttersnipe of Dublin's dirtier
streets should be crouching in the cellar under the kitchen of
a Totnes house. Yet no change, for the cellar was a slum, with
filth below them and terror overhead. A big change among the
changes of many-coloured life, and far from a pleasant one.
The many-coloured dome had turned dark, and above it chaos
and old night had begun to reign again. Millions were crouching as they were crouching here. The monstrous ego squatting
in Berlin or Berchtesgaden was making millions do what they
were never born to do; an ego with a senseless, smiting arm
stretching from Berlin to the Volga, up to the Arctic snows,
and down to this little town of Totnes. All were being bitten,
and no brazen serpent, now, to heal the bites: nothing but the
making of an aeroplane to equal Hitler's and a bigger gun to
smash the gun that he was firing. Where were the bombs falling?
It mightn't be long till they were falling here, so what was the
use of worrying out a guess? But still they worried, and still
they guessed, while the baby slept and the two boys sitting on
the floor nodded forward in tendentious sleep; nodded till they
stretched themselves out, and were covered with the blankets
and the overcoats worn by Eileen and himself.

All were miserable and cold now; even the children were
moving uneasily under the blankets; as if the clothes had taken
into them the coldness of the damp from the floor under them
and the walls around. He could stick it no longer. There was
little safety here, anyhow. If a bomb gave even a glancing
blow to the house, it would go stumbling down on top of them,
and all would go down to dusty death by suffocation. Sean had
liefer die under a tree, behind a hedge, or walking fast or slow
along a road. He looked at his watch – near half past two, with
the burring drone of the aeroplanes still sounding overhead.
He couldn't stick the numbness of body and bone any longer.
A cup of tea! Would it be wise to leave the cellar? Wise or
unwise, he'd go. What better way to die than to be brewing tea
when death came? He went up, made a pot of tea in the
scullery, and brought it down to the perishing family. Jasus,
wasn't it sweet! Whisht! Heavy steps coming down the steps
outside; a desperate scraping as the boots slipped down most of
the way; a catching of breath, and a hurried curse; then a
knock at the cellar-door.

—Who's that?

—Me. 'Arry, and in came a Home Guard, in steel helmet, full uniform, and rifle in hand.

—Near broke neck on steps, he panted. On watch for paratroopers; expec's 'em drop anywhere. He rubbed his neck; near broke she acomin' down. Know where th' bastards is bombin'? Plymouth! They're pastin' Plymouth. Swarmin' over she, an' only a few ack-ackers defendin'. He sipped from a cup of tea. Th' bastards! Sean noticed the hand holding the cup trembling. Jus' relieved fr'm guardin' bridge. Poundin' Plymouth, poundin' she to bits!

The Siren sounded the All Clear at last; the Home Guard hurried off to rejoin his comrades; the blankets and children were lugged up out of the cellar, and were guided to their beds, Sean and Eileen elated that no bombs had fallen, and that sleep was before them for the rest of the night. No sooner had they begun to remove their clothes than the Siren sounded the Alarm again, and the whole weary, wasteful performance had to be borne once more. Down, down in the cellar cool again; down in it till half past six before the All Clear sounded, rising from it once more, weary and worn and sad. To hell with it! Sean had learned the sound of the Nazi planes, and he and Eileen decided that for the future Sean wouldn't rouse them till he heard the Nazi planes circling directly overhead, and sensed any danger of an attack, let the Siren sound how it might. They decided, too, that they would stay in a room, and seek the cellar no more.

Sean did most of his work at night when all were in bed, and the house was soundless. One night, typing away at a biographical chapter, he thought dimly that he heard the snarling burr of Nazi planes, but was too busy to care; and, anyway, if there was any danger, the Siren would send its wail to him. He was sitting at a big table, in a ground-floor room, facing towards the Plymouth road. Suddenly a shattering explosion shoved him and the chair a good way away from the table, the typewriter lepped up a foot from its pad, glass of a window crashed out on to the floor, the hall-door shook violently, and the whole house shuddered. The family came rushing down, covered with anything their hands first found, and all gathered in the hall, for planes were dropping bombs very near. Some had fallen a little way up the Plymouth road, in a field bordering the roadway, making a huge crater, and sending a row of houses opposite into a panic, so that the windows twisted, the

ceilings fell, the doors buckled, and a little child was near
blinded by the dust of a ceiling falling all over her. Had the
bombs dropped thirty yards farther east, they would have
fallen on the road, directly in front of the houses, and then
there wouldn't have been many left alive within their walls.
Again, and once again, shattering explosions, tossing the door
about, shaking the house, and sending the hall where they
crouched rocking so that it seemed ready to change its shape
like a crushed-in cardboard box. Night after night it went on,
till it seemed concussion was the natural form of the earth's
emotion.

Night after night, Plymouth was pounded, till one thought it
must have swallowed itself up in its own flame and its own
erupting dust. At night, even after the Alarm had gone, and
planes were circling viciously about in the sky, the people living on the Plymouth road would stand outside staring at the
tremendous glare of fire filling the south-western sky, just a
few miles away, showing plain where Plymouth was burning;
burning amid the sharp rumbling of exploding bombs; a sky
that seemed to say that hell was no longer beneath us, but
seemed to have ascended and to reign where heaven used to be.
Evening full of the aeroplanes' wings. In the broad bosom of
that red, flaming plentitude many a Nazi airman died, many a
British mother's son, many a British sweetheart's boy, found
death, too, in that red sky-glow made by Plymouth's burning.
Light at evening tide.

> Last night as I lay on my pillow, last night as I lay on my
> bed,
> Last night as I lay on my pillow, I dreamed that my Bonny
> was dead.

So he is, lass: a dream come true.

In the flame beneath, of which that in the sky was but a
shadow, men died with a quick curse, or before a sudden
prayer had finished; women stretched themselves over screaming children as the walls came toppling down on them imagining their arms of flesh to be fit props to keep the tumbling
stones away from smiting their little ones.

When the Heinkels, the Junkers, the Dorniers, and the div-
ing Stukas had shed all their bombs and departed, smoke-
harried men and women sweated and cracked their muscles to

reach, here and there, a faint cry heard somewhere at the
bottom of a tangled ruin; daring to add some of their own lives
to the already dead in an effort to dig out a living soul from a
heap of smouldering débris. All kinds went down in the Plymouth bombing; many a sprig of a Tess of the D'Urbervilles,
many a pair of blue eyes, many a Farmer Oak, many a
Sergeant Troy, a Marty South, a Diggory Venn, Bill Brewer,
Jan Stewer, Peter Gurney, Peter Davy, Dan'l Whiddon, Harry
Hawk, old Uncle Tom Cobley, an' all; good souls, gay and
morose, sensible useful souls – all thrust together in the terrible
companionship of violent death.

A friend of Sean's, an ack-ack gunner, home for a few days'
rest and a few nights' sleep, half staggered to a chair, on a visit
for tea to empty himself of the thoughts he had had while
helping to hit a bomber darting through the clouds, and snatch
him down to death; his eyes red with staring into flame, so
worn out that his crimson-topped forage-cap remained on his
head throughout his visit.

—Looks like Plymouth's gone, he said, looks like they 'as
done it to she. Yes, Sean, mister, looks like she's gone. He
seemed to be sinking into deeper exhaustion through rest in the
deep chair. Yes, mister Sean, he went on, now too tired to try
to open the slitted eyes, Plymouth's woeful place; don't 'ee
never go near she again, for 'tis death's front parlour now.
Day after day, week after week, us was at guns afirin' up,
afirin' up, afirin' up, till all us wanted from Nazis was chance
of a little sleep, sleep. The few guns us 'ad was tired, too,
afirin' up an' up. No rest for guns, no rest for 'em afirin' of
'em up. No, mister; keep on your toes, an' keep afirin' up was
hourly order. Seen whole skyline agoin' down; houses, docks,
churches, chapels, shops, just athrowin' theyselves down flat
on knees, on faces, alyin' flat in flame, with us afirin' up, afirin'
up, afirin' up! Ten blows for one, us'll give the bastards yet;
ten blows for one!

The gunner seemed to drowse, his face haggard, his skin
bitten into visible pores by the sharp smuts flying about and
around the smoking city; his hands restless, the fingers moving
about among the buttons of his tunic, up to his cap, along his
chin, and down to the tunic again; his eyes closed, though the
darkness made the flames he had passed through much more
visible still. Sean gently took from the gunner's mouth the
cigarette threatening to burn his lips, and put a fresh one in its

place, the soldier never once trying to open an eye; still, save
for the hands giving flickering touches to his tunic buttons,
down, up, down again, darting unsteadily from the top tunic
button to the tiny ones on his crimson-topped cap, down again
along the row of tunic buttons, up again to touch the chin, and
down again to the buttons on the tunic, his nerves showing in
tiny crinkling waves under his skin, stretching, and then crinkling again. A rough-cast face disturbed, clear-cut honesty its
one testimony to grace: his whole soul now a crunching cry
for vengeance.

—Th' shelters was useless, Sean, came in a murmur from
the depths of the chair, and the tired hazy eyes flickered open
to a half-slit; a fool's fart would have knocked they down.
Blasted to bits all tumblin' down with they fallin' buildin's. An'
fortunes was made out of they, Sean; fortunes. Doesn't bear
thinkin' on. He stretched himself, made half an effort to rise,
and lay back again. When us started firin' up first, us tried to
hum The Old Hundredth, but us couldn't get further 'n the
first line – you know, Sean, All people that on earth do dwell.
No go. All people was afightin' each other. Kill, kill, or be
killed! He wrenched himself from the chair, the hands still
flickering over and along the buttons. When the old mind gets
tired, Sean, mister, I says to she, I says, There's a war on,
mate, an' don't 'ee forget it. Us must get home for a rest. A
rest is all us's needin'; a long, long rest. Thanks for tea, mister
Sean, an' for the happy talk; does one good, does she. But the
tired body slid back into the chair again, the weary eyes closed
once more, the flickering hands went more slowly from button
to button, and the tired soldier dozed.

Here was a chap who should have been guiding a plough, or
driving a tractor, now spending years of his life, in sun, rain,
frost, and snow, at the arse of a big gun, firing up to the
firmament; loading shells instead of loading hay; trying by the
probing light from a magnified candle to nick an enemy in the
higher air, and send him tumbling down. Asleep now, and
harmless, even pathetic; but dreaming it, dreaming harm,
surely; encouraging himself to hold on till the time came to
give ten blows for one. Here, a father seeks a son, there a son
seeks a father; there a mother scrounges in the ruins for a
child, here a child is wailing for a mother; a husband burrows
for a wife, a wife watches others burrowing for her husband.
All were hunting for the dead. Give a glance, and go, mate. No

time to look; there's a war on. Ten blows for one. Vengeance is mine, saith the gunner.

Stick it, grim gunner: the time is coming when for every home demolished in Plymouth, ten will sink into rubble in Hamburg and Berlin. They may blast our streets away, but we will blast away their cities; level them so that not one stone will be left to balance itself on another; the people who once trod entranced through cities, sure and proud, will seek refuge in their ruins, like conies seeking shelter in the rocks. Nothing left for them but holes and corners; scream it out, gunner – holes and corners! Smother the terrible testimony in the drumbeat of bombs exploding!

Sleep on, grim gunner, and take your peace; and dream your great dream. The time cometh and is at hand, when your gun shall be idle and silent, cloaked against the weather; when you may sit calm on a bench in the inn, drinking your beer, and chuckle, gunner, when you hear the German kid scream and the kid's mother scream, and the kid's father yell in agony, for the cities and the towns where they have their habitation shall fall upon them, splintering their bones and squashing their ripe flesh till it is flesh no longer; and you shall laugh, grim gunner, for there shall not be a corner in city or town, be it never so small, that shall not be inflamed with the terrible blaze from a bursting bomb. Then you will have time and breath to sing All people that on earth do dwell, remembering God's mercy is for ever sure.

The tired eyes twitched half open, and the gunner's soul urged the gunner's body out of the chair's comfort. He stood up, a little crookedly, blinking at Sean, the fingers still playing wistfully with the buttons.

—Must go, he said. Want rest, long sleep; yes. Don't 'ee worry, no, don't 'ee worry, Sean, mister; we'll bust they bastards soon. Carry on.

He moved crookedly to the door, and went out, Sean going with him to the garden gate to watch him walk towards town and home; watch him walk unsteadily, with occasional jerky pauses. He faced round, suddenly, shook a fist in the air, and shouted, Don't 'ee worry; us'll get they bastards soon! Then he turned, and went on shakily, as if uncertain where he was going; as if he were walking in a half-sleep, as, almost certainly, he was.

Life kept on going into new years, and Christmas was cele-

brated more scantily than in former times. The decorations on
the Christmas tree were shoddy, and had abandoned their
scintillating brilliancy; peace on earth to men of goodwill had
swindled into a mocking injury of the inquisitive Oh, yeah,
brother! The bells of Christmas had croaked themselves into
silence. Harder times than those of Dickens were upon all like
a pall without a break. Spiritual ack-ack guns throughout days
of national penitence kept afirin' up, afirin' up, petitions for
help, but heaven seemed to be far and away out of range.
Aforetime, kids had seen apparitions in Lourdes, kids had seen
apparitions in Fatima, kids had been apparitions even in little
Knock; but, now, the time seemed to have dimmed their eyes.
Most probably, they were shivering with cold and fear in some
Nazi concentration camp, or were hiding in an Anderson
shelter, or crouching under a Morrison table, biding away from
the bombs. No apparition appeared in Westminster over the
anglican abbey, or over the roman catholic cathedral; none was
seen anywhere; none. Even the Angels of Mons, it seemed,
had dwindled into old-age pensioners. The skies were too
dangerous now for angels to be knocking about. The baby girl,
Shivaun, who had been carried down to the cellar in a clothes-
basket, now was a sturdy kid, running round and prattling
away; even attending a nursery school: but still the bombs
were falling, and the blackout as keen and wearisome as ever.

On a bright, brisk morning, after the children had gone to
school, Eileen and he were busy washing up the breakfast
things, when, halfway through the work, they heard the rasping roar, continuous and angry, of an aeroplane, somewhere
above them; a roar that filled the scullery so that they couldn't
hear each other speak.

—Ah! shouted Sean into Eileen's ear, one of our aeroplanes
in trouble!

He rushed to the window, flung it open, and stretched out to
get a clearer view of the sky. Yes, there were one – two – three,
flying by, skimming the O'Casey roof and the roofs beyond,
flames spitting out of every fuselage. Then came a long, shattering explosion, shaking their nerves, and rocking the house
under their feet and over their heads; an explosion that seemed
to grow louder as it rumbled fiercely along.

—God, the house's falling! shouted Eileen.

—Come along to the front of the house! he shouted back,
the explosions turning the shout to a whisper; and the two of

them ran from the back of the house to the front room facing
the road; but this room was rocking more violently than the
other.

—Out of the house, into the open! he shouted, catching her
hand and hauling her to the window, but push and push as
they would it wouldn't open to them. Then, suddenly, they saw
that the hasp was on the window, and ten men couldn't have
pushed it up. Holding each other's hands, they stood in the
centre of the room to laugh splendidly at the frantic and
ridiculous efforts they had made to open a bolted window by
main strength; the snarling rumble of the explosions forgotten
in a hilarious sense of humour; laughter that sounded through
the explosions shaking out a window, sending down the
greater part of two ceilings, and loosening the trembling house
in all its joints.

They unhooked the hasp, flung up the window, and ran out
to shelter beside a loaded lorry standing alone, without a
driver, in the centre of the Plymouth road, the air all round
full of a biting acid smell of fumes mixed with burning wood
and scorching brick. Half the railway station was in ruins, the
bridge had been damaged, walls flung down, Totnes main street
was a river of glass, and all the roofs around were battered,
broken, and slit with machine-gun bullets. A number of persons were wounded, and an Air Force officer, just released on
leave, and waiting at the station for a train to take him home,
was killed; wending a way home, he went too far; stepped over
time into eternity. No wound showed on him, not even a
scratch, but his lungs within had been burst asunder by the
blast, as two strong hands coming together would burst a toy
balloon. When the raid was over, soldiers returned to the lorry,
and told Sean and Eileen that they couldn't have selected a
more dangerous place to shelter, for the lorry was loaded with
explosives. Another fine laugh for them, sitting by the fire that
night, the blackout up, the danger past for the present.

Through it all – the bombing, the blackout, the drills, the
departure of loved ones into a paramount and pungent danger;
the arrival of telegrams to some family telling it briefly that a
loved one had vanished; the lengthening of the Roll of Honour,
and the swelling lists in the local papers of simple rhymes, like

> Time passes, shadows fall;
> Love and remembrance outlast all;

for nothing dies but something mourns: through them all, life went on, harder now in its everyday problems, so that, with ration-cards and allocated points, with a heavy scarcity to select from, the housewife was ever in a maze of figures that toppled to a tangle as soon as they were settled to a tidy-looking sum. Many an old woman, an old man, or a young girl, go along silently, now; no longer eager to stay for a gossip; wordless where they used to babble; two have lost a son, one a lover. But still life hurries on, too busy to halt for a moment of mourning. Too much mourning to mourn at all. The wintertime is the hardest, when the blackout lasts too long, and makes the gayest heart moody. Winter's bosom-pals, the cold rains, fierce winds, nipping frosts, and sullen snows have been with us far too long; and so all welcome the snow-drop slowly and sturdily pushing its white way up through the cold earth and the rain-sodden grasses, its stem of gentle green bearing its tiny white flag of promise that though winter be still here, spring's not far behind. There they are in a drenched meadow by the Dart, or on the moor, demure and thoughtless, but confident under the grey, grumbling skies of aged and agued winter; tiny and fragile angels of the annunciation sent by spring to tell all that life will soon be new-born under sunnier skies, and sit in the lap of an ampler earth.

The snowdrops send a stir through the hearts of many living in the little houses stretching themselves along the hedgy roads, nestling under the shoulders of the hill, or hiding away in the deeper dip of a valley. The people murmur among themselves, saying, Soon they snowdrops will be adottin' they woods, an' maybe clusterin'; an' us'll go gether them. They wonder if the broad fields will nurse more of them than they did last year. Women too old for uniforms, or privileged by family burdens; girls too young for uniforms, and many chil-dren, will search out their oldest clothes and strongest boots to be found in press or box, to equip themselves against muddy or snowy road and sodden woods; and among the countryfolk will be a sprinkle of those who have been blown thither by the red, flaming winds that turned their little city homes into deso-late confusion. They will fetch out old baskets, and trim them anew, so that the blossoms may be carried back without bruise or blemish. Some will sigh for a pair of wellington boots, for the grass will be high, and will be plump with the rain that has fallen so fast and so often, making foot, ankle, and knee numb with the sappy wet, and will saturate the pendent skirts of the blossom-hunters, making the skirts cling madly to the cold, perishing legs of the enthusiastic thieves. They will bear the flowers home, not to decorate a mantelpiece with a graceful tribute to the Virgin or to that angel who drove Eve from the Garden out into the snow, and who, breathing on the snow-flakes as they fell, left snowdrops in full blossom behind: they pull them out, pluck them up out of the snow to market them. They trim their stalks respectably, wrap them thoughtlessly in moistened paper, pack them decently into suitable cardboard coffins, and hurry them to the steaming train; for the well-off of London cry out for them, and they carry a good price back to those who had plucked them from their cool beds in the hidden places of the snowy woods. They droop quick in the hot breast of a London dame, and wilt as fast when they are forced to form for a minute a pool of quiet glory on the polished corner of a pompous table. Throw them in the dust: many more fresh and fair ones left where these ones fading first were snatched from the snow.

It must be that upon each tiny snowy blossom there lies now a tiny crimson stain, for where they grow, the ground often shuddered, wondering why, and they have trembled many and many a time with the sigh of many a dying Englishman, the nearby sigh of a dying Englishwoman, and the dying English child sighing a bewildered farewell to all that killed her. Their tender and reclining loveliness fits no way into the warm and cosy bosom of even the prettiest woman; nor do they sit satis-fied in the blue bowl on the polished corner of a grandee's table. They are not for the world-wise, the wasteful-minded, or the whirling dancer. This little plant with its green leaves touched with white, its white flower touched with green; these three pale sepals holding the tiny, green-speckled white cup, enclosing the tinier yellow pistil, like a midget queen, beneath her canopy, cloaked in saffron. These pale pages of their lus-trous sisters, the daffodils, may rest in peace only in the bosom of the very young when the very young are dead; to lie quiet on the young breast, replacing the red rose of life snatched from the mouth of those who died too soon. Breathless and afraid these blossoms feel, where red wine-spots stain the purity of linen, where silver glistens, where words are many and the voice is loud. Rather let them rest in peace upon the breast of the young who haven't had their day.

Through all life's twinings, its affection and animosity, the war went on; the men went off to die or came back mangled; the bombs still fell; the blackout was still as tense as ever: the tale of a wasted life was still being told. Sean and Eileen had bought a Morrison table with its thick steel top, and this had been set up in a little room off the hallway, ten feet from the front door. Under this table, Eileen, the girl of three, and the boy of six lay flat, while Sean and the elder boy of thirteen sat in the hallway, just outside the door of the room where the rest of the family lay under the steel table, whenever bombs were falling in the nearer neighbourhood. The table was said to be able to bear up brightly against the shock of a tumbling house, however big, and to preserve a cavity where those under it could possibly last out life in semi-suffocation till a rescue-squad had time to dig them out of their huge burial mound, and give them better air to breathe. A wan hope under a wan protection; but it gave more confidence than any useless prayer or any old-fashioned hymn. There they were, Eileen and the two younger children flat on their bellies under the steel table, the little girl laughing at the experience, the younger lad merry, too, but sobering when the house shook; the older lad, quiet and unmoved, sitting on a chest beside Sean, glum, though trying, too, to look unconcerned, but cocking his ears to distinguish the nationality of the aeroplane engines throbbing, snarling, throbbing overhead; his work laid out on a table in another room, abandoned when the raid came, waiting for him to come back to writhe towards a competent interest in it again, when the raid ceased, and the All Clear sounded; his heart in his mouth whenever a bomb fell near, and the explosion made the windows jump, and the hall-door, a few feet away, bulge in and out, with a rattling snarl as rapid as a frantic roll beaten by a frantic pair of hands on a tightly-laced drum. Oh, in war, there is neither song nor sermon. Oh! let the winter go, let the spring hasten, let the summer come, let the autumn linger, and let this damned war die away out of life; let Hitler and his chums die with it; and all who may ever want war again, die too; so that we may have time to look at, ponder over, and enjoy, our desolation.

SHAW'S CORNER

A LETTER came when stars were paling, came from Charlotte Shaw; a letter that was kind and homely; a letter that was law; written in that style of handwriting so oddly like that of her great pard; the confident manner of its phrasing sending out the idea that the invitation was a minor command to come when you're called; inviting Eileen and him to lunch in White-hall Court. Indeed, an invitation connecting itself with a visit to G.B.S. was a command that few would like to disobey or ignore. A visit to him always made Eileen's heart and his own beat a little faster. Mrs Shaw liked Sean, but seemed to like him in a bitter way; a shrill kind of attachment. She looked upon him as a somewhat refractory fellow, and was too anxious about him. She had resented his silent refusal to accept the offer of her husband's mediation in the contest with the Abbey Theatre over the rejection of his *The Silver Tassie*. She seemed to think that Sean's choice to fight it on his lone was something of a snub to her great husband. She was eager to direct him in the way he should go, through literature, through art, through drama, through life. She had an earnest admiration and deep respect for some things that Sean wouldn't stop to look at twice; and she vehemently resented his demolishing regard for George Russell's works, for she placed Russell firmly before Yeats, taking him to her bosom as Ireland's most brilliant, spiritual, and powerful avastar. Avast! Her cheeks glowed whenever she muttered the magic symbol of A. E., as if this diphthong had within it the whole kind kingdom of heaven. To Sean, he was Ireland's brazen Buddha. One sentence criticizing anything said or done by Russell would tense the curiously soft face into a flint-look, cold anger sparking from its flushed compression. Numerous times, she had commanded Sean to honour and obey the genius of A. E., but Sean had smiled and registered a refusal in solid silence.

Another writer she had tried to force into his esteem and affection was the scholarly Miss Helen Waddell, a fellow adorer of George Russell. Mrs Shaw sent him Miss Waddell's

The Wandering Scholars and *Medieval Latin Lyrics,* calmly commanding him to give direct attention and whole-hearted admiration to the works. They were the works. But Sean side-stepped away from Mrs Shaw's peppermint-explosions of You Must read and re-read them till you Understand them, and so gradually get to realize how fine they are, and get to Love Them. Come with me and be my love. But Sean hadn't the time, Or the scholarship. Anon, sweet wag; anon, anon!

Later on, she tried to make the philosophy of Gerald Heard a pulse-beat in his mind, but he slipped away from Heard without even hearing him speak. Mrs Shaw used every call to lunch to mention something he should do or not do, or name a book he should read which would wave him along some one-way road of spiritual life and mental wisdom; her great husband gazing at her all the time, silently, with a patient, quizzical face. He had such an affection for her, and she was so necessary to him in his going out and his coming in, that he rarely tried to cross her; or, maybe he thought it best to let the advice given be left or taken, according to the nature of him or her to whom it had been offered.

Once at a lunch, with Charlotte at one end of the table, Shaw at the other, Eileen at one side, Sean facing her at the other, the group looking like a four-leaved shamrock, Mrs Shaw, grim-faced, waiting for the lunch to be served, and the maid to go, Shaw chatting about the sharp spring air that tingled the cheek and nipped the ear. Sean had long noticed that Charlotte ate heavily, a great pile on her plate, thickly covered with whatever sauce went with the main dish; that she leant forward determinedly to swallow whenever she filled a forkful, using a sluggish energy to bring it to her mouth and get it down quickly, quietly rebuking him because he ate sparingly, never allowing a heap on his plate; for, however hungry he might be, a piled plate shoved away any desire to eat. Mrs Shaw felt the cold keenly, and she sat over her plate, hunched up, a shawl round her shoulders, and an electric fire beside her chair – symptoms, probably, of the dread disease that, later on, shoved her into the grave. Shaw sat erect in his high-backed chair, eating his baked eggs and vegetables, and drinking his milk with graceful ease; chatting away, evoking a burst of laughter from Sean, a rippling one from Eileen at some witty comment given about some former incident, startling Mrs Shaw away from her attention to her plate, and delighting the

great man himself, who leant farther back on his stately chair
to give a musical laugh himself. While Sean was eating his
share of apple-tart, Mrs Shaw suddenly asked him what he
was doing now.

—Nothing at all, at the moment, he said; for he had no wish
to undergo a catechism of what it was about, how it was growing, and when it would end; he added: Nothing at the
moment; I'm afraid I am an idle man just now.

—Too busy quarrelling, she said, rather viciously. I hear you
have quarrelled with Agate now. You will have to learn a
better way of conducting yourself. You will get nowhere by
these senseless disputes.

—Not even into heaven? queried Sean, not knowing what to
say to this sudden assault, and trying to put it aside with a
hasty laugh.

—It's no light matter, she said. Quarrelling with people this
way, you will have enemies everywhere. Why do you do it?

This was unexpected, and damnably embarrassing to him.
Eileen, more embarrassed even than Sean, lifted her head,
smiling uncomfortably; bent her head, lifted it again, hoping
that Sean wouldn't burst out in resentment at Mrs Shaw's re-
bukes. He had, apparently, been led into a trap: brought to a
private, personal lunch so that Mrs Shaw could go at him to
her heart's content. She didn't seem to realize that she was
doing now what she was condemning him for, with the advantage of being the hostess, and so making it hard for Sean to
reply. Silent for a moment, he then said, If a critic judges a
writer by what a writer may say to him or even about him; if
he denies merit in a work because of dislike for the author,
then he's not a critic, but a dastard.

—There you go again! she said, angrily. You must learn to
be more agreeable to critics. You mustn't go on disturbing important people in this reckless way; you must be made to check
this reckless urge towards opposition. You must control him,
she added, turning suddenly on Eileen; you must advise him,
and modify what he is inclined to say; while Shaw sat straight
up in his chair, listening; silent.

—Sean is too honest, ventured Eileen. He says things in a
very blunt way. It seems unpleasant, I know, but I think he is
right.

—He isn't right! said Mrs Shaw, emphatically. He's too
peevish, too peevish altogether. You shouldn't encourage him.

She turned swiftly towards Sean again. Why do you do it?

—Why do I do it? echoed Sean, trying to think out what he ought to say to such an attack by such a woman. Somehow or other, I am made to do it. Your own husband did it, and does it still, Mrs Shaw.

—There you go again! she said, and the too-soft face crinkled with vexation. You quarrelled with Yeats, you quarrelled with A. E., as great a man as Yeats, and, in some respects, a greater one – no, you don't think so, I know, she said quickly, sensing Sean's rejection of her claim; and now you've quarrelled with James Agate.

—I didn't quarrel with Yeats, said Sean, quietly; I differed from him on a question of drama; so, too, with Agate: I withstood him to his face because I thought he was to be blamed – if he doesn't like it, he can lump it.

—You see, you stay obstinate! No one will have a good word for you if you go on in this irritating way. Why do you do it?

—I have to, said Sean; I can no else. Something within me speaks before I am aware of it, and the harm is done. Sean was trying to be good-humoured. Maybe it's the prompting of what some venture to call the holy ghost.

—What do you exactly mean by the holy ghost? The voice was sharper than before, and the soft face was flushed and even quivering a little with anger. You must learn to define your words before you use them. Just what do you mean?

—He means, said Shaw, in a calm, even voice, never moving the white, clinging hands from the back railings of the high chair; he simply means, Charlotte, that he has got something and I've got something that you haven't got.

Sean had been several times to lunch with them when they had lived in Adelphi Terrace; and he had wandered round the district, remembering how many great men had lodged and dodged about the streets: Garrick, Pepys, Turner, and even Peter the Great. Dust of time was everywhere, and mustiness clung to hall, stairway, and room. Streets crowding after each other's heels everywhere; houses pressed so close together that few found space to breathe in. How we cling to old and dying things! To things Doric, Corinthian, and Ionic, as if these were to be the everlasting architectural for all ages; as if no new thought of building could infuse human imagination with forms as fine, and far more suitable. And for family worship

no finer forms of furniture than those of Sheraton, Chippen-
dale, and Hepplewhite; lost now with the fop, the dandy, the
curtsy, the low bow, and the jewelled snuff-box. All gone;
gathered up and taken away by the groping hand of time. The
hardier things about them stayed, table, chair, and ceiling;
snuff-box, necklace, and sword; stuffed into a museum, and set
out in ritual tier and row; the men and women themselves no
more than the scintillating dust of England.

Sean entered by the wide-open doorway, climbed the stairs,
fumbled a long time with the chevaux-de-frise, spears against
uninvited probers. He got it open at last, passed through, and
was guided by a maid into the presence of the great man and
his wife. A vast experience to the shy and inexperienced Sean;
but the genial twinkle in the sage's questioning eyes, and the
soft, motherly welcome of Charlotte dissolved the nervousness,
and Sean's nature fused pleasantly with the Shaw household.
At a lot of these lunches, curious customers gathered to meet
the Shaws. Only on a few occasions did Sean see sweet
feminine face and form and hear elegant or sturdy talk from
visitors. Looking like human goofies (Sean himself among
them; for once Shaw had asked John Dulanty, Eire's Ambassador, How lovely Eileen Carey had come to marry such an
ugly fellow as Sean. Although it was little known, and few
thought it, Shaw, like every intelligent Irishman, had a keen
eye for a good-looking woman.) 'Mostly, Mrs Shaw's cronies',
a handsome young visitor once whispered to Sean. How singular, Sean thought, Eileen and a handsome young Russian
named Duiska looked, caged among so many gnarled and un-
couth guests, gabbing away importantly to Mrs Shaw and her
white-bearded sage. Shaw alone put brightness and daring into
the current remarks, though they forced him to give opinions
of persons and things, long ago dead, and never before the eyes
of the present generation. The faded puppets of long-dead
dramas, Balfour, Bonar Law, Bannerman, were marched about
and handled, by this one, by that, as they munched and
munched meat and swallowed wine round the round table.

At one of the lunches there were a man and his wife who
were crooked as cods in a pot. Both were lame, and each
carried a stick to help them over a stile, one veering to the
right, the other to the left, as they toddled along. The man's
voice sounded like the sound of a saw going through a rusty
nail embedded in wood the saw was cutting, and whatever

humanity was left in a sourpuss was evicted by a black patch
over one eye. His wife sang the praises of some osteopath,
who, she said, had straightened her into what she was now,
Mrs Shaw nodding in agreement, and mentioning that her own
bones had been put into a smart conception of what they were
originally meant to be by another osteopath. The husband
assailed Shaw with some old history of something that had
sucked from political life and usefulness a man named Sir
Charles Dilke in the days of Gladstone, forcing Shaw to prod
his mind back to a reconception of, and to comment upon, an
event that had died, and lay like a log, deep buried under the
loam of time. Shaw was plagued with persons insisting on
hearing his opinions past and gone, who came with pick and
spade to disinter the near-forgotten dead, and make them look
lively again: the encumbrance of the remembrance of things
past.

At a lunch given by Lady Lavery (whose face appeared on
the first issue of Ireland's national pound note), wife of the
painter, Shaw entertained everyone present with racy accounts
of incident after incident, while Lady Londonderry, Mrs
James MacNeill, wife of Ireland's High Commissioner, and
others, enjoyed themselves; the magnificent head of Augustus
John, moving slowly on his broad shoulders, gazing at the
company, the brilliant, piercing eyes seeing all in anything
worth seeing, noticing nothing where there was nothing to
notice. Afterwards, when most had gone, and Mrs Shaw with
Mrs MacNeill was upstairs looking at a recent painting, by
Sir John, of a prelate – Archbishop Mannix if he remembers
right, he who had led the hostility to Dr O'Hickey, in Maynooth, the time Mannix was President of the College – Shaw
walked firmly up and down the dining-room, pausing for a
moment to say to Sean, Great strain on one this necessity to
keep talking during the time of a luncheon.

—Why the hell do you do it? asked Sean. Is it vanity, his
mind asked, silently; is it just trying to shine? Shine out, fair
sun! We're all doing it, doing it, doing it.

—They all expect it of me, Shaw said; and one can't sit in
silence, staring at the others.

—Why not? queried Sean. If the others can stick it, you
can; and, if they can't stick it, they'll talk themselves, and save
you some of the strain. Augustus John talks only when he
feels like it. Unless talk comes spontaneously to me, I'm dumb.

I don't make conversation at lunch a question of conscience.

—That's sound advice, said Shaw, halting in his patrol, slanting back his remarkable head, and letting out a musical laugh. Shaw stops talking – what would the world say!

Sean wondered if Shaw really took all this in so as to sit more silent sitting at a foreign table, reserving his queer, salient talk for the time he would be at his ease sitting at his own. Under those bristling eyebrows, behind those brilliant Irish eyes, over that thick-ended nose, under that frosty pow, thinning thickly now, the alert, witty, and peerless mind peered out at the present, peered into the future; almost faultless, utterly unafraid. Oh, Shaw, there is not your equal now! When shall we see your like again!

Chesterton prancing about, commodore of the cosmos, wrote a book setting forth Shaw as a connoisseur of mistaken opinions and belief. In a debate, Shaw was always merciful to Chesterton. Miss Ward tells us that 'each would sacrifice his life rather than hurt the other'. Bosom-pals. Not like Cuchullain, and Ferdiadh, who loved each other as few did; yet in the fight of the ford, each strove to wound the other; and though they halted in the evening to bind up each other's wounds, they kept hard at it till one of them was killed. Shaw was merciful to Chesterton as anyone might be to someone angling obliquely for a possible conversion; and Chesterton was fulsome with Shaw in a childish effort to show how close the roman catholic church came to Shaw's idea of religious and social life. Keep the door ajar. Indeed, Miss Ward is clearly puzzled as to what to say about their differences because she doesn't want to make them too pronounced. She, too, was helping to keep the door ajar. She says 'Chesterton was, however, in agreement with the ordinary citizen and in disagreement with Shaw as to much of Shaw's essential teaching. And here we touch a matter so involved that even today it is hard to disentangle it completely.' Hedging! Today? Yesterday, today, and for ever, Miss Ward.

Shaw was a member of an expanding universe, Chesterton of a narrowing one. Chesterton grew in childishness as Shaw grew in grace. Bawling out that he was the one man who understood Shaw, Chesterton showed, in his first few comments on the dramatist, that he didn't understand a thing about Shaw's idea of *John Bull's Other Island*. Shaw didn't bother, for you couldn't tell a thing to Chesterton. He was incapable of assimilating anything outside of himself. Shaw sought out chances to face things, Chesterton rushed after every chance to avoid them (Dreyfus!). It is funny to think of him trying to reflect Tolstoy, Blake, and Browning from the mirror of his shifty mind. It's a wonder he didn't try to write about Joyce; but Joyce beat him, for he was too great a catholic for Chesterton's mind to manage. Hide him from me, heaven!

Fear, ever behind Shaw, was ever in front of Chesterton. According to his sister-in-law, he feared sickness, or even to speak of it; hated to think of, discuss, or debate death, except in its relation to fanciful murder done by faraway denizens in his lurid detective fiction. Like the title of one of them, he himself was the sign of the broken sword. Chesterton, to maintain his cosmos of cosmic comprehension, of God, of man, and of all things, from everlasting man to tremendous trifles, had to proclaim that, to him, Shaw was an open book, and that he alone, had the hand to close it. But in his jump into cosmic comprehension from what he thought to be the kernel of the church, he became but another old woman who lived in a shoe. We are told in the life of this tremendous trifle that Chesterton showed 'deeper thought' in his play, *Magic*, than Shaw did in his, because, evidently, he 'believed in the love of God and man [as if Shaw didn't], he believed in the devil and that love conquers diabolical evil'. See the conquering zero comes. He dismisses every writer greater than himself with a gentle, recessional wave of the hand from a cloud of the love of God – Ruskin, the Brontë sisters, Tennyson, Tolstoy, and, of course, George Moore (but not a word about Joyce); takes them down as one would china figures from a shelf, gives each a chestertonian spit and a catholic polish, and puts it back again; all of them, in Chesterton's mind, abashed that they had not kept right on to the end of the road to Rome. But the newer roman catholic writers, Mauriac, Waugh, Grahame Greene, seem to doubt the power of love in conquering diabolical evil. Their thoughts seem to go too damned deep for words. With them it seems there's no love left anywhere to conquer anything.

Seeing how popular he was, how he splashed his concepts about in paper, magazine, and book, his rush to get his words recorded, so mad and so breathless that it took a litter of publishers to print his books; seeing all this, it is odd that so few (if any, bar his wife) followed him into becoming a *persona gratis romanorum*. One would imagine he'd have marched in at the head of a crowd. He doesn't seem to have caused even an *honoris causa* conversion. He fiddled for Shaw, as did many others. The roman catholic church would have got a tremendous kick out of Shaw's conversion to the faith – their faith. Many of them thought that Shaw had already got flashes of the truth as it was in Father O'Flynn, and they hoped on to the last. Flickers of faith. Would Shaw become a Catholic Movie? Once, a letter from Mrs Shaw to Sean, asking him to lunch, told him a Father Leonard would be there, the letter's tone implying that the priest was a familiar figure to the Shaws; but Father Leonard didn't come, and Sean never knew what kind of a bloke he was, except that he was an Ess Jay; never heard his name again. Probably a number kept praying for Shaw's conversion. All together – pray for the wanderer, pray for him! What a catch he'd be! If he would only come knocking at the door. Knock, knock, knock. Whisht, is that him? Oh, if he only would venture under the portals of St Peter! At times, he seemed so near, then, in a laughing moment, he was farther away than ever. Miss Maisie Ward tells us that when visiting Shaw and Wells, the two 'able and indeed brilliant men betrayed not only an amazing degree of ignorance concerning the tenets of Catholicism but also a bland conviction that they knew them well'. If Miss Ward had talked to the parish priests, she might well have found that they were more ignorant of the tenets of catholicism than were these two able and brilliant men. Dr McDonald, forty years Professor of Theology in Maynooth roman catholic college, tells us how on a ship heading for Belfast, he met a young doctor, a Scot, who was astonished at the small amount one had to accept in dogma in order to become a catholic. The Scot asked time to consider what McDonald had told him, and, in the morning, he asked the Professor, in all honour, to tell him that if he explained the faith to the priests of Ulster as Dr McDonald had explained it to him, would the priests recognize it as the faith that each and all avowed. 'As an honest man', adds Dr McDonald, 'I was forced to admit that they would not.' Miss Ward sighingly complains about the laughing way in which Belloc and Chesterton tried to answer Shaw's and Wells' denials of the doctrine of The Fall. 'Perhaps', she says, 'they did not realize where the beginning must be made in instructing otherwise instructed men on the subject of Catholicism.'

They didn't know the beginning, and, seemingly, they didn't know the ending either. They did not know because they were not told! Miss Ward adds, rather pathetically, 'Has any Catholic ever explained the philosophic meaning of Transubstantiation to Shaw?' Answer her, answer her! Not a damned one, apparently, Miss Ward. Since Dr McDonald, forty years Professor of Theology in Maynooth College, found the going hard, rejecting a lot of common and high-brow catholic teaching, including Belloc's and Chesterton's Fall, is it any wonder that Wells and Shaw found the coming harder?

How men like Belloc and Chesterton could think that such sensible, secular minds could seek shelter under the roman dome of dogma is difficult to understand. But Shaw's gentle way of turning aside roman catholic supplications for submission left him open to the patter of pietistic hope. He might do it. He might, he might do it!

Multitudes of minds have been explaining the meaning of the philosophy of transubstantiation, the semi-catholic philosophy of consubstantiation, and the philosophies written round the other church tenets, for the last thousand years, or more; yet they stand still, waiting, unexplained, even to the roman catholics themselves. Indeed, the whirling controversy goes down even to the origin of man himself, all along, down along, out along way. Looks like Chesterton, Belloc, and Miss Ward spent a good deal of their lives stretched out comfortably on the plush-covered, cushioned roman couch of traditional thought; and didn't notice many things; or were dozing deeply when they happened. Not so St George Jackson Mivart, who died when Sean was already twenty years old. Mivart was made a Dr of Philosophy by the pope of 1876, four years before Sean was born; and MD by the University of Louvain, in which he was given the Chair of Philosophy of Natural History; then in a blaze of blackened roman candles, he was excommunicated by the roman catholic church four years before his death. Among others, here are a few things said about this brave man by Dr McDonald, Professor of Theology in Maynooth roman catholic college: 'Here, in Mivart's *Primer of Philosophy* – given to me, mockingly, by Dr Walsh, afterwards Archbishop of Dublin – was what was being said every day, quite near us; not by lunatics or demons, but by men of great scientific attainments, who deemed it a duty to say what they said. The book stimulated me in a way I never felt before.

It was the beginning of a new life – the life which I have led ever since, and which I am likely to lead while I live at all. Few things pained me more than that Mivart, to whom I owed so much in the way of religious and scientific instruction, should, at the close of his life, have had such a struggle and have suffered such eclipse; that he did, throughout, what he deemed his duty, I cannot for a moment doubt; neither, however, do I doubt, that he was wrong objectively, in attributing to the Church, as definitive, what she never taught definitively; but that such a man should be plunged into such misery by non-definitive teaching – a fate which I myself barely escaped, if by God's grace, I do escape it – shows how good men, by ultra-conservatism, may be doing the devil's work when they are most zealous for God and religion.'

The church that had no room for a Mivart could hardly have the strength to squeeze out a place for such as Shaw, such as Wells; no room in the bin. No room, really, even for Dr McDonald, who fashioned out his own faith (as he tells us) far away from the mouthings of infallible fools. It is odd that neither Chesterton nor Belloc ever mentioned McDonald's name. Chesterton was forty-six when McDonald died; he was in Ireland after the world war, plunging into the roman catholic world there, but, apparently, never heard a whisper (or, if he did, kept his mouth shut) about one of Maynooth's most remarkable priests. It is odder still that Dr McDonald never mentions this prancing champion of catholicism on his white horse, or when, in lighter moments, he was doing his comic catholic can-can, though Chesterton was famous in roman catholic Ireland, and his sayings were being quoted by priest, poet, and peasant. But then, we are told that 'his awe and reverence for a priest were enormous', and that he would listen, 'head bowed and hat off, to anything a priest might say, however fatuous'. Add that this was a man who didn't like to speak of sickness, didn't like the mention of death, put Walt Whitman out of his house, and refused to let Ibsen in, as well as declaiming against giving a vote to a woman – hardly a competent guide, either in secular or religious philosophy, to such a man as Wells or such a one as Shaw. How Belloc and Chesterton could for a moment imagine that such sensible secular minds would jump for shelter or crawl for shelter under the roman dome of dogma is difficult to understand. Still you never could tell what thought might change the

thoughts of the devil's disciples. Shaw's gentle way of turning
roman catholic supplications aside left him open to the patter
of pietistic hope. He might submit. He might do it, he might do
it. He jarred at times, though: like the unintentional way he
hurt a hopeful mother superior, who, when he had gone, ex-
claimed What a horrid, blasphemous fella! When I asked him
would he join up with us, he replied, Yes, I'd like to; but think
what a terrible thing it would be if the world had two popes!
Setting up an equality with the Holy Father. The villain! Still
he might, might do it.

> The dame made a curtsy,
> The dog made a bow;
> The dame said, 'Your servant',
> The dog said, Bow-wow.

The odd thing was that the probing minds of Mivart,
McDonald, Wells, and Shaw were, in fact, coming closer to
God, while, it seemed, the minds shrinking away from question and quiz, turning their backs on pillar of fire and cloud,
were covering their eyes with their hands, rather than see or
sense the back parts of God as he passed by on his way to
others. Those thinking to hold up the church were knocking
her down, those apparently knocking her down were holding
her up: perhaps, now and then, heaven likes a joke.

Shaw's *pied-à-terre* in London was a roomy and comfortable
one, and for all that it must have heard, many times, many
great arguments about it and about, the whole impression it
gave out was one of commonplace serenity; a cushioned recess
for the mighty mind. Here was nothing vulgar, nothing modern either, in furniture, picture, or stone, except the painting of
Shaw himself by Augustus John, hung so high that the eyes of
Shaw or of his wife never met it during their sitting down or
standing up in the room. The head had to be thrown back on
the shoulders to see it, and Shaw never, far as Sean knew,
pointed it out to a visitor. Let it hang there quietly out o' the
way. Eileen's eye caught sight of it the moment she entered the
room, and halting to stare, she cried out, happily, A John!

It was amusing to see the half-startled way Shaw turned up
his head to squint at the picture, turning his head down again,
to wait patiently till Eileen and Sean had ended their look at it.
Perhaps it was too lyrical, too far away from the cloudy em-

phasis of a photograph, too sensuous, though the sensuousness was a gentle mingling of lovely silvery greys and gentle blues, giving it a look of gay loneliness; and from these lyrical greys and gentle blues peeped impudently the wise and humorous face of the dramatist and the fighter. A suggestion from Eileen that it should be placed where the eye could see it comfortably evoked no comment from Shaw and but the short statement from Charlotte that G.B.S. didn't like it well enough to change it from where it was. Ricketts was about the furthest that Shaw got towards the enjoyment of the painter's art. He preferred the ghastly picture of himself done by John Collier to the lyrical impression of himself done by John. It would seem that he had gunned the art of painting away from him by a multitude of shots from his camera. What a great loss this lack in the Shaws was to Ireland! With their wealth how many fine pictures they could have gathered to be presented, some time, to Eire's National Gallery, or to the Municipal Collection housed in Parnell Square. His friends didn't help him any, for few, if any, cared a damn about Raphael or Renoir. Few of those pictured beside him had shown any desire to mingle their souls with the old painters or the new; indeed, some of them – like the Webbs – were as deaf as the mole is blind to all art and all literature. They spent their working-hours and leisure sorting men and things out in tier and row. They never sought out a second for a song and a dance. What would the Webbs have thought had they seen Joyce suddenly indulging in his mad, amazing, wild-man dance on a bridge of the Seine? Shaw would have wondered, and laughed; the Webbs would have hurried away, for it wouldn't have been either possible or seemly to have tucked away such an item into a pyramid of statistics. Dublin workers, had there been any there to see it, would have remained hushed for a few moments, and then they'd have hilariously joined in – hoosh the cat from under the table! Joyce, for all his devotion to his art, terrible in its austerity, was a lad born with a song on one side of him, a dance on the other – two gay guardian angels every human ought to have. And what is the universe but a dance of orbs? Brooks Atkinson in his *Once Around the Sun* tells us that the Dog Star's Procyon is rushing towards us at the rate of two and a half miles a second; and many other stars are rushing away; this way, that way, in the expanding universe: so if we go wild at times, as Joyce did, we are errant in magnificent

company. Life will be on a high plane when life becomes a song
and a dance and a serious thing.

Music. A harpsichord. Shaw's crest and arms. A lovely one,
encased in polished yellow wood, standing in a prominent part
of the room. Shaw's heart was here. He was blessed with a
deep love for, and a deep understanding of, the melody, intri-
cate, rippling and majestic, that flowed from, and thundered
out of, the magic weaving of sounds by Beethoven, Brahms,
Wagner, and Mozart. These were his God be praised. These
glories balanced safely his lack of feeling for the glories of
painting in the past and the present outspread of its experimental valour. Shaw had deeply what Sean lacked altogether.
Not altogether, maybe, for he could, at least, love the melodic
bars in opera, oratorio, and symphony. But Shaw had the
knowledge of music in brilliant abundance, and this, maybe,
gave him his serenity, as it, maybe, did to Joyce, too. The
lullaby to irritation and anger in David's harp still sang
through the music of the day. It wasn't, of course, that Shaw
was always serene. He very often felt the flame of indignation
alight within him; he felt anger at stupid things said and cruel
things done; and he felt the sick heart when fools assailed him.
He could calmly set down hard things without a quiver in a
bristling eyebrow when writing of revolutions; but he was always damnably reasonable: 'Even in the first flush of the
Soviet Revolution, the Soviet was more tolerant than we were
when our hour came to revolt. We frankly robbed the church
of all it possessed, and gave the plunder to the landlords (a lot
of them catholic, by the way). Long after that, we deliberately
cut off our archbishop's head. Certainly, the Soviet made it
quite clear to the Russian archbishop that if he didn't make up
his mind to accept the fact of the Revolution, and give to the
Soviet the allegiance he had formerly given to the Tsar, he
would be shot. But when he very sensibly and properly made
up his mind accordingly, he was released, and is now, presum-
ably, pontificating much more freely than the Archbishop of
Canterbury.'

Music helped to keep Shaw calm, and made a fine dramatist
of him, for music sings in most of his plays. Oh, lackaday, that
Sean had so little of its solace! One had to be a constant
practiser, or a constant listener, to know or feel anything right
about the form and style of beautiful sounds which we call
music. How is the ordinary man to enter into an intelligently

emotional enjoyment of music? Sean could think of but one way: listening. Listen to the band, for that was what an assembly of eminent musicians really was, though given the lordly, and deserved, name of an Orchestra. Now that their three children were constant listeners to Beethoven, Mozart, Bach, and the rest, flowing from the wireless, the gramophone, and, more simply, from the stately piano they had in their best room, he was often sprayed with beautiful sounds. But it was but a lovely baptism. Too late, now; too late. He would never be able to go farther than the porch of the temple; never see the lights gleaming on the altar; never hear the full hymn sung.

Had Mrs Shaw lived longer, Shaw would have lived longer, too. She cushioned away a lot of the hardness of life for him. She was his woeman of the guard. She travelled a lot, following the sun for warmth, and he went with her; for boat-decks, cabins, and foreign lands with her were better than Ayot St Lawrence without her. Constant comfort and companionship departed from him with Charlotte. He tried to take it cheerily, but he was just an old boy whistling in the dark. In a letter to Sean, he said he was all right, but damnably lonely. A lone one at last. The state of a lone star; and to remain damnably lonely till he departed too. Though they had their differences. Once, sitting pleasantly by the fire, just four of them, Shaw, Charlotte, Eileen and Sean, chatting generally about the drama, Mrs Shaw suddenly asked Sean which did he think was G.B.S.'s best play; Sean replying, immediately, that it was *Heartbreak House*. Shaw's face lit up instantly, and he took his elbow from the mantelshelf to give fuller attention to what Sean had said; but a cloudy look settled on the face of Charlotte.

—Do you? said Shaw, delightedly. That's odd. Few do, though I think myself that it is my best play. Charlotte doesn't like it.

—Nonsense, said Mrs Shaw to Sean: *St Joan* is the best play G.B.S. has written.

—No, no, said Sean, innocently and fervently. *St Joan* is his most popular play, maybe. It is a lovely play, but a compiled one. *Heartbreak House* is deeper, far more original, and nearer to life. It is as a fine symphony with flaws in it is to a perfectly modelled folk-air. There is no heartbreak in *St Joan*; she burns too triumphantly. G.B.S. knew this, and so he added the Epilogue.

—It cannot compare with *St Joan*, said Mrs Shaw – a note
of finality in her voice. I don't like *Heartbreak House*.

Shaw saw that there was disorder in poverty, and he liked
order, said to be 'heaven's first law'; he saw that there was
disease in poverty, and he liked health; he saw that there was
death in poverty, and he loved life. He was the first saint to
declare that God no longer liked to look upon the face of the
poor, so different from the Jesuit, Vaughan, who, well fed,
well clothed himself, said that the poor were God's own aris-
tocracy. What voice has shouted Dope? Banish poverty from
our midst and from our ken, and with it her foul breed of
deformed men, deformed women, deformed children. Force
the Christians to seek divine election through their own efforts
and development, and suffer them no longer to feel they are
jolly good fellows by doling out to others what they never miss
themselves. Take the wine away from them, and let them drink
a little water for their stomach's sake. To the Lyons with the
Christian rich! Shaw is the workers' War-cry!

There is sense for everyone in Shaw's Corner who hates the
ulcerous misery of poverty. He was one of those who never
hesitated to say into the ears of the man isolated by wealth,
and in the ears of the multitude, that what are called man's
petty and insignificant needs are related to the stars. 'Men
honoured Christ', he said, 'so long as he remained a charming
picture in a golden frame, or hung helpless on a varnished
cross; but men begin to yell with alarm when the picture
leaves the frame, or when the figure comes down from the
cross to become a moving, terrible force in the world.' The
picture is out of the frame now, the figure is off the cross, and
Christ now marches in the surge forward of the masse-men.
Blok saw him march through Leningrad at the head of the
Red Guards, and he has appeared in China amid cheers; today, too, his shadow falls on Africa: Lo, I am with you always
– March! Left, left, left!

Some critics say Shaw was no poet (indeed, Sean remembers
arguing against this precious aversion of men and women to
others, having greater gifts than their own, in Dublin, thirty
years ago, with Sarah Purser, a notable lass of the city of that
day); that he was one almost incapable of emotion. Hens cack-
ling, cocks crowing, at the eagle's whistle. There is poetry in a
lot of his plays, emotion in some of them, and laughter and
thought in all of them. A fine synopsis of active and poetic life

– tears, laughter, thought, and song. He will live in the life
following his own for his jewelled courage, his grand plays, his
penetrating wisdom, his social sense, his delightful, effective
criticism of the theatre of his day, his fight for Ibsen, Wagner,
Brahms, his uncanny knowledge of children, his battles for
womanhood, and for his brilliant leadership in the thought of
man.

A great man, but not great enough for the closed shop of
saintship in the Christian church. Indeed, a name to be mentioned with great caution; and so the churchmen slip down to
the hell of mediocrity. No, no; not Shaw. What a scandal it
would have aroused had Shaw been allowed to climb into a
pulpit! Bernard Shaw in the pulpit of Westmonaster Cathedral. Monastrous! Do stop him from playing such fantastic
tricks before high heaven as make the angels laugh. Church in
danger! The gates of hello are prevailing against her! Even
the figures in the stained-glass windows are climbing out to go.
Mention a more suitable name. Here's the Prefect of the
Sacred Congregation of Rites, and there's the Reverend President of the Anglican Convocation; so, mention a more suitable
name – we're listening. Johnny Appleseed, sirs. Who's he, and
what did he do? Done millions of miracles, sirs; scattered
appleseeds wherever he went. Appleseeds? You don't know
your catechism, son. Don't you know what the apple has done
to man? *Mala mali malo malu, melo contulit omnia mundo.*
Oh, sirs, I am sorry. It seems to me as sweet as honey. Oh,
Plautus! Oh, preserve us! Well, mention another – we're
patient. We're eager to have as many saints as *per se* possible.
Hiawatha's a name, sirs, I mention with glee, for the way to
make honey he taught to the bee; to Red Men, he gave agriculture, and more – he cur'd them whene'er they felt sick or felt
sore. A pagan chief he must have been, and we've no room for
pagans here; we drink no wine, but sit and sip the sober excel-
lence of beer. No dionysiac thought or laughter can enter here,
now or hereafter. So get you gone, you brazen smarty, and
lecture to life's cocktail party!

If not saints, then bishops! What a grand bunch they'd be on
the bench – Shaw, Joyce, and Yeats! Stop them! Rerum
novarum oram pro noram. Maanooth is in an upsoar. Oh,
catholic herald, come blow your horn, before a wild oak comes
from the little acorn. St Patrick's coming down on a winged
horse. Was there ever such a one as the Bull from Shaw; was

there ever such a one as the Pastoral from Yeats; was there ever such another as the Encyclical from Joyce! They'll ruin and maruin us. Oh, soggart, aroon, is it dhreamin' I am as I'm standin' up stiff in a medley of fear, for the heads are all harps and the harps are all heads in the things that I see an' the things that I hear. We're betrayed! Who's that running about like a kingaroo? Belloc. What's he shouting, what's he shouting? They Do Not Know Because They Are Not Told. They don't; we do, don't we – oh, boy! What are the three boyo bishops doing now? Blessing the people. Blessing them – what with? Shaw's blessing them with his plays and Yeats is blessing them with his poems, and Joyce is blessing them with the comic laughter of a brooding mind. They'll destroy us. If they're let go on, they'll quench the *ignis fatuous* of the faith! They're doing God down, harming heaven; taking all the smoothness out of it, and the velvet away from under our walking. The Universe is going mad. Such things to happen in Catholic Times! And we thinking they were stretched out among the Defunctorum, with the tablet of non este fideles over them. Under the silentio luna. What's Father O'Flynn doing that he isn't here to help? Let him come to the fore now, and bring his wonderful way with him, for it's well wanted. They're the devil's disciples. Undermining truth. What's that bounder, Yeats, saying? Would that the Church were Anything but Merely Voice. Oh, they do not know because they are not told. They've been told often, but they won't listen; they refuse to hear the voice of truth – the gang of hearetics! What's Yeats saying now? That he's fallen from himself because he hasn't seen for a long time the Prince of Chang in his dreams. What Chang, which Chang, whose Chang? Is this Chang in the cullender of saints? No, no; he isn't. I guessed he wasn't. It's these free libraries is doing all this detriment. Shut the doors, Richard! Where's the Catholic Herald? He's on the rumparts of infidelium proclaiming a dies irae erin on all shinners. It's too late now. Oh, Leonore oh oh ora pro woebis. What's Shaw saying, saying? Saying that no church shall ever have a creed. Wants to take our one remainder, leaving us without a screed. We're in a bad way, Mick. What's the other boyo bishop, Joyce, doing? Taking down verbatim a discussion between the Mooksee and the Gripes. What's them? Are they civil or religious disorders, or what are they? No one knows? There'll be nothing here now but the wind and the rain, and chilly water under every tired foot halting for a rest. Even the older dogs know the road no longer. These three boyos are whispering their strange thoughts into every Irish ear, and every Irish ear is cocked to hear them. This land will soon be nothing but a weed in a garden of noses – no – poses. Oh, what am I saying! Soon be nothing but a nose in a garden of weeds. Oh, I'm going mad! Impetuous heart, be still, be still.

—Conthrol yourself, Mick, and let some sound of sense get into what you're saying. More things grow in Ireland than the three-leaved shamrocks. Say what you like and pray how you may, there'll always be a gay song deadening the sound of a *de profundis*. It would be a big, bright blessing in disguise if even a few of our bishops had some of the imagination of Yeats, a tittle of the wit and deeper sense of Shaw, and a little of the royal ribaldry of Joyce to test our thinking.

—I won't listen. Are you letting yourself emerge into their meaning, too?

—And if I am? It's near time we got something fit for a man or a woman to read; something having a jolt in it as well as a jingle. Your heaven seems to be responsible for a helluva lot of rotten literature.

—Don't say that; you mustn't say that, man! What we read is safe reading, and that is our only need. We must have virtue at all costs; and no inquiries, no questions. D'ye hear me talking? No inquiries, none at all, I'm saying!

No, no, it wouldn't do. Unsettling saint; never do for us. Let St Peter go back to his sedia astoria in Rome, and Patrick to his stone stand on Tara's Hill or Croagh Patrick. The names mentioned aren't a quarter good enough to be thought of by the roman catholic church, or even good enough to win a thought from an anglican pulpit. They are man's saints; our saints, registered in the wide church of humanity; if not for social service, then for heroic virtue in the integrity of their art: the people's choice.

Yeats got a large medal from a Swedish artist, and was so dazzled with the design that he decided to form an Irish Academy of Letters. A circular, signed by some prominent Irish writers, was sent out, appealing to others to become founder Academicians or associate members. The circular came to Sean signed personally by Bernard Shaw. Shaw was asking a favour from Sean; the first favour ever asked, and Sean saw himself threatened with the hardest refusal he had

ever had to face. Shaw had fought by his side in the Abbey
Theatre controversy over *The Silver Tassie*, and now Sean had
to refuse the one favour the great man asked of him. He didn't
know what to say, though he knew what he would do – refuse
to join. Indeed, he had sent a laughing, critical article about
the scheme to *The American Spectator*, and its editor, George
Jean Nathan, had replied, saying it would appear in the next
number. Sean didn't like institutions powered to decide what
was good literature and what was not good: they had made
too many mistakes before. They were inclined to look kindly
on those who flattered their own work. He spent a long, long
time thinking out a loving letter in whose core was a firm and
final refusal. The letter of refusal was sent to the sage, but no
answer came back. It was but an incident in a busy life. No
malice touched Shaw's nature; he was the most forgiving man
Sean had ever met. Nothing mean ever peeped out of his
thought or his manner; the noblest Irishman of all Irishmen.
Sean and he met many times again, but neither of them ever
once mentioned the Irish Academy of Letters.

Later on, when the O'Casey family shifted down to Devon
to be near the school Eileen had chosen, on Shaw's emphatic
recommendation, for the children, they rented a house that
was the only one vacant for miles around that could shelter
them in a partially suitable way; a pretentious place, originally
built by some lower-middle-class snob who feinted towards
being an ape of his betters. The landlord didn't like the look of
Sean, or mistrusted anyone trying to make a living by writing
(small blame to him for that), and demurred about agreeing to
the tenancy, demanding credentials as to the prospective ten-
ant's character and good repute. As to his character, Sean told
him he would ask no one to trust it, for he couldn't trust it
himself. Though he knew many who would readily give him a
bad name, he knew no one who would give him a good one.
This made the landlord more dubious, but he brightened up
when he was promised a guarantor who'd pay the rent, if Sean
didn't. The landlord agreed to allow the tenancy if the name
Sean gave proved to be satisfactory. Not wishing to bother
G.B.S., Sean wrote to Mrs Shaw, and asked her to do him this
favour. Almost immediately, a letter came back asking them to
lunch in Whitehall Court to talk about the matter. After lunch,
before a fine fire, Mrs Shaw started questioning; asking how
much a year the house would be, including rates, if Sean was

working at anything; if a play, had it any prospect of production; while G.B.S. leaned over the back of the chintz-covered sofa, listening to all that was said by Mrs Shaw sitting on the sofa's centre. Sean was put through a means test, his face flushing, his nerves urging him to walk out of the room, out of the house, his necessity riveting him to where he stood listening.

—Oh, give it to him! Suddenly ejaculated Shaw from the cloud of questioning. He has told you all you need to know. Mrs Shaw stopped dead, and immediately changed into a gracious readiness to do all she was asked to do.

But all for nothing. When Sean handed out the news that Mrs Shaw would stand as guarantor, the landlord let a snort out of him, jumped from his chair, ran to the farther end of the room, and almost shouted, It's no good; I'll not take any woman's guarantee! I won't let you into the house on any woman's name. I'll let no woman meddle in my affairs!

Oh, Jesus! First Mrs Shaw's hesitation and distrust; now this old-fashioned fool's rejection of a name Sean had gone to so much trouble to get! So Sean had to write to Mrs Shaw telling her that her signature would not do. G.B.S. then took over the guarantee, first indulging in a spicy correspondence with the landlord's solicitors, and a subsequent letter told Sean that the business had been carried through:

4 WHITEHALL COURT, LONDON, SW1
17th October, 1938.

MY DEAR SEAN,

Your landlord, being a dentist, has developed an extraction complex. He proposed a lease in which I was not only to guarantee all your covenants, but indemnify him for all the consequences. I said I did not know his character, but knew enough of yours to know that the consequences might include anything from murder to a European war; so I redrafted the agreement. The lawyers, knowing that their man was only too lucky to get a gilt-edged (as they thought) security, and that his demands were absurd, made no resistance. I mention it as you had better watch your step, not to say his, with the gentleman. Anyhow I had a bit of fun with him. I seem to have picked up completely. The anaemia was not really pernicious. I am glad to learn that the two miniature O'Casey's are happy among the young criminals at

Dartington and that their mother is now one of the Beauties of Devon. Charlotte sends all sorts of affectionate messages.

G. B. S.

The fun Shaw had had cost Sean guineas he could ill afford, for the lawyers charged for all the letters. But the great-hearted G.B.S., Sean thought, imagined he'd have to pay, not only the costs, but the rent as well, and so he thought he might as well have a good laugh out of the loss. Sean thanks heaven, feasting, that G.B.S. never had to pay a red cent of costs or of rent. The Agreement is with T. Cannon Brookes of Cannon Brookes and Odgers, London, who cried out that he wouldn't part with it for anything. T. Cannon Brookes is a direct descendant of Napper Tandy (the one who Met with poor old Ireland, and shook her be the Hand, according to the famous ballad of *The Wearin' o' the Green*. Napper Tandy afterwards became a general of France's Grande Armée, and lies buried in Bordeaux), with the Napper Tandy nose which he has handed on to his tall son, and whose little son is sprouting the same nose too.

Then came the long, sad shock of Charlotte's illness; the gradual distortion of the stout body, the sinking away from association with the companion she had loved and guarded so long. The great and sensitive man had to watch the life of his wife declining day by day; the flag of companionship slipping down the staff. She is very much deformed, he wrote to Eileen. Though the day ends the same way for us all, there is infinite variety in the place, time, and manner of its ending. There was a great deal of goodness dying side by side with Charlotte Shaw; and the greatest good was the care she gave to the people's champion. Still she was there while the shadow of herself lingered in the home; there beside him. But shrink from it as he might, he had to let her go at last. She is dead, G.B.S.; ay, indeed, she is dead right enough. Shaw's Corner suddenly expanded into a wide and desolate world. One was taken and the other left. Put a brave face on it, man. I will, I will; but icy death that has taken Charlotte has touched me, too, as he passed. My wife is dead. She was called Charlotte; a good woman, a very good woman; and, now, she's gone. Alone, at last. Oh, Charlotte, where art thou, and why art thou silent, thou pulse of my heart? The place is full of shadow even when the cuckoo calls. The summer is icumen in, but it will always be winter, now. Life is like a withered tree; what is all the world to me; life and light were all in thee. I am very busy trying to answer the thousands of letters of sympathy coming from the four quarters of the earth. It will take months; I am very busy. Ah, my heart is sair, I darena' tell, my heart is sair for somebody. Busy yes busy. A fistful of dust about the garden blows. I said to the rose, the brief day goes. Silence everywhere. The housekeeper talks, the maid talks, the visitors talk; but there is silence everywhere. Silence in my own heart. I wander lonely as a cloud, a lone, lorn critter. The brief day goes. She was told; she had her day; the day soon goes. The evening star is gone, the shine has faded from the morning star.

> I'm here alone, I'm there alone;
> All that was here is here, yet all is gone;
> The star that glittered, the sun that shone.

> Visitors come and go,
> To laugh, murmur, and crow;
>   All has been said and done.
>   Death faces a friendly foe;
>   Tho' there's still things I'd like to know.

>   I'm withered to creaking bone,
>   And I potter round here alone.

>   A few more years shall roll,
>   A few more seasons fade;
>   This mind of mine, if it shall last
>   Behind death's lone façade,
>   Shall question many things mismade:
>   Shall question unafraid.
>   Oh, Charlotte, well-beloved, I hear you
>   calling me.

Eileen and Sean sent several letters to him to assure him that he was far from being forgotten, but no reply came to the letters, and both were troubled. Sean wondered if they had been kept from him (afterwards, Shaw seemed to confirm this, for when, on a visit to Ayot Saint Lawrence, Eileen told him she had written some time ago, the old man said she must be mistaken, for he got no letter). Then Sean thought Shaw might be too tired or too busy to be bothered with him. Later on, a letter from George Jean Nathan, the American drama critic, told him that he had written to G.B.S., enclosing one of his books, but had got no acknowledgement. They all puzzled over the reason why Shaw could be so silent. Later, Sean forwarded to Shaw a letter from a Dublin friend, Peadar O'Donnell, editor of *The Bell*, pleading for a Preface to a book written by an ex-soldier of the Irish Republican Army. This brought an affectionate reply from G.B.S., saying he had written to Peadar pointing out why he couldn't write the Preface, adding that Peadar couldn't have had a better introduction than one from Sean. Then came word from George Jean Nathan, saying Shaw had acknowledged the book, and had written 'Attaboy! Write a thousand of them. I like your stuff, and rank you as Intelligent Playgoer Number One!' So all smiled again, George Jean in New York, the O'Caseys in Devon, for all was well with the glorious sage of Ayot Saint Lawrence.

After they had sent him, at his request, a portrait of the family, Eileen on his invitation went, with John Dulanty, Eire's Ambassador, to have tea with him, caged now in his own home, where they had a fine time, John Dulanty brimming over with stories, Shaw commenting on them with many a musical laugh, Eileen adding her own merry laugh and good humour to the party. But the day soon goes. Some time later came the news of the accident; he had fallen while pruning a plum or a pear tree, and had broken a thigh. And he was ninety-four; there was small hope now, said Eileen, he is so old. No, no, said Sean, though, in his heart, he feared that Shaw, at last, was on the way to the land o' the leal. Carry him off to the hospital, where, it was said, the great man was quite chirrupy. It is odd to think of so many unable to see that this manner was assumed by Shaw to veil his shyness, to conceal his hatred of having to be helped by others; and strangers, too. To be helpless and dependent on others was a taste of horror for Shaw. Meagrely patched up, Shaw returns to his home, and soon after, hearing that she is in London, Shaw asks Eileen to come to see him. She goes, and that night her voice from London comes down to Devon over the telephone to say, Sean, Shaw is dying! Can you hear? G.B.S. is dying.

—Nonsense! went the voice of Sean from Devon up to London. You're imagining things. He's no more dying than I am.

—If you saw him, Sean, you'd know he was dying.

—He'll rally out of it. He'd rally out of anything.

—Not out of this, Sean; not out of this. When he looks at you, death looks at you, too.

Some days after, Eileen heard from John Dulanty that Shaw would like to see her again, but she put it off, having to give a lot of time to two of her children who are with her in London. But the thought that she should go down again to Ayot Saint Lawrence keeps coming into her mind. She should go, she shouldn't go, she couldn't go. She would ask John Dulanty as to whether she should or should not go; for she feared to disturb Shaw, or receive a snub from those who had charge of him. She journeyed down to the Ambassador's office, but he was out. That settled it: she would not go. The secretary asked her to come the following day, and Eileen, murmuring that she would, decided that she wouldn't. Anyway, it was hardly likely that Shaw really wanted to see her. He had always like her greatly, wondered sometimes why she had married such a one as Sean, at times gently teasing her about it. He liked her intelligence, not only of her mind, but also of her heart; so natural, vivid with friends; so real and generous with children. She understood as many didn't the odd, sparkling mind in the weakening body of Shaw; the mind still gay and as unpredictable as ever under the shawl of age. But she wouldn't go to John Dulanty's office tomorrow, and so would never see the bold G.B.S. again. But in some strange way, the thought that she should go never left her mind, and on the morrow, she went down to the Ambassador's office, and met him as he was going out for the biggest part of the day. He came forward, saying Ah! I want you! He told her Shaw would very much like to see her, adding that, if she hadn't come, he would have written to her. Like Sean himself, John didn't believe that Shaw was dying, saying so to Eileen, and adding that when he was in Ayot Saint Lawrence a week or so ago, the old man was in fine fettle; but Eileen still fears that she is right, and that Greatheart, Captain Valiant, is dying; that the last moments of this battler, this lover of laughter, are saying farewell to the world and us all.

The Ambassador tells her to ring up to see if a visit would be all right at the moment. The housekeeper answers Eileen, goes away to ask Shaw, and comes back to say that Eileen is to come at once, for Mr Shaw would very much like to see her. So Eileen goes down to stay for a few minutes, but remains for

a long, long time with the departing Titan. He is slowly leaving
the ken of the world, chatting in whispers so low that Eileen
has to bend down close to the gentle face to hear what he says,
sinking into a doze occasionally that was the shadow of coming unconsciousness.

He was lying in a sloping position in a bed against a wall, in
a ground-floor room; lying there, waxen-faced, calm and patient; his eyes, bright as ever, shaded by the bushy brows,
common-sense alert in them, humour still aglow in them: living to the last. Another bed, narrower, lay alongside a wide
window, looking out into the garden, sanctified now with the
dust of his Charlotte; the flowers and walks he loved hidden
away from him for ever. Looking round while he dozed,
Eileen saw on the wall a big photograph of the upright Stalin,
full face, handsome and jovial, and, nearby, one of Gandhi –
both fine fighters, like Shaw himself, fighters in different ways;
equals in ideal and outlook, fundamentally three in one: the
world's peoples have spoken by and through the three of them.
Eileen panted a little, very quietly, so as not to disturb the
dozing Shaw, for the room was very hot, vainly assailing the
coldness of death creeping over the life of the losing leader.
The young woman and the old man; the one in life's centre,
the other about to slide away from its oldest circle. The keen
eyes slowly opened again, and she bent low to catch his whispering chat.

—I'm going, at last, Eileen; and I'm glad of it.

—Nonsense, G.B.S. You'll rally out of it, and live for us all
a long time yet.

—No, no, Eileen; no longer. I want to die. What good would
it be going from this bed here to that bed there; and all the time
to be handled by those I don't know; by strangers? No, it is
time for me to go; and he slid into a stilly doze.

—Are you there, Eileen? Are you still there? he whispered,
coming back to the world again for a few moments.

—Yes, I'm still here, Eileen whispered back. Tell me if I bore
you, or if you wish me to go away.

—No, no, he said, in a hasty whisper; stay till I sink into a
deeper sleep.

—A sleep will do you good, she said; you'll be better then –
not rightly knowing what to say.

—No, I'll never be better, he whispered back. Then the bright
eyes closed again, and the long, lean figure lay still, the hand-

some hands, transparent now, lying quiet on the quilt. Eileen
waited till the eyes opened again, the wan but still powerful
face turned towards her, and a gentle smile creased the whiten-
ing lips; I have no desire to live longer. Could you stroke my
forehead for a little while? – it seems to soothe the pain; and
she stroked the high forehead gently, feeling that Shaw imagined himself back in his childhood, with his mother watching
over him.

—It is very pleasant to feel the touch of a soft Irish hand,
and to hear the sound of a soft Irish voice. He was going from
the world with his comrade-fighters, Gandhi and Stalin, watching from the wall. A quizzical smile flickered over his face. It
will be interesting, anyhow, Eileen, to meet the Almighty.

—I'm sure, G.B.S., that He and you will get on well together.

—I'll have a helluva lot of questions to ask Him, and the old
humorous look lighted the wasted face again.

—Wait for Sean, she whispered; wait till he joins you, for he
is a bit of a fighter.

—I'm a fighter, too, and the whisper became emphatic; but
here my fighting is finished. It's up to Sean, now.

—Sean is too old, said Eileen quickly; he's seventy, now.

—Well, then, it's up to one, or both, of the boys, if their lives
aren't wasted in another war.

Quietly and softly, he stole away into a sleep, and quietly
and softly Eileen tiptoed out of the room, leaving him looking
as if he were already dead. Outside, she talked for some time
to the nurse. Then, suddenly, the bell, fastened to Shaw's
shoulder, rang to bring attention. When the young nurse went
in, he asked her if Eileen had gone, and was told she had not,
but was about to go. He said he'd like to say goodbye to her.
She went back, sat down by the bedside, and with a lovely smile
that flashed back into his face the younger Shaw to view again,
he said, Goodbye, Eileen, goodbye; give my love to all the
O'Caseys. She lingered there over the goodbye till the great,
tired soul sank into sleep again, a deeper sleep than before;
then she stole from the room, and left Shaw's Corner, and left
the great householder in sleep, that he might be free to go forth
to meet death, to give death welcome, and see death bow before his greatness.

He died two days later. These were his last words: That
youth might not be wasted in another war. Kind man, brave

man, wise soul, indomitable spirit of the indomitable Irishry.

Many tries have been made to press down the world-stature of Shaw. Critics have derided his plays; politicians have jeered at his socialism; defenders of institutional religion cocked noses at his philosophy. Little chitterers reaching up puny hands to pluck at his knees and tumble him down. Life can't change. Oh, unchangeable, sinful, sinner human nature! Original sin has got us all by the short hairs! With Grahame Greene life is a precious, perpetual, snot-sodden whinge. With Shaw, a poke from a living, forward-thrusting hand – pip pip! Theirs a pat from a hand damp with death.

Every character in every play is a puppet, in so far as every character does, or says, what the author thinks it should say or do. There is no part in any play, bad, good, or great, which is independent of its creator. The author says to his character, do this, and he doeth it; come, and he cometh. Of course Shaw often uses the characters in his plays to voice what he thinks about man and his methods; but no more so than dramatists who are no more in skill and creation than, physically, a tom thumb is to a giant. They all weave their own opinions into what the characters in their plays say. Some critics say there is no poetry in Shaw's plays (how often have the Dublin bravos signed this in the air with a sawing hand!); and no emotion. There is poetry in the very description of the Syrian sky at the opening of *Caesar and Cleopatra*, in the way the Bucina calls, in the two great figures dwarfed between the paws of the Sphinx, in the rush of the Roman Legion into the Palace, halting to cry Hail Caesar, when they see him sitting alone with the Queen of Egypt; poetry, and emotion, too. There is poetry and fine emotion in the scene on the banks of the Loire in the play of *Saint Joan*, and in the Saint's sorrow when she sees that while the world venerates her at a safe distance, the same world wants her no nearer; here is ironical emotion, shot with sadness stretching out to the day that is with us, for, with Christians now, it is not, Get thee behind me, Satan, but Get thee behind me, God. There are poetry and emotion in *The Devil's Disciple*, a heart-sob, indeed, at the end of the first scene when Essie, the natural child, finds a friend, and cries to show her joy, to get the devil's disciple's blessing in Oh, yes, you may cry that way, Essie. Indeed, the whole play is shot through with emotion, and he who doesn't feel it is neither critic nor man. There is poetry and emotion in *Candida*;

poetry of a minor key in the way the doctors regard the
thoughtlessness of the artist, Dubedat, rising into a major key
at the death of the artist when the play is ending; it flashes
through every scene of *Heartbreak House*; and stands dignified
and alone in the character of Keegan in *John Bull's Other
Island*; the poetry and emotion gleams out in the revelation
that God is close to Feemy Evans, the fallen woman of the
camp, though the respectable humbugs wouldn't let her finger-
tip touch the Bible. The English critics are afraid to feel: Eton
and Harrow seem to have groomed them against the destitute
dignity of tears. They are cross-grained against any visible sign
of emotion. The Irish aren't. George Jean Nathan in his preface to *Five Great Modern Irish Plays* says, 'Perhaps the out-
standing mark of Irish dramatists by and large is their shameless emotional candour. They write what they honestly feel,
however possibly embarrassing. The Irish alone as a play-
wrighting nation appear to appreciate the human heart for
what in all its strange and various moods it is, and the Irish
alone with a profligate beauty and a lyric artlessness permit it
to tell its true and often aching story.' Emotional expression in
Shaw's plays is seldom shameless; but it is often plain and
outspoken, reaching those who haven't locked humanity out of
their hearts.

His comments upon the theatre of his day stand dauntless
still, though almost all the plays he saw and spoke about are
dead, and vaulted now where no man's mind can reach them.
The Notorious Mrs Ebbsmith, sore disturbed, stormed for a
day or two, then sighed, and gave her queen-seat to Lady
Wayneflete. Michael's Lost Angel stretching out arms to keep
away intruders, was hustled out and off by the wild sanity of
the Devil's Disciple; and all the mouthing crew of cant and
humbug hurried off to hide from purging laugh and biting wit
of Shavian play and Shavian preface. He was the greatest
British playwright of his age; none equalled him then, none
equal him now. None of those who learned from him have yet
thrown a wider chest than his own. Dead though he be, none
can yet venture to sing the *Nunc Dimittis* of Bernard Shaw,
either as prophet or playwright.

What time has been wasted during man's destiny in the
struggle to decide what man's next world will be like! The
keener the effort to find out, the less he knew about the present
one he lived in. The one lovely world he knew, lived in, that

gave him all he had, was, according to preacher and prelate, the one to be least in his thoughts. He was recommended, ordered, from the day of his birth to bid goodbye to it. Oh, we have had enough of the abuse of this fair earth! It is no sad truth that this should be our home. Were it but to give us simple shelter, simple clothing, simple food, adding the lily and the rose, the apple and the pear, it would be a fit home for mortal or immortal men.

That was one of the great and courageous virtues of Shaw – he made the most of life. The earth was his home, and he loved it. He was at home among the mortals. His epiphany was the showing forth of man to man. Man must be his own saviour; man must be his own god. Man must learn, not by prayer, but by experience. Advice from God was within ourselves, and nowhere else. Social sense and social development was the fulfilment of the law and the prophets. A happy people made happy by themselves. There is no other name given among men by which we can be saved, but by the mighty name of Man. It was wise and good of Shaw to give himself no grave.

SUNSET

VICTORY DAY was born in a bluster of bells. Confined
within the cell of silence during the years of the war, they rang
out now as if every ringer were a Quasimodo swinging from
the ropes. All of them; everywhere: bells of St John Lateran,
of St Jim Clatterin, of St Simon Slatterin, of St Finian Flat-
terin, of St Nicholas Natterin: bells of St Mary's, bells of St
Clement's, and bells of Old Bailey; bells of St Martin's and the
big bells of Bow. Hellsbells brazen bounding about, with Saints
George, Andrew, David, and Patrick, bowing acknowledge-
ments. Sean stood, half deafened, in the midst of the din from
the bragging bronze, a din that would have caused Dickens to
clap his hands over his hearing; a din that would have
prompted Keats to write about bells tolling as he did of those
that rang in his day:

> The church bells tolled, melancholy sound,
> Calling the people to some other prayers,
> Some other gloominess, more dreadful cares.

The bells were trying to be merry now – harder, faster, pull,
pull, pull! Ding dong dell, Europe's in the well. Who knocked
her in? Hitler's scurvy sin. Who'll pull her out? Ah, therein
lies the doubt; no one knows a thing about the rightful way to
pull her out, said a brawny boy scout, musing by a scout re-
doubt. Ring out, wild bells, to the wild skies. Belling the ruins.
Weeds are growing where stately buildings stood. Sit down
solitary amid silent ruins, and weep a people inurned and their
greatness changed into an empty name. Ring out, wild bells, to
the wild sky! God is clapping his hands! Christians, awake,
salute the happy mourn! Ring out the hot war, ring in the cold
war! Hitler, the world's blunder, is a withering handful of
ashes sourly sinking within a world of ruins; the great cod-god
gone. Mussolini is hanging, head down, naked, from a hasty
gibbet, his glory gone, his bawling jellied in his battered brain;
the end of the huddling half-god.

It was indeed right to peal the bells, to try to feel gay, to dance a measure in honour of the silence which came when the cannon's mouth was shut; to cheer for the joy of peace that was the sweet voice, the luminous cloud. For a moment, forget the wounded, the maimed, and leave the dead to bury their dead, while the people snatch a fearful thrill from a moment of peace: and so the people of Totnes rejoiced, the Mayor in his red robe, the Town Clerk in his black gown and white wig, the Town Sergeant in his embroidered coat and his new cocked hat, and all the people with them; the little children, the young, the middle-aged, the old, in their best attire, trailed down the hilly main street under the setting sun, under the evening star, trailed down carrying torches, Sean's wife and his little girl among them, singing a song to the hour that had brought them victory and peace; and in the midst of the torches' light, the music of a band, the riotous peal of the bells, his old age stands, serene and bright, and lovely as a Lapland night. No, no; not quite, for the look of the land without and the feeling of the heart within mock the loveliness of a Lapland night, laugh at the serenity of old age.

Wherever we may stand in England, there are ruins around u⁻ and the breath of old age is thickened and harried with aggressive smoke; smoke coming between us and the light from the torches; envious smoke, blurring even the sound of the song. The smoke from ten thousand ruins is rising, sullying the silver solace of the evening star; the flames are flickering round the blackened stones still. Poor me, poor me! The dead lie down beneath the ruins, the dead that are blackened and burning still. Has anybody here seen my Jesus? Has anybody seen my Lord? Poor me, poor me! Did He see the smoke, did He feel the fire? A sky of smoke and a floor of fire. The roadways gone, no pathway left. Did He hear from the blast the sigh of the burst one? Did He hear the scream of a mother maddened for a child that was but is not now? Has He seen a woman's fingers scraping timber and stone away from the ruin of her man? Or a man's sad finding but flame and a fuming and a line of dead where his home had been? Oh, I see too much, know too much. Many dead here, many there; many maimed and many marred. Oh, Jesus, trouble's going to bury me down! Where is my young son? My younger daughter? Where is my young husband? My young wife? Bring me the black cloak for my body, the black hat for my head. Poor me, poor me! Give me many tears to waste away this ache. Oh, has anybody here seen my Jesus? Has anybody seen my Lord?

When the gatherings had dispersed after the Victory Toasts had been drunk with wine or beer, and the people had gone back to the chair and table, England sat down to count the cost, and couldn't do it – the quicker the rush to the horizon of recovery, the faster it scurried away. All she had left was her pride and a hot cross bun. Her last glittering foreign investments had been snatched from her glands. The once wealthy England was now like Mrs Squeers measuring out tea, sugar, meat, cheese, eggs, and coal, so that most might get a little lick to preserve the longing. Gloomy honours appeared on her flag – Mend and Make Do, Eat Less, Wear Less, Do Without; their one uplifting thought – others are worse than we. The British People, fearsomely heroic throughout the uproar and bustling bloodiness of war, now had to be heroic through lean years, years that dragged them close to the snarling snout of want. Let the people sing, said one fellow; put out more flags, said another; but the people were in little mood for warbling, and bunting was needed for patching shirt and shift so that the poor body might present a respectable façade to the gaping world. The broad straight road had disappeared, and England now walked unsteadily over a crazy pavement. Tomorrow had vanished, for the day that was had in itself more than enough to think of, so help us God. The women defiled themselves into a queue stretching from one end of England to the other. Through the summer hot and sweating, through the winter's damp and desolation, the women were inching, inching along in a never-ending queue. It often took a woman months to grab hold of a coat, a pair of knickers, a pair of shoes for a child. A-hunting we will go, a-hunting we will go! The sharing out of points and rations became a geometrical problem. The nation was living on its spare parts. After the querulous quietude of the queue, there was the rush home to wash, to sew, to cook, to get the children to school; more than ever now, the indomitable housewife became the pushed-about pathfinder of life. If women were not what women are, the world would perish overnight.

Some Irish sent up a titter, thinking that England would soon be as the old Bards had foretold – trudging through frost without a shoe on her foot. It was no laughing matter for the English, and, soon, the Irish found that it was no tittering matter for them. England down meant Ireland up no longer. A poor England on her flank was as big a menace as a wealthy England had been. England was no longer such a responsive market. Coal was Ireland's big need, but England could spare but a paper-bagful. Constirnation! No miracle, no novena could bring to Ireland the coal she needed. No coracles appeared carrying miraculous draughts of fuel. Depend on yourselves. Shinn Fane. Burn everything except English coal. Turf turf turf! Oh, Eire, turf is the only wear and smile in thy cry. The dear's cry — turf on me left hand, turf on me right one; turf before me, turf behind me. De Valera and his cubinette were in a state of ecstatic coalition. It's turf that gives me heart all its joyous elation. Fianna Fail was dancing the baile baile. There's nothing we cannot do without it.

> I met with Napper Tandy, an' he took me by the hand,
> This turf'll be the one an' sure salvation of the land;
> Three things we've got'll keep us great, an' speed us on our
>   way —
> Our turf, our Irish Sweep, and shawls of gallant galway gray.

In the hundreds of rotten, leaky, Irish schools, the happy children were learning all about the evolution of the idea of a sod. The old bog road's thick with cheering crowds on their way, trot trot trot to bother the bog; a slawn on every shoulder, all singing the new national anthem — *The Bog Down in the Valley O.* Turf is what'll enlighten our darkness. Listen, before yous begin digging: did yous hear that they're going to build the new catholic cathedral outa turf? D'ye tell me that? Ay, roof and all. Ay, and they're going to make all the new bishops' croziers outa bog-oak so's to keep things in harmony. I'm telling you turf's a thing'll never peater out. Let England keep her coal — it's a turf stage. Let turf electrify the land. The whole land under turf-ray treatment. Electric teashocks everywhere. Staggering thought! Electric hares and prayers; electric spires and lyres in the new land of shrines, sepulchres, and shams. Electrical vibrations in the Lenten pastorals short-circuiting sin and shocking souls into ample nodes of *senora pro nobis na hEireann.*

The sun is halfway under the horizon's rim, a sad decline when it symbolizes the lost loveliness of life's full day. Pale gold and paler green but thinly garland the sober livery of the evening's end. The day is dying drowsily in a lovely bed. The night is near. Swift to its close ebbs out life's little day. Life's day ebbs swiftly, but life's day is not a little one: it is big with grandeur and may be bright with glory. Oh, twilight, stay with us another hour and keep the last and loving light of day from fading!

A rumble of low, blaguardly thunder from the right. Rowdelum Randy, the insinity divinity tinkers are at it again: a first production of *The Silver Tassie* causes definite desolate protests in Vienna, and a first production in Berlin almost provokes a riot, though the comedy was shouted, the cry against war whispered, and the crippled Harry prevented from crushing the Silver Tassie in the last act; all to avoid offending roman catholic churchmen, in fear of committing a breach of the cold war. Rowdelum Randy: a Dublin friend, working in Birmingham, going homeward once more on a holiday, brings a copy of *Drums Under the Windows* with him, lends it to his brother, who reads it in the quiet of the night, and leaves it beside his bed when he goes to work in the morning early; the mother enters to make the bed, picks up the book, reads a little of it, thunder shakes the house; she rushes to the fire, burns the book, and rushes to get the priest to bless the building. He blesses it, and the dangerous vibrations from O'Casey's book are bent back; push, push, lads; bent back to poor old Pagan England again. Wipe the sweat from your face, lads; wipe your face; the sweat away. With all this rumbling of thin thunder, comes a soft limelight love from many letters bloated out with Dublin Catholic Truth Society's tracts, like *Tolerance Thumbs Up Too Much of a Good Thing*, by the Reverend Daniel Lord, SJ; the booklit lanterned with a *nihil obstat* and an archiepiscopal *imprimi potest*, with the news that the booklit is reprinted by the kind permission of The Queen's Work, St Louis, USA; tailed by a warning that 'this edition must not be sold in the United States or Canada'; and a coda reminding all that 'this booklet is to make God known and loved', and that 'you cannot serve him better than by passing it on to a friend', or 'if you cannot find a friend, leave it to Providence (thumbs down!), and deposit it in a theatre, a bus, or a park seat'. Deposit is good. Deposit account. Make him known. Give him plenty of publicity. The heavens that declare his glory, and the firmament that showeth his handwork aren't enough by a long chalk: we must floodlight his glory with booklits.

Some British reviewers seem to have a coy way of avoiding any touch with an author commenting on what they may have written about his work. Those who aren't rich enough to have an ivory tower, shrink into a shell. When *I Knock at the Door* came out, Oliver St John Gogarty shrank away from its candour, and, writing in *The Sunday Times*, said he was gravely shocked at what he called 'the unlocking of the heart'; and instanced the habit and example of the Chinese of reticence and silent fortitude. This, too, when the red flare of revolution had appeared in the Chinese valleys and the Chinese hills! But Oliver St John Gogarty hadn't heard a word about it. The time of Chinese reticence was over. A letter telling him all about it was sent to the paper, which, refraining from publishing it, forwarded it to the reviewer, but Oliver never replied: practising personally his own gospel of reticence. The willow-pattern plate must not be broken. Silence. Silence never betrays you.

Sean was mystically confronted by another ghostly silence on the part of the celebrated poet, Mr Louis MacNeice, when he made some comments on a review of his book, *Rose and Crown*. In the review, Mr MacNeice said, 'O'Casey assumes that everything Roman or Latin is alien to England. Odd for an admirer of Milton. In refusing to hear anything good of the Middle Ages, O'Casey is equally perverse. As a playwright he might have remembered that there were once Miracle Plays and that some of these were very gay.'

Gay? Oh, God! Old and gay! These Miracle Plays are moulded from episodes in the Scriptures, few of which were gay; none of them very gay; The Fall, Expulsion of Adam and Eve from the Garden of Eden, Killing of Abel by Cain, Israelites in Bondage. And Mr MacNeice calls these gay! Even the events culled from the later Testament, and made into plays, aren't what would be called gay. Such as Massacre of Innocents, Flight into Egypt, Temptation of Christ, The Betrayal, Remorse of Judas. To call such entertainments gay would seem to say that Mr MacNeice has turned humour all tapsalteerie O. Most of them are clumsy and terribly dull – including the worshipped preciousness of *Everyman*. Even these, though, were frowned on by the church! 'It is forbidden him by decree to make or witness miracle plays, because miracle plays, once begun, become gatherings and sights of sin.' Even this poor, dull gaiety was condemned by the church of the Middle Ages. Thou mayest kill, an thou will, but thou shalt neither dance nor laugh. But the ghostly frown was no extinguisher of the peasant dance round the maypole, or of the lover's desire for his lass, or the lass' desire for the desire of her lover; for these were life, and the church could not kill life.

Perhaps Mr MacNeice confused Miracle Plays with Morality Plays coming to us afterwards. It was only when life started to pull itself out of the Middle Ages that we come to more human thought peppered into the Morality Plays, a very different genre from the Miracle Plays. Even these couldn't be called 'very gay', containing, as they did, more of satire than of merriment. By far the best of them is Lyndsay's *Ane Satyre of the Thrie Estaitis.* Here we find little laughter in the Pauper's story of how, when his old feyther died, the landlord took his grey mare, the vicar his best cow; the same vicar took his second-best cow, and got the Clerk to take away the Pauper's clothes, after his wife had died of grief, leaving him only with a groat, which, we are told, he intends to give to a lawyer as a fee to win, through the law, justice from the church; to which, when he hears it, Diligence replies, 'Thou art the daftest fuill that ever I saw; do you expect to get remedy from the clergy by means of the law?' Diligence knew more about the gay customs of the Middle Ages than does Mr MacNeice.

Sean admired Milton, not because of his Latin, but because of his English, despite the fact that Milton was Latin Secretary to Cromwell. In the Preface to the First Edition, the Editor, Humphrey Moseley, says, 'It is not any private respect of gain, Gentle Reader, for the slightest pamphlet is now adayes more vendible than the works of learnedest men; but it is the love I have to our own Language that hath made me diligent to collect, and set forth peeces both in Prose and Vers as may renew the wonted honour and esteem of our English tongue'. Aha, the English tongue! Who cares now about Milton's Latin Elegiarum? His Latin illusions are but the tiny Latin buttons on an English suit of serge. Milton was as English as Hobson, the University's carrier in the poet's day. He was an English oak that sent out a few sparse sprays of the gadding vine. Born in Bread Street, buried in Cripplegate, Milton was a great Republican, and, to Sean, an Englishman to his heart's true core.

Sean in his ignorance couldn't understand the orgiastic idea that there was something inherently divine, poetical, and tremendous in the Latin language; that among the battling lan-

guages around, it was an Emanuelian manifesto of human
speech. Strong an idea today as ever it was. We are told that
all the monarchical titles on Elizabeth the Second's Great Seal
of England are shrouded within the wonder of aloofly-warbling
Latin words. The language of Bible and prayer-book, of Shakespeare himself, wasn't classy enough for the great, grandiloquent Seal of England. No, sor. At one time it was everywhere
and everything, separating the people from all life outside of
their hovels of clay and wattles made, their spare-ribbed pig,
their shabby cow, and their woeful patch of arable stone. It was
the earth, the zodiac, sky, sun, moon, and stars; hail, dew,
thunder, and lightning; it was the signpost to heaven for all.
God spake it, and the devil, too. It is still plastered over many
things: on banners, coats of arms, army slogans, of navy, of
air force; signposts to an earlier grave. It forms divine mottoes
for diocese, city, and church bell. Bold-faced, it bears a preface
on a raw book of Dublin street ballads. 'Looka, lad', said
Molière once to Sean, 'a laudation in Latin is of marvellous
efficacy at the beginning of a book.' It puzzled people for centuries, and plundered them of knowledge. Sean had heard it
mumbled beside a coffin, and had seen wistful and weary kids
intoning *Tantum Ergo* and *Salutaris Hostia*, little members of
a Latin hymn-class in a Dublin school, a music-master leading
them on, the parish priest present to prod them on, an irritated
gob on him because of the children's hesitation over unfamiliar
and foreign words.

Latin, they say, is the soul of all literature, and Virgil the
soul of poetry. Soul of Rome! Shakespeare but a player on
pipes of reed compared with the outspreading symphony of
poetry composed by the honey-spouting Virgil. Are these
appellants for Latin right? he wondered. A big claim, with
very few to verify it. Of the thousands of millions of people
crowning this earth with human life, how many are there who
could lie back on divan, sit straight in a chair, and enjoy the
poetry of Virgil? Very few. And of these fewer still who could
translate him in such a way as to show him shining to those
who read him in English. Are there even a few who could do
this? Ne'er a one, ne'er a one. Who could give in English sense
and English music the rolling O of Virgil, imitating lamentation for the falling stones of Troy? Or all the Ss combining to
give the hiss to the snakes destroying Laocoön and his sons?
Ne'er a one – not even James Joyce. And why Virgil alone?

There's reason to believe that heaps of poems by other Romans perished because they hadn't the influence of grander persons to help in preserving them. When an emperor stands by you, the world does, too. Folk-lore and the songs of the people died with these other Romans. Many, or some, of those might have had with us, had they been more fortunate, as great a name as Virgil. He wasn't the only one who sang fair and sang to the music of man's soul.

Ford Madox Ford says of Horace's *Dulce ridentem Lalagen amabo, dulce loquentem* that they are 'the most beautiful words ever written about fortunate love'. He adds that they cannot be translated, and then says they mean 'I shall love the sweetly-smiling Lalage'! He goes on, 'There is no word for loquentem; it means "conversing", or more in French "devising"; it certainly doesn't mean "chattering" or "prattling"'. No? Then what the hell does it mean? Indeed, Ford Madox Ford says of Propertius' poem of his Cynthia sinking to death in the Ionian Sea that 'no translation can give the poetic feeling or equivalent of the extraordinary beauty of the Latinity of this poem. Faced with the incomparable, ringing, marble, bas-relief of the Latin, you will be overcome by paralysis. [Poetri-omelitis.] The English with its harsh sounds and soft, gluey effects of meaning as compared with the clean Latin, can hardly ever be marble or ringing.' The same writer says somewhere else that he has always held that the most exquisite poetry in the world was contained in the following four lines of Tibullus:

> *Te spectem, suprema mihi cum venerit hora,*
> *et teneam moriens deficiente manu*
> *flebis et arsuro positum me, Delia, lecto*
> *tristibus et lacrimis oscula mixta dabis.*

Well, there's a marble slab for you to make what you can of. Indeed, the whole of Latin literature is but a cemetery of marble slabs jutting up here and there to show the passer-by what he may be missing. Footman, pass on! Latin has slunk into the silence of the grave. Canned into cold storage, with no one able to rede the labels on the tins. One wonders if the Latin be so high and the English so low; if the Latin language be really so grand and glorious as Ford Madox Ford, here, and T. S. Eliot, there, make it out to be. Certes, in translation, it is

more like plywood than like marble. It has no ringing sound in
it, not even the sound of Gregory's swashing blow. Shakespeare himself (probably, like Sean himself, because he didn't
know it) usually uses Latin to raise a laugh. Sad sight, sad
sound, sad sense. But if it be such a mighty language, why did
it die? Why did ye die, why did ye die; Conn the Shaughraun,
why did ye die! Time was when the English Parliament's
marble halls constantly heard round ringing Latin phrases,
when members bullied each other with quotations from Virgil,
Propertius, Lucretius, Horace, and Ovid; long, long ago; oh,
long ago. Now, they quote themselves. Why couldn't they keep
the Latin poets on their laps? It couldn't have been Com-
munism that ordered their liquidation. Latinity was a warm
thing in the schools and colleges the governing class attended;
gave them their Latin cue; and sent them forth with a loqua-
city half as old as time. Perhaps it died because, when we grow
up, the world is too much with us. The fact is, life leaves us far
too soon. It keeps us busy. We haven't the chance, even if we
had the wish, to spend a lonely life reclining by Windermere's
Lake or on the banks of Loch Lomond, sipping fiery or mellow
Scotch, or lowering wild Falernian wine, chanting Virgil. We
have to watch our muttons.

The one claim that Latin poetry is all it is said to be seems to
be the claim that a translation can never touch the beauty, the
regularity, or the dignity of the original. No one can contradict
the claim, since, if we could, we should have to know the Latin
familiarly and well; which few of us do. Is this lady latinum as
fair as they say? Come now, press your hand to your head,
and think – SPQR or USAR or USSR? Latin civilization has
downed us into a literary demurity. Ovid, Horace, and Virgil
peep over the cotswolds and the quantocks with the rising of
every sun, and we are tired of them since they have to speak to
us by signs. Latin has put English into a toga, and English
looks damnably affected in the garb. When a car was invented
holding more than a couple, it was called an omnibus, so
frightening the people that they short-circuited it into bus,
which is bad enough, and not near so good as folkwagon; so
agon-bite of inwit is more piercing than qualm of conscience.
Anyway, reduced to a translation, Latin pales off into a ghost.
None of them Sean ever read equals a poem by Yeats or a
sonnet by Shakespeare. What's this now? Just caught a
glimpse of it: *Everyman's Encyclopaedia*, in its article on

Latin, says 'Latin is not naturally suited to the writing of
poetry. The Romans were not themselves an imaginative race,
and the long, sonorous Latin words do not fall easily into
lyrical metres. In the hands of Horace and Virgil it received its
finest form as a poetic instrument.' Now, what bounder said
that? Some guttersnipe! Not an Eton or a Harrow laddo, certainly, or even a Grammar School scholar. Oxford giving a
Doctor of Civil Law degree, *sonorus causa*, to the United
States Secretary of State, told him, in rich Latin, that he was a
jolly good fellow, a gay honour few would have known about,
if it hadn't been put into English the following day by the
British Press. A few must have smiled and nodded their heads,
and nodded at one another when they heard the Latin rolling
along like ole man river, as Roman Senators did when Cicero
spoke Greek.

Still the Latin hasn't the gift of turning itself into a charming English changeling, and the purple stipple given to it by
them who know it must be taken for granted. But the English
translations of Latin hymns and poems in Miss Waddell's book
are as flat as pancakes, without salt, sugar, or spice. It is very
odd that an awed honour is still given to anything which
comes hopping lamely out of the Latin. Sean was one with
Whitman's regard for this persistent reverence for something,
chiefly because that something was unfamiliar to the general
man. Whitman didn't like it, and the old man sang out for
American preference, his wide-brimmed hat covering Manhattan, his beard flowing out in the winds of the world:

Come, Muse, migrate from Greece and Ionia,
Cross out please those immensely overpaid accounts,
That matter of Troy and Achilles' wrath, and Aeneas',
    Odysseus' wanderings,
Placard 'removed' and 'to let' on the rocks of your snowy
    Parnassus.

And uncles Remus and Romulus, too, me lad, for we have
had a fine fill of them all, and some of us want to turn to
sturdier native fruits and wine of the mind and spirit, for our
nature's inclined to be cloyed with

That soft bastard Latin,
That melts like kisses from a female mouth.

Bona roba of literature. It was always pathetic for Sean to see Grammar School lads shoving Latin verbs and nouns into their memories, things which they didn't enjoy and could never understand, for, when they broke loose from school at last, Lucan for them was lost, Seneca dead as a doornail. Thousands of them leave school yearly, but one never sees a Virgil or a Horace in an ageing grammar school hand; nor, for the matter of that (to move to the lords of Latin) do we see a Juvenal or a Catullus in the hand of priest, monsignor, or bishop; no, not even an abbreviated copy of the Aquinas' *Summa* in the original Latin; more often, probably, a detective tale in a back-pocket of their pants. Sean remembered telling a priest of a friend, known to both of them, that he had gone into the priesthood, and received the comment, 'Aw, he mastered the Latin grammar'. Well, the Latin is more than a grammar, a lot more, if it's a language at all. The most of these have just enough to read the Canon of the Mass and browse over the breviary: a quick browse often. Lord, they have taught them Latin is sure waste.

Latinlore twisted the neck of art for years so that she couldn't whisper that there was anything else in the world. For instance, the statue of King Billy in Dublin looked more like an illegitimate Caesar than it did an English or a Dutch king, and pictures painted by Poynter and Alma ta ta Tadema showed Rome at its worst, giving her a decline and fall that Gibbon never meant her to have. Johnson spoke to Frenchmen in Latin (though the Frenchmen couldn't understand him) because he wouldn't speak to a mere Frenchman in a foreign jargon. Some of the literary men of the time bescreeched him to write Goldsmith's epitaph in English, but the learned one refused 'to disgrace the walls of Westminster Abbey with an English inscription'. Said Emerson, 'the barbarians who broke up the Roman Empire didn't come a moment too soon'; and it is near time present-day barbarians broke up the literary empire she left behind her; for, as Stobart says, 'The great Latin writers are truly and really classical, apparently, because they did not write as they spoke or thought'. So, apparently, the Latin left to us is purpled Latin never spoken by the bulk of the people, by those watching the circus, those ploughing the fields, those tramping the roads – legionary, centurion, or even captain; the little left is the Latin of those who were afraid to write as they spoke or as they thought.

And translations, however good, won't do, even for the Latin wearing a toga with its purple stripe. Says Stobart again, 'Latin, of all languages, least permits of translation. You have only to translate Cicero to despise him.' Good God – Cicero; no! And thousands of our schoolboys blue in the face trying to do it. But a louder voice than Stobart's – that of Ford Madox Ford – says 'I carried six lines of a poem by Propertius in my head for fifty years before I ventured to translate them, and then, comparing them with the original, found they didn't fit, and violated the dignity of the original'. For fifty years. Fifty years agrowing! No use of knocking at the door of original classics; there's an ironical curtain between them and us; their pictures don't suit our hallways; their drums no longer sound under our windows. None or few of the translations, read by Sean, seemed to come up to those made from the Gaelic. Even the satirical poem or two in Miss Waddell's collection can't compare with the satires of MacConglinne, for instance; and even *Adeste Fideles* or *Tantum Ergo* are thin things compared with the passionate faith and courage expressed and recited in *The Deer's Cry*, better known or unknown as *St Patrick's Breastplate*; or St Ita's lovely little lullaby to herself with the Infant, Jesus, on her breast,

> Jesu, thou angelic blossom,
> No ill-minded monk art thou.

Or Crede's lament for Dinertach, whom she loved, when he was brought in wounded before her from the battle of Aidne,

> There are arrows that murder sleep
> At every hour in the bitter-cold night.

In a review of *Rose and Crown*, Louis MacNeice, the well-known poet, said 'O'Casey assumes that everything Roman or Latin is alien to England. Odd for an admirer of Milton.' Not a bit odd. O'Casey would like very much to know Latin himself, but, before it, he would put any living language of Europe as far more important. Latin isn't any more alien to England than it is to France, Germany, Hungary, or Russia. As a dead thing it is alien to all things living. It is a bright thing for scholars. For instance, if Coulton hadn't been such a one, he could never have written his books on the Middle

Ages, and Sean could never have enjoyed them. But even University Fellows don't commonly talk Latin among themselves. They used to; they no longer do so. Neither do the priests; not even the cardinal priests. At one time, Latin was the expressed power of the Church and the State, hiding everything from the common people, giving the things of the Church and the State a grandiloquent air of divinity. It had a divine rite of its own. But the English language was its enemy; it fought the Latin ceaselessly, gaining strength every time it touched its own good earth. Even the Anglo-Saxon Latinists – Clerks Adhelm, Alcuin, and Bede – couldn't stop the English manner and spirit from jumping about in their dignified Latin prose and poems; time and change finally confining it to a few words on the arms of the lords, ladies, and bourgeois gentlemen, and the brassy cap-badges of the serving soldiers. Even many members of the roman catholic faith have declared their wish that there should be less of Latin and more of what they call 'the vernacular' in their church services. After all, The Lord be with you is as good a fellow as *Domine vobiscome.*

Fitter for the purple-flushed ones in college, school, and home to love the languages on their own doorstep, tongue of Scot, Cymru, and Gael, than to hell-bend over ones as dead as any dead thing can be. The English language, after many hoary centuries, is vivid, valorous, strenuous still, and glowing for them, to them, who use it, respect and love it; and, hard as it may sometimes be, it can often melt like kisses from a woman's mouth, and a lovely mouth too. So the English first and foremost, though, but for the Latin, we shouldn't have known about Hercules, who with his club killed Cerberus, that three-headed *canis*, and calmly strangled serpents with his mighty *manus.*

As the comments on Oliver St John Gogarty's review of *I Knock at the Door* in *The Sunday Times* remained unanswered, so the comments on Mr MacNeice's review of *Rose and Crown* in *The Observer* remain unanswered to this day, this day. The rust was silence. Perhaps they feared there was a red ray in the comments; or, more likely, they thought the comments to be silly, and, out of charity, decided to do the commentator no further harm. Maybe it was the pity that gave before charity began. We shall not quench the smoking flax. Clever and delightful poets, both of them; but one didn't know much about China, and the other didn't seem to know much about Miracle and Morality Plays. Still there was a kinship between him and Louis MacNeice in their outlook on drama. Mr MacNeice writes in the *Radio Times* in 1952, 'I have attempted in *One Eye Wild* something similar to what I did in two earlier programmes. Both of these were experimental and tried to combine two techniques, those of realism and symbolism.' Attaboy!

Sean was now near to the door again, about to go out of life's house by the same door as in he went. It was a wider door now than when he first knocked at it. A few more drinks. As he drank, change in all he saw. He felt hustled. It wasn't that change was here: that is no new, no startling thing. Changes were busy before the first man was able to give his first indicative grunt. Changes moved through all the changes, through the Plantagenets, the Tudors, the Georges, through the slow, plushy years of the Victorian satisfaction, yawning up its gratitude to God for trying to keep things as they were; saved from self-satisfaction by its group of great men and women, and many fine things done in their time. It wasn't the changes that hustled him; it was that so many changes have come so fast; so fast that he and all the old come halting on behind. Science has presented life with more life than present life can comprehend or hold. Worlds in bunches away beyond the Milky Way, and worlds alone in space; with new worlds unfolding themselves beneath the microscope and within the atom; new worlds still hidden from the myopic eye of the microscope and the equally myopic eye of the telescope nosing among the stars. New worlds of vitamins, cells, viruses, moulds, chromosomes, isotopes, superseding spermaceti for an inward bruise; new worlds for all, with a new world of democracy thrown in, garlanded with glory and with danger too. Aristotle is becoming a ghost.

The sun is more than halfway beneath the horizon's rim, and its pale gold and pale green garlands are paler now, paler, and turning grey. The day is dying, dying drowsily in a lovely bed. Swift to its close ebbs out life's lambent day. Oh, twilight, stay with us another hour and keep the last and loving light of day from fading!

OUTSIDE AN IRISH WINDOW

THROUGH it all, how fared my sweetheart when a boy; The little Dark Rose; Ireland to you, sir? Nicely, thank you all. In the midst of the heavily-hanging hollyhock, the broad sunflower, and the tiger-lily, the shamrock had dimpled its way through life, untouched, except by the morning dew. The people went down Sackville Street as if nothing was happening next door; though tens and tens of thousands of Ireland's sons and daughters flocked to seafights and landfights, so that in every place where tiny crosses stand, Irish names are found. Ireland had her own problems, her own life to live, her own death to die. Busy saving her soul. She was growing holier day by day, according to statistics, 50 per cent this year above the norm; not good enough, but encouraging. All Ireland's temporal activities had been placed under saintly protection – Textiles under St Clotherius, Building under Saints Bricin and Cementino, Brewing and Distilling under St Scinful, Agriculture under St Spudadoremus, Metal Work under St Ironicomus, Pottery under St Teepotolo, Fishing under St Codoleus, Book-making under St Banaway, the whole of them presided over by the Prayerman, St Preservius, a most holy man of great spiritual preprotensity, who was a young man in the reign of Brian Boru, and who passed to his rest through a purelytic seizure the day he tried to read the first few lines of Joyce's damnable *Ulysses*.

Ireland had developed tone, too: gentlemen had their morning coats and tall hats, judges their red robes, senior counsels flung black silk gowns over their shoulders and planted fine white wigs on their law-loaded heads; and formal etiquette was made obligatory in all formal gatherings, causing acute distress to those put down into a low category, though they all belonged to the old and honoured clan of the great Dull Cash; and the President trotted about in the manner of the old English Viceroys, surrounded by his gold-braided Blue Hussars (at present in pawn to save something that might help to balance the Budget), lifting the taller to anyone bidding him the top of

the morning; cloppety clop clop through the streets of Dublin,
aidescamp on either side of him to keep the wind away.

Aidecamp, aidecamp, look after me ease,
Protect me from touch of the commoner's pleas,
Please, and their fleas;
Aidecamp, aidecamp, protect me, do, please,
From the savage mavrones and the wicked machrees,
And from Sweeney, there, swinging, mad, out in the threes!

This is Sackville Street, sir, and that's Mr Costello speaking
outside of the Bank of Ireland, and he telling the world that
Ireland's greatest need today is dollars – can you see clear,
stranger? And hear clear, too? Right: the curtains are drawn,
but they're thin, and the window's wide. First get the dollars,
stranger, and all the rest will be added – ahem, amen. There, in
front of Parnell's statue, stands Dev, and I hope you hear him
saying that Ireland's the foremost spiritual state in all the
world. So we are. The very ships that leave our harbours now
have strings of coloured lights a-swing from mast to mast,
exactly like rosaries, stranger, so that, when they're lit up o'
nights, the deckhands and stokers can say the rosary in tune
with the hum of the engines. We're not like England, with her
mouth open against fasting, and the same mouth shut against
prayer. Turf and theology, stranger, were our two main props
throughout the quiet years of the war. That youngish woman,
crying on the back doorstep? Oh, that's the Widda Malone
whose two kids, a boy of five and a girl of six, were whipped
away from her, one being put in an Industrial School, and the
girl in a Convent School, because the Widda couldn't keep
them properly on her pension of sixteen shillings a week.
There was a tinkle of a murmur about it, some interfering gets
saying that if the Widda had got what it would cost the convent and the school to keep the kids, she'd have been able to
keep them in clover. Taking the children from their natural
guardian, the gets said, because the woman pleaded for the
kids to be left with her, and the kids yelled to be let stay with
their mother. Wasn't Christian, the gets said. The kids'll soon
be made to like where they are, stranger, for a cane's a fine
convincer.

That fine, out-stepping fellow on the other side? A bishop,
stranger, who'll stand no nonsense. When a City Council and

its architect chose a site for a new school, a site he didn't like
and thought unsuitable, he soon and short told them to build it
on a site of his choosing; and when the Council decided to
keep to their own selection, he soon and short told them they
were behaving in the Continental manner of disrespect for
their priests; a gentle warning that sent them running to vote
as one man, bar the architect, for the holy bishop's choice. The
bishop's ring rang the bell.

That imposing-looking laddo, over in the corner, leaning on
the edge of the mantelpiece, in the tweeds, in danger of taking
fire any minute from the maroon waistcoat he's wearing? Sh!
you'll waken Mr Doyle. Wait till this lad coming up the
street's passed us, for one's got to be careful these days. Oh, it's
only Dan. Sh! The sayin', 'You'll waken Mr Doyle', 's a way
we have of warning. Morra, Dan.

—Morra, Mick.

The laddo in the tweeds, stranger, is Ireland's literary copper
cockoo. No one knows how he landed among the poets and
writers. He just suddenly appeared. He perches in a clock-case
office in *The Irish Times*, one of Ireland's National Dailies.
Every Saturday as the clock strikes the hour of a dark rosaleen
dawn, the portcullis shoots up, and me bould cockoo steps out
to give his private views about writers, poetry, and prose, without conception, without respect of persons. Once, he says,
'Looka', he says, 'Looka that Padraic Fallon fella writing that
deplorable series called his "Journal", in *The Bell*, where what
he doesn't say, and the manner in which he doesn't say it, is
the most interesting part of his thesis. It is not altogether
fanciful to regard his extraordinary capacity to talk a great
deal while committing himself to the bare minimum of communication. All our writers dislike taking up a position without first ensuring that all possible avenues of escape are open.'
The grim, copper cockoo paused to let this sink into the listening souls. Have you got that much cockooed? Right. On we go
again: 'The Irish writer, that boneless wonder, is an expert at
wriggling. He will not be committed; he will not be taken quite
seriously, because he does not really take himself seriously. He
adopts not a position but a pose. Thus Mr Fallon's rollicking,
rambunctiousness; Mr Clarke's arch pranks among pierrots
and ancient Irish monks; Mr Iremonger's grim detachment;
Mr O'Farachain's metrical acrobatics are all sleight of hand.
The escape tunnels are all safely secured. Even Mr Patrick

Kavanagh, when he comes to writing prose, is the deftest side-stepper of them all.' Have you that much cockooed down, stranger?

—He's got it down all right, Mick.

—Right. On we go again: 'In Ireland the critical faculty – critical in its denigratory sense – is hyper-developed. In a society firmly based on the principle that "what goes up must come down", everyone waits maliciously with beady eyes cocked for the collapse of the next victim. The almost audible sharpening of knives, the gleeful anticipatory chuckle of those ranks of Tuscany who make a lifetime's occupation of forbearing to cheer, would make the strongest think twice about exposing himself in the arena. The only future would seem to be a literature of Artful Dodgers.' Mavrone for Ireland and for Irish Writing! There y'are, stranger – a sad state of affairs.

—I dunno, Mick. What do we want writers for anyhow? They only create confusion.

Oh, St Anthony Guide, St Anthony Guide, is O'Casey to go back to this? To become, maybe, a Member of the Acodemy of Blethers. A high extinction. A good death, Bona Mors. Dignified defunctorum. Immortelles all. No flowers by request. Lay them to rest where the shamrock's growing. Little field of renumbrance. Each little tablet over each little head. And you'll remember me. We will try; till we go ourselves. Looka that one writing in the corner, stranger; from here you can see what is being written. 'Stay where you are, O'Casey, in England, where, if there isn't wisdom, there is sense, and some decency of manners.' And the other writing in the far corner – read: 'All the new plays would have been better had they remained senseless on the typed-out paper. Dublin has changed so much! Pseudo-intellectuals, social climbers, racketeering politicians and business men, all squabbling and scrambling for power and position.'

Isn't that a right one, Mick! The ignorant get, even if he is known well among literary gents and ladies, to defie his country!

—That noise, stranger? Echoes, only echoes, The land's full of them. Isn't it, Dan?

—It is that. Mostly wailing echoes after the emigrants. Won't you come home, won't you come home? Come back again; come back some time. The heart-cry of the Gael! Heard so often that the very echoes of the land have learned them. Hasn't she, Mick?

—She has that, Dan. The one you're hearing now, stranger –
come over nearer, bend your ear down, for we speak of such
things seldom. The one you're hearing now like quiet thunder,
is the echo of the hurried patter of boots over the pavements. It
came out of – listen, for this tale's a whisper. A week ago, the
International Affairs Association (what the hell it's doing here,
I don't know) heard the editor of the roman catholic paper,
The Standard, giving a lecture on 'The Pattern of Persecution
in Yugoslavia', with the papal nuncio, Monsignor Mickey
O'Hara, sitting nice and easy in a front row. At the end, Dr
Owen Skeffington proposed that the meeting be flung open for
a discussion (always a dangerous game), and the meeting voted
in favour of the idea. Up sprang a country gentleman, named
Hubert Butler, who, low and behold, began to talk of the part
Cardinal Stepinac took with Pavelić, the Fascist leader, in forcing them of the orthodox church over into the roman ditto.
Yep, yep! stir your stumps for your spiritual good, till you're
all mangled and ironed out into good, hearty roman catholics.
Go on, yep! to your sure salvation! At the nonce, up bounced
the noncio, and out he flounced, beset with such indignation
that he forgot to bang the door after him. Close the meeting
quick; oh, quick; no more talk; no, none! What you're hearing, now, stranger, is an echo; the echo of what happened
immediately after. The echo of the thudding of boots worn by
them racing along to the nuncio's dwelling to apologize for
what had happened; and to beg his big blessing. It's been echoing here, there, ever since – hasn't it, Dan?

—It has that; and, if you listen cautious, stranger, you'll
hear within it a curious strain of music which an anthropolo-
gist said is the tune known as *The Man Who Struck O'Hara*.
Bar a few fluttering letters in the Press, no one spoke. Better
let it lie. The thing was like a harp in the air – everyone
listened, but no one heard. No poet or peasant spoke. Thersites
said nothing; Miles na Gobaleen said nothing; Quidnunc said
nothing. Neither priest nor parson spoke. Didn't notice a
thing. The whole of Ireland was undergoing a retreat. Silence.

Later, it was discovered by someone that Dr Skeffington was
to be principal speaker at a meeting organized by the Students'
Union. Some members of the Vocational Committee who had
control of the Union, had a chat, without calling any formal
meeting, and decided, mum con, that Dr Skeffington's name
gave a dark decoration to the Student's programme, and that it
would have to exit (excuse me, stranger, using Latin, but it

comes natural). So, on orders from the Vocational Committee's members, the name of the clever and well-known Doctor
got the sign of the cross-off from the programme. Didn't it,
Mick?

—It did, Dan. At the night of the meeting, the Vocational
Committee and their butties took over the Hall, let their
friends in, keeping out even the distinguished persons invited
by the Students, locked the doors, and guided the meeting in
the way it should go. Didn't we, Dan?

—Ay, did we, Mick, without a whisper from the Students,
afraid of the catholic cleric's ecclesiastical punchios; and the
lecture on 'Can the Individual Survive?' would have gone fine,
only for the get on the platform who condemned the banning
of Skeffington, using honeyed words that made the meeting
agree with a vote that the banning was wrong.

—Sh! You'll waken Mr Doyle, Dan. We don't want that
shame known, stranger. You see, if Skeffington and his pal,
Butler, were left to open their gobs to bewilder us, there would
be no freedom of thought left in the country from one end of it
to the other. If the blithers aren't prepared to voicify wholesome opinions, then they must be made to keep their mouths
shut. We're working towards a population of holy, practising
imprimaturs, stranger. Hear that bugle-call in the distance?
The *Dies Irae*, Reveille of the Maria Duce, a most commend-
able body, filling a long-felt stunt. We must insist on proper
reverence to our bishops and our nuncio. Why, looka here, just
imagine, our Ministers, Ministers, mind you, scorning the
jestice of ceremonial dress, attended the Eucharistic Congress
in soft hats, soft hats, mind you, while at the secular Ottawa
Conference they were there in all the sweet attire of morning
clothes and silk hats, an indecent dereliction, making Oliver
Gogarty, the poet, write the lines.

> Who wore soft hats for Christ the King,
> And toppers for King George.

you see, stranger, if things were let go, where would we be?
Just think of the happy picture of Christ reviewing a Guard of
Honour of Ireland's best in morning clothes and toppers!

What's what, stranger? That blaze in the distance? Oh, that
– that's the blaze of burning books. Little Mary Cassidy, a
county librarian, has warmed the whole country by the burning, off her own bat, of 443 books, 'because they were unfit for

publication'. Sniff! This one smells bad, too! To the stake with
it! Bought and burned. A woman of much importance. The
bishop's book-keeper. What a lovely job. What a lot of thrills
one might enjoy reading so many books that have to be burned.
Reading sub nosa. We're putting a proper shape on things.
Every foreign artist coming over here has to show his points,
especially Americans; some have had to sing either 'I Am a
Little Catholic', or put on the uniform of a catholic boy scout,
and do a saunter down O'Connell Street, to show all and sundry how he defers to the devotion of the land. I'm saying,
stranger, that it won't be long till we're a land of saints again.
A land of perpetual prayer, a perpetual spiritual Tostal – Ireland at home to God! We've made a great beginning, and soon
every levee at our President's Residence'll be nothing less than
a levee of saints. Eh, Dan?

—A laudable entherprise, up to a point, Mick, up to a point;
but it's soldiers we want now, an' not saints, seeing that we're
in the throes of talkative preparations. All our generals and
colonels, coupled an' crossed with military experts, are arguing
here, there, how best to act if tens of thousands of Russian
parathroopers came dropping down from the Irish skies on to
Tara's Sacred Hill, or on to the Mountains of Mourne that
sweep down to the sea. You haven't to think twice to see the
pickle we'd be in then. That's our present problem; though
some don't seem to realize it. D'ye know what that ignorant
eejut, Muldoon, the Solid Man, said when he was told that the
Russians could come down from the Irish skies in swarms?

—No, then, I don't, Dan.

—The venomous eejut said it would be betther and fitther
for us to guard against the swarms of green flies and swarms
of black flies that dhrop from the Irish skies and destroy the
crops!

—Did he, now? Such persons should be arborized into
places where they couldn't be heard talking, Mick. Go on,
Dan, me son; go on approvin' of us.

—You see, Mick, we're too small to fight the Russians on
our own. It isn't that we haven't the courage.

—You're right there, Dan. He's right there, stranger. We
have the courage, right enough. Let me like a soldier fall,
wha'? You're right, Dan; we're twice too small; we'd have to
have help.

—No use either, Mick, of looking to allies too far off from
us, like France or Italy – they'd take years to come.

—So they would, Dan, so they would.

—You see, Mick, Ireland's so important, that, in a war, Russia would need to take her over in an hour; an hour, Mick. Does that ring a bell?

—Yis; a whole peal of them. But then, wha'?

—Well, man, we'd have to get help at once, at once.

—Then what about England, Dan?

—England! Why, man alive, she'd be fighting for her life, and couldn't let us have even a policeman from point-duty!

—Well, then, wha'?

—America's our only man, Mick. Organized battle on our part wouldn't be worth a damn; a guerrilla war no good either.

—So what, Dan?

—What we need, Mick, is swarms and swarms of jeeps.

—Jeeps, be jeepers!

—Yes, jeeps, Mick; each with a driver, a spare driver, a commander, and a wireless-operator. Every able-bodied man in Ireland in a jeep here, a jeep there, with a sten-gun, a hammer and pliers, head-phone, and a jeepsie walkie-talkie – that's the one solution, Mick.

—And a trailer to every jeep, Dan – you forgot that.

—Aw, man, use your brains; think a little! How the hell could a jeep jump a hedge with a trailer attached?

—But, Dan, what would the ordinary cars and pedestrians do and the roads buzzin' with jeeps? You haven't thought of that; I don't like the idea at all. Man alive, there wouldn't be a man, woman, child, or chicken left alive in the country. No; count me out.

—Aw, think again, Mick. Your thoughts aren't exact enough yet to gather it all in: Looka, if they were all done for aself, wouldn't death on our own roads be better than exportation be the Bolsheviks to an unknown destination? Take that in, Mick.

—I am taking it in; you're not the only one who can take things in. What exportation are you walkie-talkiein' about?

—Looka, Mick, the expert put it plain before us all; the military expert, mind you. A nation like Russia that holds fifteen millions and more in concentration camps, and has eliminated twenty millions more and more be vast and frequent purges, man, wouldn't cast a thought about eliminating thousands of Irishmen, women, and children, the expert said, or wait to think twice about exporting the rest of us. It would be only child's play, he said, to the Russians.

—A thrue saying, Dan; thrue for me, thrue for you, thrue for all. Pity all this wasn't said to the eejut laddo with his swarm of green flies an' swarm of black flies.

—It was said, Mick.

—It was, was it? I bet that bet him! An' what did the Solid eejut say to all them homers?

—And where, said he, would the Bolsheviks find the ships and the trains to cart our people to exportation, four millions of us? he says: Siberia's a long way off, if you ask me, he says.

—Huh huh; that was a sensible question, Dan, and a sensible remark for the eejut to make, anyhow.

—How was it a sensible remark, and how was it a sensible question, Mick? Where's your brains, man? The Bolsheviks wouldn't be dreaming of Siberia, man, and the Isle of Man only a few feet away from our own green border.

—Aha, Dan, I bet that had him bet. He hadn't had the imagination to think of the Isle of Man – the eejut!

—Divil a bit it bet him, Mick.

—No, Dan?

—No, Mick; sorra a tremor it took out of him. He just let an eejeeotic laugh outa him, saying, Counting the millions of relatives of them in concentration camps, with the millions of prisoners themselves, an' the millions more of relatives of them who've been purged, he says, making in all hundreds of thousands more of bitther enemies to the Russian Government, then the nation that can stand to that, and then send millions of more paratroopers flutthering down through the skies on to Erin's lovely shore, is invincible, says he, an' we're wasting our time thinking out a way to fight them.

—An' did he say that, now? Wasting our time! Isn't that shockinly reaving! What about our well-known love of country? Why didn't you counther him with that, Mick?

—I did, so I did.

—An' how did the eejut react to it?

—Looka, says he, prodding me in the chest with his fore-finger; looka, he says, if the Bolshevik land is the kinda country you're saying it is, then the Russians that'll dhrop from our Irish skies on to our emerald sod will be, says he, some poor divils seekin' asylum.

—Seekin' asylum, is it? What, a lunatic asylum it is he must be meanin'.

—No, no, man; an ordinary asylum, an ordinary asylum.

—What ordinary asylum? There's no ordinary asylum. When a body says We've taken a certain party to the asylum, we mean a lunatic asylum, don't we?

—Yes, yes, but—

—There's no but about it, Dan. An asylum's an asylum – there's no but about it.

—Yes, there is.

—There isn't. I'm telling you!

—I'm telling you there's different asylums; for instance, a deaf-and-dumb asylum.

—Maybe, but the parathroopers dhropping from our skies won't be deaf an' dumb, will they?

—I know they won't. For Jasus' sake, don't thry to be as big an eejut as the other fella!

—Who's an eejut?

—You're talking like an eejut now.

—You're talking like an eejut yourself! A fully fledged one! Wantin' to flood the counthry with jeeps! While you're at it, will you kindly tell us who's goin' to provide the hundred thousand jeeps to go gallopin' around and lay us all out, dead as mackerel, on the roads of Eireann; every man-jack of us and every woman-lizzie of us that hasn't the good fortune to be sittin' safe in some of them! An' if we put into every one of them, as your expert advises, a dhriver, a spare dhriver, a commander, an' a wireless-operator with his walkie-talkie, addin' all them stretched out flat an' dead on the roads, will you tell us who's going to look afther the common things that have to be daily done to keep the counthry goin'? Aha, you're silent now! That's bet you! An' listen, another thing: While America might be dhroppin' the jeeps, what's to prevent the Bolshies at the same time from dhroppin' their parathroopers an' filling the jeeps as they touch down, to let them go scamperin' all over the roads, takin' over the Turf Board, the Tourist Association, the Hospitals Sweep, the Court of Chancery, the Catholic Young Men's Society, the Protestant pulpits, the Abbey Theatre, and the President's Residence, forcin' the unfortunate members of Maria Duce to do point-duty at street corners an' crossroads; an' ending, maybe, with the plantin' of a Red Flag in the hand of St Patrick's Statue standin' helpless on a windy hill in the centre of the lonely Plains of Meath! That's what your jazzin' jeeps would do –

provide the Bolshies with a rapid an' logical means of loco-
motion throughout the whole of our unfortunate counthry!
Isn't that so, stranger – God, he's gone! The sensible man
wouldn't stay to hear the ravin' of an eejut commendin' jeeps.
Well, I'm goin' too!

—Goodbye, Mick. Think it all over; take your time. Say
what you like, but cantherin' jeeps on all our roads alone could
purse the land into safety.

Woman and war – two terrible dangers. Wherever she goes,
rings on her fingers, bells on her toes, she trails behind her
devotion that should go to God, destruction that should never
come near Man. What's that, what's that! Lightning flashing
before her, thunder rolling behind, and a voice from the midst
of them. What voice, whose voice? McNamee's voice, bishop
of Ardagh and Clonmacnois's episcopal Pistol thundering out
the Rule that No Dance must last beyond twleve o' the clock,
no Bar to be in any Dance Hall, no revelry in Lent in Clonmacnois today, or in Ardagh either.

A hand's stretch away, in Sligo,

> Among hydrangeas and the falling ear-rings
> Of fuchsias red as blood,

Catholic energy and art painted a picture of real life, when a
girl went to work for an unmarried farmer, aged fifty-six, with
the blessing of her parents, but against the will of the clerics
and their henchmen; an occasion of sin – the priest objects;
so, one morning early, when the hoar frost was out, the first
postman of the morning found the girl in her shift chained and
padlocked to a telegraph pole, too frozen to moan, or give
signal of life; while the farmer stretched himself out in his
kitchen, bruised and bloodied as red as the fuchsia's ear-rings,
from a beating given in the cause of honour and virtue, though
no untowardness had passed between him and the girl; but the
danger had been there, so the clerics stayed dumb, and the
police folded their arms till the district became calm, and a
hush hush came down among the hydrangeas and the falling
ear-rings of fuchsias red as blood. Where Yeats lies buried, far
away now from fuchsia and hydrangea, and from the over-
blown bleat of the clerics; but still in County Sligo, in Drum-
cliff; still there, but quiet, and resting.

Barrum, barrum, barrum; Yeats' drum tapping as in his

play, *The Resurrection*. A rattle in the wood where a Titan
strode. Barrum, barrum, barrum.

> The herald's cry, the soldier's tread,
> Exhaust his glory and his might:
> Whatever flames upon the night
> Man's own resinous heart has fed.

Is there a heart among us now with enough resin in it to
provoke a flame that would roast a spud? Tiny holy candles
flickering around Ireland, fainting wills-o'-the-wisp; woeful;
but ne'er a torch; ne'er a one blazing anywhere.

> Heads bent, we go; go stumbling on
> Where others ran:
> A pray'r for me, a pray'r for you,
> And pray'rs for Jack the journeyman.

What's that? An eagle's whistle! And another, a number of
them! Jasus, there are eagles flying among the grey tits and
the flat snipe! Brennan's still on the moor. There are brave
men and women in Ireland still; and will be, will be, always,
for ever.

AND EVENING STAR

THE sun has gone, dragging her gold and green garlands down, too; gone from the sky, leaving him to live in the glimmer of midnight, to share the last few moments of life with the tender loneliness of the evening star. Soon it will be time to kiss the world goodbye. An old man now, who, in the nature of things, might be called out of the house any minute. Little left now but a minute to take a drink at the door – deoch an doruis; a drink at the door to life as it had been with him, and another to whatever life remained before him. Down it goes! Slainte!

The whole earth's a place of never-ending arrivals and departures; Glad to see you is but the echo of goodbye, Sally, goodbye, Sue. Still the interlude, strange interlude, was a fine and exciting one. He had lived and fought through twenty years of the nineteenth century and through more than half of the twentieth, and ginger, i'faith, is hot in the mouth still. Good going. The evening star was the one lantern to his feet now; the morning star would never again be bright for him to see. It was sad, but within him sadness faded quick, and the evening star was beautiful. It was a long look-back to the time when he remembered wearing the black-and-red plaid petticoat – a little rob roy; and he sitting on the doorstep of a Lower Dorset Street house, watching the antics of the older and braver kids let loose on the more dangerous roadside; in his ears the sound of lorry, dray, and side-car, with their iron-rimmed wheels, clattering over the stony setts of the street; in his nose the itching smell of dusty horse-dung. A long look-back to the time, kneeling cold, on a chair, looking out of the window to watch the rain pelting down on the pavement, each impact of its falling watery lances forming tiny, swirling circles that his mother said were pennies. He had been rich while the rain had been falling. Not the Father, the Son, or the Holy Ghost; not the sun, the moon, or the stars were this kid's, or that kid's, gods; but the penny. The kid who went to the catholic catechism, or the kid who went to the protestant sunday-school, worshipped the penny. As it had been then, so it was now – though no longer a kid in a red-and-black plaid petticoat, but an old man: he still stood at the door waiting for pennies. Most artists do. They stand at the door, on the pavement, hat or cap in hand, hoping some god may prompt some passer-by to sling a penny into the patient, waiting cap.

Odd why so many thought authors with any name must be very rich fellows. He himself got appeals to help a charity by fishing up some forgotten trinket from some long-neglected drawer. Dip a hand down, said one request, and you will probably pull out a pair of gold cuff-links, a gold cigarette-case, or a gold watch, long hidden away from memory. Pull away, and up she rises! Lucky dip! The old figure developed from the kid in the red-and-black plaid petticoat never could, and never would be able to thrust down a careless hand and pull up a gold watch from a neglected drawer. A civilization in which millions are hard put to find shirt or shift, harder set to find a house to live in, that condones a condition permitting a fortune-flushed hand to pull a forgotten gold watch from a dusty drawer, is a civilization needing the curse of God and the hammer of man to its changing.

When Sean was twenty, the first tweed cap, worn by Keir Hardie, came suddenly into the House of Commons. Gents empanelled in glass-encased offices, looking over ledgers at God, didn't bother even to look up. The one tweed cap among the crowd of glossy toppers caused a disturbance, but only one of loud laughter. Bah! Pooh! Who is this so weak and helpless; who is this in yonder stall? A miner; went down into the pit when he was ten; never got a spot of schooling. Must be very embarrassing to Black Rod and Sergeant-at-Arms. It is, and to the Constable at the gate, too; doesn't quite know if he should permit a tweed cap to come in. It is trying. Comes from some god-forsaken place in Wales, I'm told. How'd he manage to get here? Freak election. Helped by that red-headed fella who writes plays and things – Shaw's the name, I think. Ephemeramental. Eh, you, tweed cap – whom do you represent? Me, sir? Yes, you, sir. Oh, I represent only the miners, railway-workers, men at the plough, men behind the counter – all earning a living by hand or brain; in short, sir, the people of England, Wales, Scotland, and Ireland; and in a way, the world.

Curious how religions, ancient and modern, harp on the

futility of life. How they fill it with pain, uncertainty, and woe.
Brief life is here our portion; life is but a walking shadow; life
is but an empty dream. Even Buddha, gentle as a dewdrop
upon a lotus blossom, sitting without a stir under the Bo tree,
calls men away from this life. They find it damned hard to go,
for no man is so old as to believe he cannot live one more year.
Even if life be all that Buddha made it out to be,

> *Ache of the birth, ache of the helpless days,*
> *Ache of hot youth and ache of manhood's prime;*
> *Ache of the chill, grey years and choking death,*
> *These fill your piteous time.*

Kneel down, and say your prayers, and be off – there's nothing to keep you here. Yet man finds it hard go to, and so he
does. 'The pleasure of life', yells out a rebellious Elizabethan,
'what is it but the good hours of an ague?' Truth in this, too,
but is it all the truth? Not to him. There are many, many
beautiful things in life, but life is too short to see and enjoy
more than a few of them. Now that is sad if you like. There
are honest men here, and women still as fair as the evening
air clad in the beauty of a thousand stars. Must we close our
eyes for ever on the holly tree in berry, or the rowan tree in
berry and in bloom? It is the many beauties of the earth that
make life hard to bear, knowing that life must end, and all the
beauties of the world say farewell to us. Oh for permission to
be old and gay; thousands of years, thousands of years, if all
were told.

There was struggle still under the quietness of the evening
star, and he, longing to sit down in a deck-chair to enter into
what Yeats called 'the red flare of dreams', found he had to
keep busy defending his corner in life. Nothing to be frightened
of, for some poet has said that 'all things declare that struggle
hath deeper peace than sleep can bring'.

A young Irishman, named Patrick Galvin, who, he says
himself, has written thirty poems, a few short stories, and has
produced a magazine of his own, has leapt into view on the
London-Irish scene, whipped off his coat, and has offered (no
holds barred) O'Casey out to fight; prefacing the contest with
an open letter to the *Tribune*, then sent on to the *Irish Democrat*, a copy of which flew down to Devon. 'I've seen your
three one-act plays', the letter says, 'and they have, to my

astonishment, confirmed in me once for all the suspicion, pre-
viously held at bay, that you are not a Socialist.' Oh, what a
fall is here, my countrymen! Am I right in deducing that the
whole theme and setting of *The Hall of Healing* derive from a
fifty-year-old memory?' Quite right, lad, and I told you so
myself, which you could have seen had you taken the trouble
to read *The Irish Times* of December 28th, 1951. There your
deduction is given an *Imprimi potest*. In a letter to the editor,
O'Casey says, 'Dear Sir, Little did I think when I wrote *The
Hall of Healing* that the conditions of fifty years ago in the
dispensaries of the poor would be the same today'. At that
time, the Mother and Child Bill was being contested in the
Dail, with the hierarchy in the close background; and things
said in the Dail, and letters and an article published in the
Press, showed that the old dispensary conditions still held bad.
The notorious Red Ticket, that exacerbated some of O'Casey's
days, was still the method of communication between patient
and doctor, and, for all he knows, flourishes still. On August
5th, 1953, a day right under Patrick Galvin's nose, Radio Eireann announced that a new Dispensary was about to be built, at
a cost of something over a thousand pounds, in Killashandra,
Co. Cavan, to replace a shack that had existed there as a dispensary for near on a hundred years. And what kind of a
Dispensary, these days, can be built for the price mentioned?
Are they building there a small cabin of clay and wattles
made? How much would it cost if it was being built for the
care of the soul and the vanity of clerics? Maybe the clergy
have got the Young Men's Catholic Association, or the members of Muintir na Tire, to work for next to nix. The old
O'Casey goes through the world with one eye open, but Patrick
Galvin seems to meander along with both eyes shut.

But let the lad go on: 'Even as caricatures I find your
characters false. As a fellow countryman of yours I cannot but
ask you to consider whether it is not a dis-service to Ireland, to
the working class, and to the cause of progress, that they
should be offered to the public ostensibly in the name of Socialism.' He goes on still: 'I have long admired your work. The
conclusions forced on me by *The Hall of Healing* have been an
unpleasant shock to me [Christ, I am sorry! S. O'C.]. I shall
now have to re-read you from start to finish to see whether
what I assess in this play as an attitude of profound contempt
for the poor – as I have heard others say, and have denied –

has been latent in your work from the beginning. Not only are your *Hall of Healing* characters frauds: The style seems to me a fraud too ... What are the rest of us to make of it (English as well as Irish, to say nothing of the rest of the world), save a new and peculiarly unacceptable stage-Irishism? Have the progressive Irish fought so long against the Stage Irishman, so convenient to their [*sic*] exploiters, only to have him handed back to them on a "socialist" plate by you who are held to be progressive too?'

Mea culpa! Please, sir, not on a 'socialist' plate, sir, no; rather on a majollican plate I hand out my plays, a plate decorated, not with galvinian socialist mottoes, but with colour and gay decoration. A few more tinderclaps: 'Had you not better in your own interests and ours, stick to the lines of sheer music-hall farce, of which *The End of the Beginning* is a dazzling example, or develop and delve deeper into the strain of Yeatsian fantasy with which you have a modicum of a success in *Time To Go*? Unless you would care to return to Ireland and find out what goes on? Your *Hall of Healing* I frankly consider an insult. To use a Dublin expression, "you were just coming the bliddy hound". The whole play was pure codology from start to finish.'

Now, sir, just a minute: The play, *End of the Beginning,* is almost all founded on a folk-tale well known over a great part of Europe. All O'Casey's children have read it under the name of *Gone is Gone*. If Patrick Galvin had searched a little in his own beloved country, which he is so eager to guard from all touches derogatory to her excellent name, he would have found the story glowing in Sugrue's (An Seabhach) *An Baile seo 'Gainn*, decked out in good Gaelic too; but these patriotic persons seem to enshrine all their patriotism in their shouting. Like the Gaelic magazine, *Iris*, which reached him in Devon, and to which he at once subscribed, because it seemed to be courageous and animated, to find that, after a few more months, it had died, because only, as he was told, eighty copies of the magazine were sold, and a heavy loss was suffered by the promoters. An Gaelic abu! *Time to Go,* oddly enough, is founded on another Irish folk-tale, but Mr Galvin can have the pleasure of seeking its whereabouts for himself.

One more criticism from the young poet, and then his trumpet coda: 'The old woman who "doesn't want much", and is managing on five shillings a week (This, God save us and guard us, is presented as the present day!).' Well, O'Casey's own mother often worked for a week for less than five shillings a week; and he and she lived for weeks on her old-age pension of ten shillings a week, which, if I can add two to two, comes to five shillings a head. Now, the galvin-gallant coda: 'I know the Irish *lumpen-proletariat* and the Irish Working Class. I know them as well as you do and much more recently. There is far more in them than you seem to imagine. I myself am a demonstration of how a man can emerge from the fecklessness and shiftlessness of the lumpen-proletariat into genuine working-class consciousness and knowledge, and I am far from believing myself to be a phoenix. [If not a phoenix, then a VIP?] The hopelessness you portray in *Hall of Healing* is out of date. Do you honestly believe it yourself? Come off it! If you and me were in some old pub for half an hour over a bottle of stout I'd either talk the indifference out of you or we'd kill each other.'

A fierce young fellow, but he'll have to go to that 'some old pub', and drink the bottle of stout alone. Rightly or wrongly, Sean ranks these letters with the ones he gets carrying little holy pictures, rosary beads, catholic truth society tracts, notes of pathetic appeals to be converted to Truth, and notes of indignant denunciation. As for Sean, were it in his power, he'd make all the young Irish poets happy, and all great.

The younger ones coming into life could never be the same as the older ones going out. He saw as he stood by the door how different this generation was from the one which had enfolded him. If the old don't recognize this, the young ones will harass them. Go down, thou bald-head! To serve one's own generation is almost as much as one can do; and no humiliation is hidden in any inability to dominate a new one. In his own three children, he felt and saw the tremendous change that had come over life since the days of the black-and-red plaid petticoat; and he himself, thank heaven, had done a few things to bring about the change – bar in Ireland, where they lingered fifty years behind the rest. The young were busy in the house of life that the old were leaving; throwing out some of the musty stuff, bringing the fresh and the new; changing the very shape of the house itself (though there were many young ones coming into life who were mouldier than the older ones going out of it); placing new pictures on the walls; knocking out walls separating one family from another; polishing everything with a newer glow; opening the windows wider.

Oh, the world was a busy place now! The one lonely tweed cap had become a great multitude such as no man could number; multitudes of all lands, of every colour, of every race. The tractor and combine, great land-gods, had appeared in the fields; the skylon and nylon had appeared in the street. The one part of civilization that hadn't changed, daren't change, was institutional religion. This was the sulky laggard in man's forward march; a dangerous and a malicious laggard; a mistress of sabbathage.

When he thought of all the common routine of life that had to be gone through – to eat, to drink, to sleep, to clothe ourselves, to take time for play, lest we perish of care, to suffer and fight common and uncommon ills, then the achievements of man, in spite of all these, are tremendous indeed. Away then with the whine of being miserable sinners, with the whine of we've no abiding city here, with the whine of pray for the wanderer, pray for me! We've important things to do. Fag an bealach! How many tons of coal have we delved from the mines today? How many railway wagons have we loaded? How many yards of textiles have we woven? How many schools, hospitals, houses, cinemas, and theatres have we built? How many railway engines, carriages, and trucks have we put on the lines? How many ships sent to sea? Fag an bealach! Work is the Reveille and the Last Post of life now, providing for man, making leisure safe, enjoyable, and longer, profiting body, soul, and spirit, having a song in itself, even when the sun sets on old age, and the evening star shines a warning of the end.

There were personal activity and personal disappointments as well as those disturbing a community. There was the perennial difficulty of getting a play produced, and, worse still, the poverty of producer and of production that inhibited any performance given. Apart from the Irish Players in their heyday, and the production of *The Silver Tassie*, all were bad, a few worse than others, and one worst of all. 'To see a bad play given a fine production', says George Jean Nathan somewhere, 'is a bad thing, but to see a good, aspiring play badly done, is to witness a betrayal of the drama.' And there are quite a few traitors to the drama among managers, producers, actors, and among the playwrights, too. Of course, the theatre, by and large, is nothing higher than a money-making game. The drama's altar isn't on the stage: it is candlesticked and flowered in the box-office. There is the gold, though there be no frankincense or myrrh; and the gospel for the day always The Play will Run for a Year. The Dove of Inspiration, of the desire for inspiration, has flown away from it; and on its roof, now, the commonplace crow caws candidly.

Whenever he ventured to think of what was the worst production of a play of his, his heart's blood pressed into his head, and all the world became red. Even critics, often tolerant of things done badly, declared it to be a butchery of a play. And one had to bear it quietly, though the heart was stung. Never before had Sean seen such an assured and massive incompetency in a producer assigned to an English theatre or such managerial support given to incompetence. He was the cockiest clacking cod Sean had ever encountered, adazzle with iridescent ignorance of the drama; a fellow who should never have been allowed even to pull a curtain up from the stage of a tuppenny gaff, yet the manager clapped him on the back continually. The play, admittedly, was a difficult one, probably a clumsy one, possibly, even, a bad one; but the shocking production failed, in every possible way, to show whether it was one, or all, of these; failed to give the slightest guidance to an experimental playwright. The fellow's gone now, making his exit by way of a gas-oven, giving in a kitchen a better production than he ever gave on a stage.

In a recent letter, George Jean Nathan refers to 'the rapidly-dying theatre'. A sad saying from such a man. Is the theatre, so long sounding the Reveille, to be heard now tuning into the Last Post? Maybe. During the production of his last play, Sean heard the Last Post clearly; but has given the fool's answer since by writing three one-act plays, and two of three acts each. George may be right: looks like the House of Satan's sinking into the turfy mud of mediocrity, with only the box-office remaining safe on the top of the bog.

Ah, some young body singing in the house of life! Sighs and songs never leave it. Beside the sigh, there is always the song. A young heart full of golden nonsense singing the challenge of love to any power in the path of a maid's way with a man.

> A sour-soul'd cleric, passing near,
> Saw lovers by a rowan tree;

He curs'd its branches, berries, bloom,
Through time and through eternity.
Now evil things are waiting where
Fond lovers once found joy,
And dread of love now crowns th' thoughts
Of frighten'd girl, of frighten'd boy.

The rowan tree's black as black can be
On Killnageera's lonely hill.
And where love's whispers once were warm,
Now blows a wind both cold and shrill.
Oh, would I had a lover brave
To mock away its power,
I'd lie there firm within his arms,
And fill with love one glorious hour!!

Then branches bare would leaf again,
The twisted ones grow straight and true;
And lovers locked within its ken
Would nothing fear and nothing rue;
Its bloom would form a bridal veil
Till summer days were sped,
Then autumn berries, red, would fall
Like rubies on each nestling head.

The singing heart. The young may-mooning. Oh, foolish
lover and foolish lover's lass, know ye not that love is corrupt
with the corustcation of original sin? A sense of beauty at the
sudden sight of some image; image of cloud, flower, fern, or
woman, lingers less than a moment. Silence the sigh, for man
has made many an everlasting thing out of a moment of time.
The lover and his lass are for ever acting on the stage of life,
and Marlowe's glimpse of fair Helen's beauty didn't die with
him in a tavern brawl. The primrose's gentle yellow blossom
dies; every season a last rose of summer sheds its petals on the
cynical earth; but the rose is always with us, and the primrose
blooms again.

He looked over Jordin, looked over, and what did he see,
what did he see? An atom bomb coming, an atom bomb coming to carry him home, carry him home, carry him home. No
angels planing over the clouds now, no sign of a cross in the
sky. Oh, Helena, Helena, have a heart, and help us! Real

things are hurting around there now – the whole firmament is full of flying saucers. There's saucers aflying in the air. Prospero, Prospero! They'll leave not a wrack behind! Don't look up, brother; keep your eyes on the ground, sister – earth's new orb is dangling dangerously over us all; botchlandt über alles. Dangle it, darling, dangle the flaming gem over our heads; over the heads of the Queen and her ministers of state, and all that are put in authority over us; over the head of the cleric fumbling for God at the altar; over the heads of the lover and his lass lying nervously under the hawthorn tree; over the mother suckling her child; over the old stepping warily towards their end. Zip! There goes a city! Send them up to heaven hot. All the saints wondering. What is this that they have done unto you?

> You haven't an arm and you haven't a leg,
> You're an eyeless, noseless, chicken-less egg,
> You'll have to be put in a bowl to beg.

The flame from the angel's sword in the Garden of Eden has been catalysted into the atom bomb; God's thunderbolt became blunted, so man's dunderbolt has become the steel star of destruction. War minions are going about giggling. We can't let it be wasted; we must use the damned thing. We can't let all our work go for nothing; and the word Inevitable is cradled within everything they say. We have the atom bomb. Twinkle, twinkle, mighty bomb, bring us safe to kingdom come; when you come with clouds ascending, doing harm that needs no mending; from the palace, hall, and slum bring us safe to kingdom come. Never worry, what the wind is, what the whether – God can stick the bits together. We have the atom bomb – get that into your head. We're ready for anything now. Warships sail with decks half cleared for action; no general wears a nosegay to soften the arrogant air of his crimson tabs; the guns are polished, primed, and pointed: we're ready for anything. Zip! any minute now. Oh, Walt Whitman, saintly sinner, sing for us!

> Walt Whitman, one of the world's good wishes
> Is the one that wishes you here today,
> To sing Shake Hands to the world's peoples;
> To listen, cock-eared, in a way of wonder,

To all that others have got to say;
Then with your own embracing message,
Lead all correctly, or lead astray,
For either is goodness with God, and gay,
Like song of a thrush or screech from a jay;
They'll mingle miles on, from each other learning
That life's delightful at work or play.
So enter in spirit the sharp contentions
Of brothers belling each other at bay,
And soften the snout of the menacing cannon
With the scent and bloom of a lilac spray.

England isn't in a good way, there's no denying it. At times, they seem to stand without breath or motion, flattening out their kidneys, as Wyndham Lewis says, with great draughts of thin beer. They haven't yet been able to come out of the dive they took in the last great war. Each English person is said to owe as much as it would take him to earn throughout a lifetime. The English do not welcome the possibility of another war. They can't absorb another one. They snap out of any talk that mentions a word of war. The more they are driven to the thought of war, or preparations for war, the more they are magnetized by the thought of peace. Most of them seem to be in the condition that if another war came upon them, they'd stand still and wait for death. Anyway, it wouldn't take long to come to them. Looks like the generals, who seem to be kept alive by the thought of war, will have to wage a little one of their own. And, indeed, most folk would be glad if none came alive out of it.

The generals don't like the look of things. They are uneasy about this ineptitude for war, cold or hot. General Montgomery's plea for a Supreme Commander to direct the Cold War met with a cold response. 'Exactly how that could be done, I haven't thought out', he said; 'it's not my job, really. I'm the Hot War chappie – if it comes. It is because we don't win the Cold War that they hand it over to Hot Wars. When the politicians get completely mucked up about the Cold War, they hand it over to Us.' Over to you, chappie. As if he were talking of hot and cold springs; as if careless of the bitterness, the ruin, the hurried burial of the messed-up dead, and the cry of woe that lies in the accursed core of the conceited and applauded villainy of war. There is no more room for any

more ribbons on the generals' tunics. The young aren't prepared to die to hang a tawdry glory out on a general's breast.

The generals don't like this. They love guns as kids love
candies. They call upon people to get ready for war as if they
were calling upon them to get ready for a walk. 'The sight
gladdens my old eyes', a general is alleged to have said, when
he saw a heap of Korean dead; forgetting that where there are
Korean dead, there will be American dead, British dead, and,
maybe, Irish dead too. The Korean dead don't lie lonely. The
price we pay for a heap of Korean dead is a heap of our own
dead; put out an eye, and lose one ourselves; a loss for a loss;
I'm dead, you're dead, he's dead, we're all dead. Every day,
every hour, there are many who will never knock at the door
again. The military mind is indeed a menace. Old-fashioned
futurity that sees only men fighting and dying in smoke and
fire; hears nothing more civilized than a cannonade; scents
nothing but the stink of battle-wounds and blood. Only today,
as this is being written, a memorial was unveiled to men who
died in the First World War. Memorializing only half done
when the tide of the Second World War swept over the work.
Looks like, if generals had their way, the tide of a Third
World War would sweep over all before men had a real chance
to see what the last war looked like. So we hang together as
best we may, going through a life that has become a corridor of
war memorials, built in honour of the young who gave their
lives gallantly for his nib's sake; with obeliskan officers standing at every corner shouting: Prepare to fight; prepare to die;
prepare to meet your enemy! Aw, go to hell, and leave our
little world alone; our little lives rounded with a little sleep;
our little streets, our little homes; we want them all, we love
them all – we'll die in our beds, you tabb'd and uniformed sons
of bitches!

Imagine it – an expert's vision of jeeps dashing about the
Irish roads while he sat here under the sunset and the evening
star. Such talk, such things, such talk, in Ireland, while the
echoes of Yeats' voice and Lady Gregory's lingered there still,
floating over the Irish Sea to glide into his own ear as he sat
listening here. The new divinity – the jeep. For all her holy
dedications, there are odd gods in Ireland today. Poor pros-
pects and poorer men. Full of green tits and flat snipe. Nothing now but hallowed hollow men. A prayer for me, a prayer
for you, and a prayer for Jack the Journeyman. Not a word

now about the Lane Pictures. One of Lady Gregory's last letters written to him – probably the last – says:

DEAR SEAN,
   I had a few days in London, arriving Sunday, leaving
Thursday, and had hoped to be able to go to see you and
make acquaintance with your wife and son. But I had a
good deal of business to go through, and I hurried home
because of my grandson having returned from Cambridge;
and his mother not having returned from the Continent. I
was very disappointed, a real disappointment. I am so seldom over here, and only went because I had promised to
attend the National University St Patrick's Day Dinner
some time ago. I had hoped to be able to say a few words
about the Lane Pictures then, and that the New Gallery had
begun, but a strike had put this off, and I thought silence
best, until, at least, the foundations had been laid. Perhaps
you will be coming to Ireland again? I hope so, and that you
will let me know. Yours as ever.

                                                A. GREGORY

Dead now, and buried, too. And the pictures buried with her.
The lowliest theft ever done by an English Government on
Ireland, in face, too, of protests from eminent Irishmen, Scots,
Welsh, and eminent sons of England herself. Hugh Lane, who
went down in the *Lusitania*, neglected to get witnesses to his
will, and, though thousands of wills made by British soldiers,
unwitnessed, were made legal, Lane's wasn't, and the Government of England's decision became God's dictum pictorum
Laneiensis. The goddamn, rotten, lousy thieves! But then the
green tits, the flat snipe, and the white-collared crows of Ireland don't care a damn about them. There are only souls waft-
ing about Ireland; souls empty save for the Pap in the Paper
Pastorals published during Lent and Christmas time. Yet
Renoir's 'Umbrellas' give a glory to God that all the Pastorals
ever written could never do. Souls sinking down to the earth.
Souls sprawling over a sweep-ticket. Four kinds – hearts, clubs,
diamonds, and spades. Hush! Voice from above; bing crosby
singing over the wireless. Oh, mighty soul, transcentdentalizer
of man! A cultured, cheering group are forming, right now, a
Society to give Bing a month's free holiday in Ireland, with an
illuminated address from Maria Duce, to be presented by Mick

McGilligan's daughter, Maryanne; right now; yessir. Shut up –
let's listen! Now.

Bing on the one end of the tape, Eton on the other. Odd
things, odd things bury themselves in life. There are numbers
of a certain class, good, often intelligent, Christians, who think
the kingdom of heaven less important than the Kingdom of
Eton's way-in, way-out. They lay an infant on Eton's doorstep
before it has learned to suck; before it has been baptized. One
sent into the world from Eton is more important than one sent
in by God. Yessir. It was never very important to God, he
could easily get on without it; it is no longer of much importance to man. The lad in the topper, eton suit, with the nice
cane, is no longer the guaranteed lord of the future. They must
now sing for their supper and fight for their place with man.
The red carpet no longer trails straight from the school-porch
to the front door of government posts. Imitation etonia sed
imitation Christi has become a cod.

Come on out of these arched and cloistered academes of
uniformity in accent, in dress, thought, manners, and super-
ficial conduct, lads, and join the crowd. There are a lot of
grand gossoons among you, but you hide yourselves in the fear
of being different from what your father was. Let the old boy
be a warning to you to change your tune. You are just feeding
yourselves on mould. Harrow and Eton no longer impress –
they are becoming comical. Forget your tony school for a
minute, and take a decko at yourself in the glass, dollied up in
your ancient dress, topper and all, and tell yourself what you
think of yourself. Your uniform isn't even slightly picturesque
like that of Christ's Hospital. You aren't dressed in it; you are
encased in it, like sacred statues encased in cellophane. Tear
off these mummifying wrappings, for sense's sake, and let your
energy and imagination loose for the good of all. Come off the
fading red carpet on to the rough road of life, where all your
brothers and sisters, without the law of a dead tradition, go.
Lads of the shiny toppers and the wide-leaved straw hats,
come off it, for life has no longer any time, any longing, to
look upon you as life's pretty pampernils. Hurry up, if one day
you don't want to be stuffed into a glass case for a wonder and
a show.

Old, oh, so old! Yet he couldn't see the logic of the calendar
or give ear to the ticking of the clock. He knew that the bit of
life-tapestry he was weaving would come to an end before

long. Soon the loom he was at would go clack clack clacking
no more; nevermore. He had to go to make room for the
young; recognize as Tennyson did that.

> Old men must die, or the world would grow mouldy,
> Would only breed the past again.

Well, the clack of his loom had always gone with the louder
clack of life. The loom worked slower now, but there was no
rust on it. It was a little tired, a little worn, for it had never
rested, and never would. The young are knocking at the door.
The old must decrease, the young increase. He hoped his children would throw a wider chest than his own. Down below,
the elder lad hammered a frame together for a picture he was
painting, the younger lad, laying aside biology for a spell, was
blasting out music from a fine second-hand trombone, the
young girl was merrily tapping out a Mozartian minuet from
the piano – all indifferent – all careless of the tumult of mind
afflicting the old codger up above, labouring over finding
words for his wonderful work. Heartless youth; didn't give a
damn how they distracted him. Thinking of themselves only.
And who else should they be thinking of, in God's name?

> When the rain raineth and the goose winketh,
> Little wots the gosling what the goose thinketh.

And why the hell should it? It is only the young who possess
the world.

Past achievements, failures, experiences, were echoes in his
ear now; all echoes under the sunset and the evening star;
echoes of places where he had lived and moved and had his
being; echoes all echoing around everywhere, in the strength of
the day, in the still deep of the night.

> Echo, I will not talk with thee,
> For thou art a dead thing.

He couldn't linger long among a crowd of echoes, however
charming they might be; there were too many things to think
of, too many things to do: things to think about, things to do
in the home, in the wider community of the nation, in the
widest community of the world. The world now was like a jig-

saw puzzle; though some had fitted the pieces well and securely together, others, in conference, committee, assembly, and what not had jumbled the pieces so confusedly that few knew even where to look for the most of them. The nations of Europe have fallen into a screaming coma. A lot of them are yelling out for help. America's feet are worn away running from one to the other. Oh, there's another one down! Prop him up, buddies! But before this guy is properly propped, two more are down on their backs; and soon there's a queue lying, dead to the world, waiting to be lifted to their feet again. The coma conquers them. Neither dollars nor machinery are worth a damn if the people haven't the will to do. A nation, though immersed in wealth and cluttered with machinery, but without a will, would surely, if slowly, die.

Ireland's idea of safety with her roads adance with jeeps was neither a will nor a way. He had just read in an Irish journal that a roman catholic dignitary, preaching in an Irish town, had condemned Communists, their friends, and their friends' friends, adding, as a sorrowful affix, that for the whole year there had been but one marriage in the town. Ha ha ha! Looks like Ireland was becoming like heaven itself, where they neither marry nor are given in marriage. Ha ha ha! Last May, the Blessed Virgin's month, before the bloom was on the rye, a letter came to Eileen from a woman living in a Dublin cottage slum, with eight children to keep. The last baby had come six years after the seventh, and had left the mother prostrate for months. Ever after she was to feel the effects of the strain. She wrote:

'My dear Mrs O'Casey, Thank you for your letter. We all had flu. Una got it Bad and I have her in Bed with Pluresy at the Moment. She is not quite as bad as she was she is a bad fighter and lets everything in on her lets hope she wont be long till she is well again. You know I am a Bad writer cant think of what to say when I sit down to write. Ill say goodbye for now Ill get this off to you and get the kids to bed love to Shivaun Sincerely Chris.'

A bad fighter, letting everything in on her! A bad character for a slum child. Written, probably in the irritation of a great weariness, or written out of a vague reason for the child's lack of toughness; for the woman, Chris, was a fine mother and a very kind one; but she had too many kids to keep and care for, and, now, with all things dearer, it wouldn't be long till thousands of other kids would cease to be fighters, and would let everything in on them. Anyway, it was far more urgent for the defence of the country to have jeeps prancing along the roads than to fill the bellies of the nation's children with the food they urgently needed. Let the kids go – we need jeeps; we do, be jeepers!

Same here, same in England. All was needed for the arms, and little needed for the man. Even in the wealthy and imperative United States, many a still, small voice cried out in solitary places. Writes an American mother to him:

'Not knowing a mother, I was brought up by a grim, hardworking father, who, bending over a noisy sewing-machine, six days a week (doing that still today at sixty-six). We were never hungry, but there were many things daily to remind us that it happened to the best of working-class families; that our furniture as well as next family's could be put out into the street; that Santa Claus wasn't abroad at Christmas time, or sitting in the grocer's shop; that the landlord was a force to be reckoned with almost on the lofty level of the Government and the Lord above. Today, they gave my little girl a bit of metal on a chain to wear around her neck. It's called a Dog-Tag [der Tag!]. United States soldiers wear it in Korea and wherever they are. That's if Russia bombs us we'll be able to identify the pint-sized remains. The stamped letters with the child's and father's names are supposed to be especially durable. Flame-tested, I guess. Neither I nor my child will ever wear one.'

There is no need to wear them. O little girl and grown-up woman. Soviet bombs will never fall on New York City, unless New York bombs fall on Moscow first. There would be no gain to either city if each destroyed the other, for both would be gone, and the world would miss them. There is no danger, no danger, for though man be foolish, men are not fools. Each great city will go on living; living in its own vigorous, beautiful way.

He was writing now in the Fall of the Year, while the leaves of the trees were taking a last flutter through the air, whispering a goodbye to life as they fell. Sere and yellow, they were useless now to the tree; they had done their work, and the newer buds beneath were busy pushing them off; pushing them away from life, never to return again. Sere and yellow leaf, fall fluttering, and fade from all you knew, carrying to earth with you some tender fragment of the summer's dream. So are many now, so was he – waiting for that gentle but insistent push that would detach his clinging desire, and send him, like the tumbling autumn leaf, sinking from life's busy tree to the dull flavour of death in the kingly dust where all men mingle in a sleep unending.

Outside, in the tiny garden, the few flowers have faded, or have been shoved from life by the sharp frost of the night before. The tall hollyhocks have toppled, leaving a few lingering rose-like forms on one dismantled stalk nuzzling itself into the chilly clay. Only the michaelmas daisies are topped with fading stars of crimson and mauve, and in the sullen hedge, hacked into rough-arrayed order, a few golden-brown blossoms still peer out from the prickly barberry-bush. A spreading bloom of a purple dahlia and the crimson disk of a single one have slunk heavily to the ground, oozy with a brownish slime that almost hides the memory of their bygone brilliancy. A short time ago, he had watched two big, handsome bees, delicately furred and red-banded, in the yellow centre of the crimson dahlia-disk, one bee in its core, the other on its fringe. Honey-drunk and half dead they seemed to be. After a long time, the furry fellow on the fringe sleepily began to press himself deeper into the yellow core of the crimson disk, his twitching legs moving about to get a firmer grip, touching the other fellow's legs in the centre, who, with the tiniest show of irritation, shoved them twitchingly aside, just as a woman in the honey-hush of sleep might sleepily shove away from her body the wandering legs of a husband. Dead the blossoms, half dead the bees, and the leaves all round fluttering down. A beautiful sadness everywhere. But in a few days the crimson disk will be there again, the purple-spreading dahlia will flaunt its pomp in the world's face, and the bees will buzz and hum and buzz again, as if the sun shone always and the frost was all over for ever. Even the winter has her many beauties, even for the old who shiver; the crisper air; the cold mists of morning, the fretted framework of the trees against the sky, the diamantling frost biting a harsh beauty into the earth's soft bosom; the stillness of the earth herself under it all, waiting for the spring. Ah, yes; to the old, spring and its budding bring a welcome as well as to the young. Sweet spring, full of sweet days and roses.

Even here, even now, when the sun had set and the evening star was chastely touching the bosom of the night, there were

things to say, things to do. A drink first! What would he drink
to – the past, the present, the future? To all of them! He
would drink to the life that embraced the three of them! Here,
with whitened hair, desires failing, strength ebbing out of him,
with the sun gone down, and with only the serenity and the
calm warning of the evening star left to him, he drank to Life,
to all it had been, to what it was, to what it would be. Hurrah!

If you have enjoyed this PAN Book, you may like to choose your next book from the titles listed on the following pages.

Sean O'Casey

Sean O'Casey wrote his first evocative and richly entertaining autobiography in six volumes over more than two decades. Each volume is essential reading for a proper appreciation of this major Irish dramatist.

I KNOCK AT THE DOOR
Autobiography Vol. I   30p

PICTURES IN THE HALLWAY
Autobiography Vol. II   30p

DRUMS UNDER THE WINDOWS
Autobiography Vol. III   40p

INISHFALLEN, FARE THEE WELL
Autobiography Vol. IV   40p

ROSE AND CROWN
Autobiography Vol. V   40p

SUNSET AND EVENING STAR
Autobiography Vol. VI   40p

Frank O'Connor

'A Master' – THE LISTENER
'Perfect' – THE SPECTATOR

A LIFE OF YOUR OWN
and Other Stories   30p
MASCULINE PROTEST
and Other Stories   30p
THE MAD LOMASNEYS
and Other Stories   25p
FISH FOR FRIDAY
and Other Stories   25p

Also in PAN is the entrancing story of
O'Connor's life from schoolboy to revolu-
tionary to librarian and his association with
the Abbey Theatre.

AN ONLY CHILD   30p
MY FATHER'S SON   30p

Walter Macken

THE BOGMAN   35p

'As quietly deceptive and as full of potential
activity as an unlabelled box of dynamite' –
LIVERPOOL DAILY POST

SEEK THE FAIR LAND	35p
THE SCORCHING WIND	35p
RAIN ON THE WIND	30p
THE COLL DOLL and Other Stories	30p
GOD MADE SUNDAY and Other Stories	35p
BROWN LORD OF THE MOUNTAIN	35p
THE SILENT PEOPLE	35p

These and other PAN Books are obtainable
from all booksellers and newsagents. If you
have any difficulty please send purchase price
plus 7p postage to PO Box 11, Falmouth,
Cornwall.

While every effort is made to keep prices low, it
is sometimes necessary to increase prices at
short notice. PAN Books reserve the right to
show new retail prices on covers which may
differ from those advertised in the text or
elsewhere.